Interactive Media

T0210679

Roy Rada

Interactive Media

Contributions by Antonios Michailidis

Includes 97 Figures

Springer-Verlag

New York Berlin Heidelberg London Paris
Tokyo Hong Kong Barcelona Budapest

Roy Rada
Department of Computer Science
University of Liverpool
Liverpool L69 3BX
England

Library of Congress Cataloging-in-Publication Data
Rada, R. (Roy), 1951-
    Interactive media / Roy Rada.
        p.   cm.
    Includes bibliographical references and index.
    ISBN 0-387-94485-0
    1. Interactive media.   I. Title.
QA76.76.I57R33   1995
004 ' .01 ' 9--dc20   95-3759

Printed on acid-free paper.

Production managed by Jim Harbison; manufacturing supervised by Jeff Taub.
Camera-ready copy provided by the author.
Printed and bound by Hamilton Printing Co., Rensselaer, NY.
Printed in the United States of America.

9 8 7 6 5 4 3 2 1

ISBN 0-387-94485-0 Springer-Verlag New York Berlin Heidelberg

Preface

This book was written for *students* and *practitioners* of engineering and social sciences, including computer, information, communication, library, business, management, and cognitive science. The topic is the relationship between people and *interactive media*. The book describes individuals, groups, and organizations. An understanding of people is critical to an understanding of the technology which can help people.

This book was written with the help of a special computer system for authoring called the Many Using and Creating Hypertext (MUCH) system. Students and researchers from the University of Liverpool contributed to the book through the *MUCH system*. Classes at the University of Liverpool, both undergraduate classes and master's degree classes, have used various drafts of this book as required reading. The book has been available to the students online via the MUCH system, and the students have provided helpful feedback for the contents of the book.

The author is particularly grateful for the *contributions* of Antonios Michailidis and Alex Birchall. Antonios's influence is most prominent in the chapters on groups, and Alex's, in the latter chapters on organizations. Claude Ghaoui coordinated the book authoring and production team, and Anthony Deakin provided finishing touches. Renata Malinowski put many, many hours into implementing suggested revisions and correcting the format, graphics, and references. Springer-Verlag via Martin Gilchrist and Rudiger Gebauer have been helpful in molding the structure and content of the book. The success of the MUCH team and Springer-Verlag with this book must be judged by the reader. Please enjoy!

Contents

1
Introduction

People need information about their environment in order to know how to react to it and to identify in their reaction what they can share with others. People want technology to support this knowing and sharing via storing, processing, and producing *information* (see Figure 1.1). The new information technologies offer exciting opportunities for individuals, groups, and organizations to store, process, and produce information.

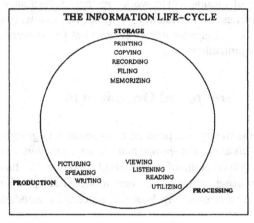

Figure 1.1: *Information Life-cycle.* The information life-cycle consists of the production, storage, and processing of information. People produce information by picturing, speaking, or writing. The information may be stored by printing, copying, recording, filing, or memorizing it. People process information by viewing it, listening to it, reading it, or otherwise utilizing it.

1.1   Hypermedia, Groupware, and Networks

Media come in multiple forms. Until recently, computers were only able to efficiently handle alphanumeric characters. Developments in information technology have now made other media, particularly images and sound, amenable to computer-based storage, manipulation, and transmission. The synchronization of media gives *multimedia*. *Hypermedia* is multimedia with links among the components and a mechanism for moving along the links. Hypermedia has a very important part to play in communication in that it serves to make sense of otherwise discrete components and conveys an overall conceptual structure.

The technology, which may be called *groupware,* has developed in the last few years to enhance group working. It is designed to harness computers and networks to give groups of workers the kind of productivity gains individual users already enjoy from single-user systems, like word-processors and spreadsheets. While groupware in some sense includes traditional database or operating systems, the groupware technology that is now emerging seeks to support information-rich, person-to-person communication. This communication may be synchronized in time or not, and it may occur across great or small physical distances.

Organizations consist of groups which work together. Coordination is necessary for organizational effectiveness and efficiency. Without communication people could not coordinate their efforts. *Computer networks* are vital to communication across time and space for many organizations.

1.2   Individual, Group, and Organization

This book considers the theory and practice of hypermedia, groupware, and networks at three levels: the *individual,* the *group,* and the *organization.* The justification for this approach is that each level manifests different problems that have to be considered in the design and implementation of relevant tools. These problems center on how information is used or, more precisely, how it is accessed, created, communicated, and reused once again.

When an *individual* becomes aware that he or she does not know something that it would be useful to know, that individual has defined a need for information. Given this need, the first step is establishing whether such information exists. If it does exist, the next step is retrieving it. Once it has been retrieved, the individual must be able to understand it. However, this apparently straightforward process can in fact be extremely tortuous and longwinded. Many barriers exist between individuals and relevant information, that can mean that the time, effort, and financial cost involved in retrieving it, effectively discourage all but the most determined. Such barriers include information invisibility, misinformation, and jargon to name but a few.

The problems of the individual with regard to information do not cease to exist when the individual is a member of a *group,* though some may be considerably alleviated. Thus the individual may find that other members of the group possess valuable information it would have been costly to retrieve through official channels; or other members of the group may be able to interpret information the individual finds difficult to understand. However, groups have problems in using information that do not exist for individuals as such. These problems center around the issue of information sharing. Solutions to these problems are various, and involve group protocols and structures. These protocols and structures determine the way information is disseminated within and beyond the group.

At the organizational level, the issue is again that of information sharing, but now it is that much more complex as it involves the sharing of information between groups, as well as between groups and individuals, and between individuals who are not members of the same groups. Individuals may be members of more than one group, the information requirements of which may conflict. Also, in the *organization* the distinction between formal and informal groups becomes important: successful organizational functioning can depend equally on both types.

The *technology* appropriate for individuals may be different from the technology for groups or organizations [71] (see Figure 1.2). Hypermedia tools, such as video editors and electronic document browsers, have been designed to satisfy individuals' needs and goals. Groupware systems, such as co-authoring systems and electronic meeting systems, support groups. Networks serve the goals and tasks of entire organizations.

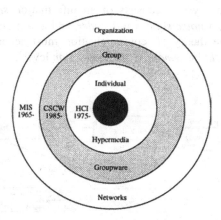

Figure 1.2: *Individuals, Groups, and Organizations - Research and Technology.* Management Information Science (MIS) is a discipline well established since the mid 1960's for the study of organizational uses of information technology. Human-Computer Interaction (HCI) is a discipline well recognized since the mid 1970's for relating individuals to applications, particularly hypermedia applications. The discipline of Computer-Supported Cooperative Work (CSCW) focuses on groups and has been popular since the mid 1980's (adapted from [72]).

The *discipline* most associated with individuals and hypermedia is Human-Computer Interaction. The study of groups and groupware occurs in the Computer-supported Cooperative Work community. Computer networks are particularly important in Management Information Science.

1.3   Communication, Information, and Media

Theories of communication seek to produce a model of the communication process that adequately describes its every mode. Such a theory links processes as apparently diverse as talking to one another, watching television, looking at a picture, or seeing an advertisement. There are two main schools in the study of communication. One school sees communication as the transmission of messages. It concentrates on explaining how communication senders and receivers encode and decode, and how transmitters use the channels and media of communication. It treats communication as a process by which one person affects the behavior or state of mind of another. The second school treats communication as the production and exchange of meanings.

A formal communication system consists of an information *source,* an *encoder,* a communication *channel,* a *noise source,* a *decoder,* and a *destination* (see Figure 1.3) [171]. A comprehensive theory of communication must account for problems on three levels: the *technical,* the *semantic,* and the *action* levels.

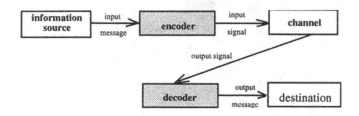

Figure 1.3: *Signal Transmission.* This basic model of communication presents communication as a simple linear process from information source to destination.

The semantic level has to do with how the transmitted symbols that encode a message manage to convey the meaning the sender of the message desires the receiver to understand. Where a message is misinterpreted, the solution is to improve the encoding of the message so that more of the meaning can be conveyed. The action level has to do with how effectively the meaning of the message that is received achieves the purposes of the sender - does it cause the desired action?

In the model, the *source* is seen as the decision-maker. The source decides which message to send. The encoder transforms the message into a *signal* which is sent through the *channel* to the decoder. *Noise* is anything that is added to the signal between its transmission and reception that is not intended by the source. Noise can arise on all three levels of communication. For instance, the static in a radio signal is noise on the technical level; homonyms can give rise to noise on the semantic level; and an unanticipated emotional response to a message can limit its effectiveness.

Information may be formally defined as a measure of the predictability of the signal, that is, the number of choices open to the sender of a message. These choices depend on the nature of the transmitter. For instance, a simple telegraph provides two signals, off and on, each with 50% predictability. This definition of information has nothing at all to do with the content of a message.

The idea that messages have a degree of predictability leads to the concept of *redundancy*. Redundancy is that which is predictable or conventional in a message. Redundancy can help overcome the deficiencies of a noisy channel. It can facilitate the communication of a novel message and can make communicating to a wide audience more likely to be successful.

Two other important concepts in communication and information theory are channel and code. The *channel* is the physical means by which the signal is transmitted. The main channels are light waves, sound waves, telephone cables, and the nervous system. A *code* is a system of shared meaning. A code is made up of both signs (i.e., physical signals that stand for something other than themselves) and rules and conventions that say how and in what contexts these signs are used and how they can be combined to form more complex messages. The physical characteristics of channels determine the nature of the codes that they can transmit.

A *medium* is the technical or physical means of converting the message into a signal capable of being transmitted along the channel. Information sources may use presentational or representational media to encode a message. Alternately, a message in presentational or representational media may be further encoded by mechanical media (see Figure 1.4):

* The *presentational media* include the voice and body. The messages encoded via these media are spoken words, gestures, and so on. These are 'acts of communication'.

- The *representational media* include books, paintings, photographs, architecture, gardening, computer interfaces, and so on. These media make use of cultural conventions to encode a 'message'. They produce 'works of communication'.
- The *mechanical media* include telephones, telexes, computers, and so on. They are transmitters of presentational and representational media.

The presentational and representational media must both come to people via their senses (see Figure 1.5). Text is seen, noise is heard. This may get complicated as, for instance, inscriptions in stone can be both seen and felt.

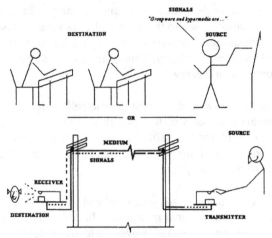

Figure 1.4: *Presentational versus Representational Communication:* The source is the originator of the message, while the destination receives the message. The teacher in the classroom (upper sketch) is using presentational media. In the lower sketch, a document (representational medium) is encoded for transmission via mechanical media.

The medium of printed paper may contain pictures, diagrams, and text, all of which are different encodings. Encoded information can itself serve as a base for another medium. For example, in a photograph of a street sign, the base medium is the photograph that carries an *image*. This image carries the name of the street, represented as text. In electronic mail, images are sometimes constructed with text, as in a sideways smiling face ':)' — this illustrates the use of text as a medium for images. When media are discussed, the differences between presentational, representational, and mechanical media should be kept in mind.

Media are a means of communication by which information is passed from one person to another. Human beings generate commitments through media and have the ability to affect and anticipate other people's behavior through media [199]. Although the content conveys information, its interpretation by its recipients triggers actions. While computers are mainly tools for human action, computers cannot make commitments.

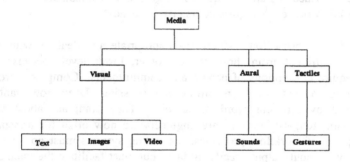

Figure: 1.5 "Organization of media in terms of human sensory abilities".

1.4   People and Technology

Every organization depends on three kinds of *processes:* material, information, and workflow. The first two are of the traditional input-output kind. Material processes move and transform materials. Information processes move and transform information. Workflow processes deal with the requests for work to be done, agreements on who will do it and when, and whether the customer is satisfied.

The field of *operating systems* has often strongly determined the kind of information technology on which organizations conduct business. The first operating systems in the 1950s allocated processor time and memory space among contending users. During the 1960s the concern of operating system designers was identifying the abstractions, such as files and directories, that could be used to construct virtual machines for users. These concerns spread over the 1970s and 1980s into mechanisms for dealing with networks of computers. Despite all the changes, the engineer still often views an operating system as a manager of work inside a machine.

The scale of time at which information is being processed has grown over the years:

- hardware electronics operate at the picosecond level (10^{-12} seconds),
- machine instructions execute in nanoseconds (10^{-9} seconds),
- computer procedures execute in microseconds (10^{-6} seconds),
- local secondary storage is accessed in milliseconds (10^{-3} seconds),
- user interface operations require seconds (10^{+0} seconds), and
- workflow processes require hours (10^{+3} seconds),

but the kinds of abstractions which are appropriate for dealing with workflow processes are different from those for the other, lower levels because *workflow processes* require conceptions of people and commitments. Computers are now for communicating and not just for recording or processing. Users now want to share files produced by different word processors. They complain about too much electronic mail. Requests to software engineers are now often for transparent and efficient support of workflow processes. Operating systems must no longer simply track the flow of input-output specifying tasks but must facilitate the management of commitments in an organization [39]. The boundary between the organization and its information technology tools is blurring.

To teach *students* about computer or information science in this new world is challenging. The basic machine models of the 1940s are adequate to deal with the traditional programming concerns but are not necessarily relevant to dealing with people as components of the information system. Mathematics and physics have been the basic disciplines which supported advances in computer science for many years, but for information systems to deal with *human commitments,* the designers of the systems must understand people. Are computer scientists to be proficient at mathematics, physics, psychology, and sociology?

A similar problem has confronted the health care disciplines. There the growth of knowledge has moved to the smaller and smaller time scales — going from the activity of humans, to cells, to molecules, to subatomic particles. Medical students can not now cope with all the information which is available and might be important. If they want to order a nuclear magnetic resonance image of the brain, or a radiated hormone level from the blood, or a gene analysis of the fetus, they may have to ask for help in understanding what the results mean. Education in medical schools is thus changing to one where students deal with prototypical patients and try to learn the principles along the way. New information technology curricula may need to follow a similar trend of teaching prototypical applications through which students learn a broad range of principles. The practitioner thus trained should be prepared to tackle new applications and learn on the job whatever is needed to succeed.

This book focuses on interactive media as one important application. The reader should learn to map types of users and their problems to the kinds of interactive media which will help the users solve their problems. Ultimately, the reader should get a better understanding of the relationship between *people and technology*.

1.5   Structure of this Book

Interactive media support the creation of *people-centered systems* that can clarify and simplify the coordination of human action. However, the new technologies have sometimes failed, especially when they were expected to change the way in which people interact. For interactive media to succeed, they need to fit gracefully into the lives of their users. The designers of interactive media systems must understand how individuals, groups, and organizations function and how technology affects that functioning [199].

The chapters of this book may be seen as fitting into three major parts:

Part I: The Individual and Hypermedia
Part II: The Group and Groupware
Part III: The Organization and Networks

These three parts clearly emphasize the *individual, group,* and *organization* on one hand, and hypermedia, groupware, and networks, on the other hand. The book includes a chapter entitled 'Human-Computer Interaction' which is in a sense about the Individual. Chapters are dedicated to groups and to organizations. Understanding people, be they seen as individuals, groups, or organizations, is critical to the successful application of hypermedia, groupware, or networks.

Part I develops a comprehensive framework for dealing with hypermedia by emphasizing the role of links in 'Chapter 3. Hypertext', timing in 'Chapter 4. Multimedia', and links plus timing in 'Chapter 5. Hypermedia'. Often in common parlance the concepts of hypertext, multimedia, and hypermedia are poorly distinguished. Part I makes clear the important differences.

Each Part of the book begins with theory and ends with applications. An understanding of the principles, models, or standards which apply to both the people and their technology supports the development of better technology. On the other hand, without an opportunity to learn about applications, people have difficulty in fully understanding the theory.

A key theme in this book is that decision-making, communication, and a common language are critical to *coordination*. Communication between machines, between a person and a machine, or between people depends on a common language. Successful decision-making often requires communication. Through decision-making people coordinate their work.

As noted in the 'Preface', many people contributed to this book via the Many Using and Creating Hypertext (MUCH) system. The *MUCH system* serves furthermore as an example of technology in the individual, group, and organizational contexts. Pictures of the MUCH system interface are provided, and in the penultimate chapter of the book the evolution of the organization which developed the MUCH system is presented as a case study.

At the heart of the *hypermedia, groupware,* and *network* paradigm is a model of technology supporting people. Hypermedia, groupware, and networks have the potential to change society. Engineers and users have an obligation to work together so that the interactive media help shape a better society.

Part I:

The Individual and Hypermedia

Media are received by people through the senses including sight, sound, touch, and smell. Multimedia are synchronized media, such as moving images with sound. *Hypermedia* is interactive or linked multimedia. Hypertext as one specific type of hypermedia is interactive text or linked text. Hypermedia helps people organize and access information. The vastly increased availability of computing power has allowed the implementation, elaboration, and exploration of the ideas underlying hypermedia [129].

The term 'hypermedia' should properly refer to the contents, such as an interactive video, which a hypermedia system presents. Hypermedia systems manipulate links between discrete pieces of media and synchronize those media in time. Often, however, the term 'hypermedia' is used loosely to refer both to the information content and the technological delivery platform. At the heart of the hypermedia paradigm is a model of the interaction between human beings and technology.

2
Human-Computer Interaction

To understand the communication between people and computers one must understand something about both and about the tasks which people perform with computers. A general model of *Human-Computer Interaction* emphasizes the flow of information and control at the human-computer interface [74]. The tasks which this chapter addresses are the basic ones of accessing and creating information.

2.1   Human, Computer, and Environment

The Human-Computer Interaction model might consist of four main components: Human, Computer, Task Environment, and Machine Environment. Two basic flows of information and control are assumed. The first originates from the *task environment*. The user is assigned to perform a task. The task sets the context and determines a number of contextual factors such as the cost of errors, the importance of time, and the criteria for successful completion of the task. The user cognitively processes the information about the task. The result is an intention that leads to some action at the computer interface (e.g. typing a command). The user's input determines some behavior of the computer, and a product might be created. The second flow originates from the *machine environment*. The computer receives data from its environment which is transformed into an appropriate form to be displayed. The user encodes the displayed information, interprets it, and responds to it with consideration also given to the task environment (see Figure 2.1).

Tasks and environments imply different requirements and impose different constraints in the specification of *user interfaces*. Tasks may be perceived in terms of the number of steps they require. Simple tasks require few steps with little control from the user. Complex tasks require not only many steps, but also involve many choices for the user. Some tasks are structured, such as filling a form, or following a predefined procedure. Other tasks are unstructured, such as browsing hypertext. Other dimensions can also characterize environments, such as information-rich versus information scarce. The design and modeling of user-interfaces must consider these factors.

The human-computer interface can be characterized across different dimensions from the user perspective. Complexity of the user interface is a function of the richness of the information exchanged between the computer and the user. *Usability* refers to the ease of use of the interface. High usability is always desirable.

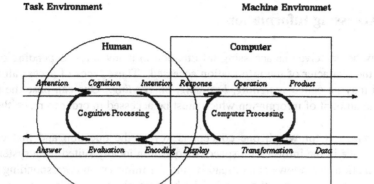

Figure 2.1: *General model of Human-Computer Interface.* The human is represented by a circle and the computer by a rectangle. Both circle and rectangle include the processes performed by the human and the computer. The overlapping area includes processes related to the interface. Arrows indicate information flow.

The *human operator* may be further characterized. Operators vary in their amount of knowledge and the type of knowledge they acquire about the system. Ideal knowledge contains information about the task and how the computer works. Nonideal knowledge contains false information that produces errors or redundant actions [7]. Operators vary in their ability to solve problems, make decisions, and perform mental tasks. The tasks require different abilities in varying degrees by the operators. Analysis of cognitive components involved in task performance are useful both in system design and operator selection and training.

The *Model Human Processor* describes and predicts human computer interaction rather than describing what actually happens in users' minds. The Model Human Processor consists of three components [25]. The perceptual system consists of sensors and buffer memories to carry sensations of the physical world into internal representations. The cognitive system consists of working memory and long-term memory and a cognitive processor. The cognitive system carries information from buffer memories into working memory and uses already stored information in long-term memory to generate responses. The motor system consists of a motor processor which carries the response.

2.2   Accessing Information

People may be perceived as accessing information in many ways, depending on their goals and the character of the information accessed. These types of access along one dimension may be called *searching, browsing,* or *reading.* One can pose the task in terms of the amount of information which must be accessed in order to reach the goal.

A *search question* for which one concept is key to the question and that concept occurs just once in the information space is a question ideally suited for a system with a search function that allows one to readily find the information corresponding to that concept. At the point where the search fails because either too many or not enough information relates to the concept, then another method is appropriate. A *browse question* has several important concepts and they relate to several parts of the information space, some parts of which are relevant and some not. If a few parts must be accessed to answer the question and those parts are neatly connected, then browsing is appropriate.

Precision is the fraction of retrieved information which is relevant to the task, while *recall* is the fraction of retrieved, relevant information versus all relevant information - both have a maximum of one [181]. Generally speaking, information access is best when recall and precision are as close as possible to one. To further distinguish tasks, third dimension is introduced: the amount of information wanted.

Search tasks need a very few parts of the information space and should be performed on a system that will provide high recall and, at least, medium precision. Browse tasks need several parts of the information space and again should be performed on a system that provides both high recall and, at least, medium precision (see Figure 2.2). The remainder of this 3-dimensional space corresponds to *understanding tasks.* Any task which requires a sizable fraction of the information space is an understanding task. Furthermore, when search and browse techniques do not lead to adequately high recall and precision, then an understanding problem arises.

The traditional media such as paper and television, have many valuable uses. *Paper* is a powerful medium whose familiarity, tangibility, and portability make it more attractive than computerized information for many understanding tasks [78]. In some cases, rather than asking whether new computerized information systems will replace traditional media or not, one should be looking for the ways in which the two can complement one another.

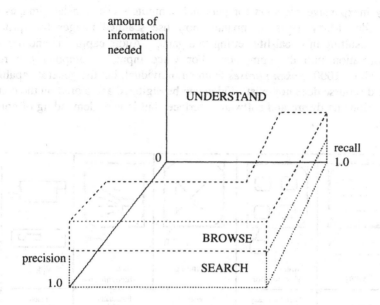

Figure 2.2: *Three dimensional search space.* This three dimension space with axes of 'recall', 'precision', and 'amount of information needed' shows that the tasks for which large amounts of information are needed are not the appropriate tasks for search or browse and that the difficult problems occur when precision or recall are low.

2.3 Creating Information

Creating information is the natural counterpart to accessing information. Entering information into the computer may itself by a challenging, though largely mechanical, step. The cognitive and life-cycle activities fundamental to creating information are fundamental to what distinguishes humans from other animals.

2.3.1 Information Entry

Of the many ways to enter information into a computer, five prominent ones include: *typing, direct manipulation, scanning, audio capture,* and *video capture* [172] (see Figure 2.3). In typing, the keyboard allows a maximum input of about 100 words per minute but is error-prone at this speed. Text-oriented documents are typically entered onto computer using this interface. *Direct manipulation* does not accommodate data entry but is otherwise a very popular means of interacting with a computer system. A user manipulates a pointer on the screen using a mouse or tracker to choose from various options provided by a graphical display. With a touch sensitive screen the user can explore by simply pointing to his chosen option.

Relatively inexpensive *scanners* for personal computers can translate images into a computer file. Many games companies now use scanned images for sprites and backdrops resulting in a real-life setting to a game. Audio capture is another way to enter information into the computer. For voice input, a computer can reliably recognize about 1000 *spoken phrases* from an individual, but the general capability to recognize discourse does not exist. Video can be digitized and stored on the computer through various hardware and software interfaces but is very demanding of computer resources.

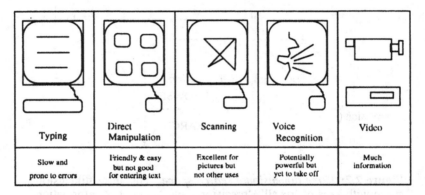

Typing	Direct Manipulation	Scanning	Voice Recognition	Video
Slow and prone to errors	Friendly & easy but not good for entering text	Excellent for pictures but not other uses	Potentially powerful but yet to take off	Much information

Figure 2.3: *Four ways of entering.* This figure illustrates four ways of entering information into a computer system accompanied by their advantages and disadvantages.

Given the high costs of entering information either manually by typing or through other capture mechanisms such as scanning, audio capture, or video capture, one is naturally tempted to wonder to what extent information can be *copied* from other places. Thus the popularity of such items as libraries of clip art. The user rather than creating an ocean scene with boats on it, simply finds such a scene from a library and copies it. The more expensive the creation of the information would be, the more attractive is the alternative of not entering that information directly but rather of copying it from another digitized source after someone else has gone to the trouble to enter the information.

2.3.2   Cognitive and Life Cycle Activities

The cognitive operations behind the creation of information have been studied for many centuries. The ancient Greek philosopher *Aristotle* emphasized that a document must state the case and prove it. Given this goal of stating a case, the creator of information must take time to consider the information available to himself and how this can be organized so as to achieve its purpose with its intended audience. Three phases of writing a document have been recognized as properly leading to the achievement of this goal, and those phases are *exploring, organizing,* and *encoding.*

In the exploration phase knowledge is acquired, brainstorming occurs, and notes are made. In the encoding phase the final product is prepared [152]. Some writers progress through this model of the writing process in a linear fashion, going from rough notes to outline to product. Other writers may begin in the middle of the process and write an outline before making any notes. *Authors* like to move freely from one phase to another and back again. In the context of goal-seeking (see Figure 2.4), the exploratory phase finds connections between the assignment or goal and the memory [84]. The organizing phase takes available information and transforms it into networks of loosely-structured information. In the encoding phase the product is revised until it satisfies the goal.

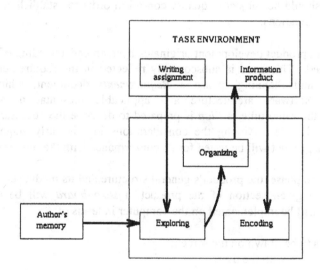

Figure 2.4: *Goal-Oriented Writing Model.* Writing process relative to memory and task [84].

Much could be said about the factors associated with information creation. One factor concerns the experience of the writer. *Novice writers* find writing a tedious chore of translating what they already know. They do little effective reorganization of their ideas and feel that after the writing exercise that they know no more than they knew before the writing exercise. *Expert writers* have the opposite experience. As they go through the various phases of making notes, outlines, and product, they continually examine what they have suggested relative to how they expect it to impact on their intended audience. Experts have a good reader model and continually adjust what they have to say after feeding it through their reader model [167]. After an expert has prepared a product, he feels that he has gained insight about ways to look at the subject of the product.

The preceding description of creating information is particularly apt for the case of a single author writing a traditional textual document. For the case of electronic documents with audio and video, the challenges are greater and the activities required of the author(s) are correspondingly more complex. One might in this situation envision a kind of *product life-cycle* that goes through phases:

1   requirements and planning,
2   design and story-board production,
3   implementation and delivery.

All the phases should be subject to quality control in order to establish conformity to the relevant specifications.

In this life-cycle, product development originates from an understanding of a customer or audience need. This need is subsequently reflected in the requirements. In the 'Requirements and Planning' phase a *Requirements* document, which includes hardware and software architecture and applicable presentation strategies is developed. At the same time, a *Plan* is prepared to describe the necessary resources and the time schedule. Among the considerations in this early stage should be already how the product will be tested for its conformance with the requirements.

During the design phase, the product's general structure and its media components are sketched. For a given section of the product, a *story-board* will be drafted that describes what will be implemented on the computer in terms of:

•   objects to be drawn on the screen;
•   interactions with the user;
•   layout;
•   audio and video sequences; and
•   logical links among the objects of a section.

In the 'Implementation' phase, the story-boards are implemented on the computer. All the logical links of the sections are installed and the media synchronized. Finally the product is delivered to its audience.

2.4   Usability

The *interface* is critical to the success of an information system. The interface should be easy to use, but there are no well-understood methods for creating such interfaces. One would like to be able to say that a certain interface style is best for a certain class of users and tasks. Many papers have been written about the user response to various presentations of hypermedia on various tasks. As one surveys these papers, the question continually arises of 'what can be said in the general case'?

One particular survey showed most strongly the importance of user types. In comparing the results of many studies on interactive media the most significant variable was the *age* of the user. When the users were young, they found interactive media attractive, whereas when they were middle-age, they were disinclined to use it.

The other most significant factor in the survey was the *motivation* of the user. When the users were highly motivated to perform a certain task, then they contributed much more to the exercise than did those whose motivation was less. While this result seems intuitively clear, adequate attention has not been paid to this factor.

2.5   Conclusion

Human-computer interaction concerns the *interface* through which information flows between a person and the computer. The models which the person has of the world and of the computer determine some of this interaction. The task at hand for which the person goes to the computer also heavily influences the human-computer interaction.

In *accessing information* searching, browsing, or understanding may be needed. Searching occurs when the task is to find information about one concept and the information space neatly presents the necessary information in one place. Browsing occurs when several information places must be visited. An understanding task requires the user to develop a detailed mental model of a large part of the information space.

Creating information involves having, in the first instance, a goal of influencing an audience. Processes of exploring, organizing, and encoding information occur. Throughout these processes the expert author reflects on the likely impact of the evolving message on the intended audience.

The *success* of a message in influencing its audience will depend on many factors, including the mechanical media, if any, used to deliver the message. For information delivery the age and the motivation of the audience may be more important in the reaction than any particular property of the information system itself. Human-computer interaction principles are critical to a proper appreciation of the directions that new information technology should take.

3
Hypertext

Hypertext is nodes of text connected by links. A hypertext system supports traversal of these links. In common usage the notion of text in hypertext includes document-like material such as drawings and photographs.

The modern history of linking information by machine is often traced to Vannevar Bush. During the Second World War *Vannevar Bush* directed the American Office of Scientific Research and Development and coordinated the activities of six thousand American scientists in the application of science to warfare and the development of the nuclear bomb. He wanted to apply science to peaceful purposes and towards the end of the Second World War perceived a problem to which the emerging technology of computing might provide a solution. He articulated the problem thus [140]:

> "There is a growing mountain of research. But there is increased evidence that we are being bogged down today as specialization extends. The investigator is staggered by the findings and conclusions of thousands of other workers — conclusions which we cannot find time to grasp, much less to remember, as they appear."

Bush proposed a technological solution to this problem in the shape of a device he termed the *Memex* (Memory Extender). This was a device in which an individual stores all his items of information in miniaturized form and which allows for their subsequent consultation and processing with great speed and flexibility. However, it was not so much the technology that was important about the Memex but what this technology made possible. Memex would provide for *associative indexing*, "... whereby any item may be caused at will to select immediately and automatically another." In 1945 Bush's ideas appeared in popular magazines in an article entitled 'As We May Think'. Such is the extent of Bush's influence that it has been suggested that Bush's Memex has provided an *image of potentiality*. Images of potentiality result when untested theories, unanswered questions, or unbuilt devices guide scientists and technologists. Bush neither tested his theory of associative indexing nor built Memex, but his ideas have influenced the work of many others.

3.1   Architecture

In this section the basic *architecture of hypertext* is presented. Nodes and links are fundamental to the logical model of hypertext. By separating this logical model from its presentation on the screen, one gains flexibility in the manipulation of the model onto the interface.

3.1.1   Nodes and Links

Formal models of hypertext may emphasize clear, systematic relationships between structure and function. The *Dexter model* succeeds in separating the model into various structural parts which have distinct functional roles. In the Dexter model, hypertext has a *runtime layer,* a *storage layer,* and a *within-component layer* [76]. The storage layer is composed of nodes and links. Nodes may be composites of other nodes. Links connect any number of nodes. Each node or link may have arbitrarily many attributes. The description of each node includes pointers to the exact locations or anchors to which its links connect (see Figure 3.1). Between the storage and runtime layers is a 'presentation mechanism' and between the 'storage' and 'within-component' layers is an 'anchoring mechanism' (see Figure 3.2). The presentation mechanism presents the hypertext to the user, and the anchoring mechanism retrieves components.

The presentation of *node content* occurs in time and space. According to their spatial presentation characteristics node context can be divided into various categories, such as nodes that provide a screen-sized workspace. A challenge to hypertext authors is to put just enough information in a node — not too little or too much.

Link types can be divided into those that directly connect nodes in the network and those that invoke programs. Virtual and Conditional links are examples of link types that invoke programs. With virtual links the user specifies the link's start explicitly and gives a description of its destination; the computer then finds some target node which satisfies the description of the destination. An example of a Conditional link is: if evidence Q is present, then link from node A to node containing Q, otherwise link from the node A to the node containing P.

A *composition mechanism* should allow the users to represent and deal with groups of nodes and links as unique entities separate from their components. It should also allow the users to access the nodes and links independently. For example, a user should be able at one time and in one action to copy a chapter of a book without having to separately copy each section of the chapter. Still at other times the user should be able to copy an individual section within the chapter.

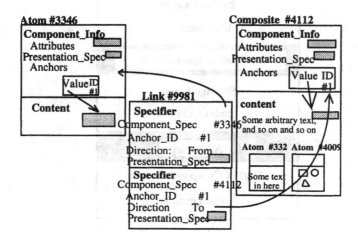

Figure 3.1: *Nodes and Links.* A depiction of overall organization of the storage layer including two nodes: atomic node #3346 and composite node #4412. Link #9981 has an anchor in both nodes.

As users interact with hypertext, they make changes to the information within it. For example, a politician may be adding information about politics to a hypertext document about a city, while an artist is independently adding information about art in the city. Perhaps the politician wants to have her version separately from the artist's version, and a versioning mechanism would support this. *Versioning* is important because it allows the user to maintain and manipulate a history of changes.

3.1.2   Semantic Models

The abstraction of hypertext as a network of concepts and relations is a *semantic net*. In a semantic network, concepts are defined by their relationships to other concepts in the network. For example, the meaning of 'hypertext' may be defined by saying that it contains media, runs on computers, and serves users. The link types in this example are 'contains', 'runs on', and 'serves' (see Figure 3.3). The nodes are 'hypertext', 'text', 'computers', and 'users'. Semantic nets are a model of memory. They lend themselves to graphic display, and their meaning tends to be intuitively clear. The disadvantage of semantic nets is that the meaning or semantics of the net may be difficult to formalize.

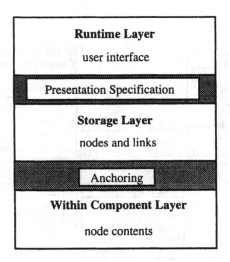

Figure 3.2: *Dexter Model Layers.* The storage layer only provides
the mechanisms to organize components (nodes) and links without
considering the contents of components, which is the task of the
within-component layer. The interface between the storage layer and
within-component layer is an anchoring mechanism which is used
for addressing locations or items within a component. The runtime
layer focuses on how information is presented to users.

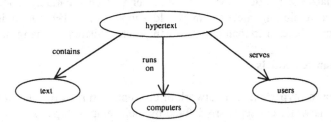

Figure 3.3: *Example Semantic Net.*

The best understood semantic net link types manifest *inheritance properties.* For
instance, if the network connects the node 'student' to the node 'person' with the link
'is a', then one can infer the properties of a student from those of a person. Inheritance
is a type of transitivity. If a student is a person and a person is an animal, then by
transitivity, a student is an animal. Transitivity also applies to the 'cause' link. For

instance, if viruses cause infection and infections cause fever, then viruses cause fever. A *thesaurus* is a kind of semantic net which emphasizes hierarchical relations and synonyms and is used in information retrieval systems.

3.1.3 Text and Hypertext

Under what conditions can text be *automatically restructured* as hypertext [58]? Two classes of text should be distinguished: clearly-structured and implicitly-structured. Clearly-structured text has obvious structural links, whereas implicitly-structured text does not.

A prime example of *clearly-structured text* is a directory. Technical manuals, dictionaries, encyclopedias, course catalogs, and bibliographies are like directories. The embedded commands in the electronic versions of these texts can be readily translated into a form that a hypertext system exploits. The documentation for the operating system UNIX has been converted into a hypertext system [22]. Each section heading within the documentation was automatically converted into a node of the hypermedia.

Implicitly-structured text refers to text whose explicit logical structure is minimal. The extreme case is an essay which has no subdivisions or other logical decomposition. A novel likewise may often be an extended stream of consciousness for which the logical structure is not suggested in the layout of the document and is not indicated by the markup language which may have been used on the computer. To translate implicitly-structured text into hypertext requires substantial human effort to make explicit the relations among components of the document [53].

To convert the logical structure of a hypertext to text form involves traversing a graph. Two popular ways to *traverse* a graph are a breadth-first and a depth-first traversal. A breadth-first traversal starts at a node and visits all the nodes directly connected to it before proceeding in a similar fashion from one of the recently visited nodes. A depth-first traversal starts at a node, visits one of the nodes directly connected to it, and then repeats this process from the last visited node. Both breadth-first and depth-first methods backtrack when a node is reached all of whose directly connected nodes have already been visited (see Figure 3.4).

3.2 Interfaces

The *interface to a hypertext system* is distinct from that of earlier 'information storage and retrieval' systems by its emphasis on browsing. The hypertext system might, however, also support searching, particularly by including a semantic net whose nodes each point to a number of computer documents. Such a semantic net in the 'searching vernacular' might be called an indexing language or under certain restrictions, a

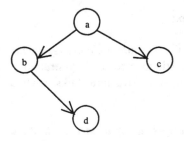

Figure 3.4: *Breadth and Depth.* For a traversal that starts at node 'a', one breadth-first route is 'a,b,c,d' and one depth-first route is 'a,b,d,c'.

thesaurus.

3.2.1   Browser Interface

In one experience a massive semantic net was first presented as a graph. The interface was too cluttered and tangled (like a bowl of spaghetti) to be useful (see Figure 3.5). To avoid the spaghetti layout, the interface was improved to include a *museum layout* that maps nodes metaphorically into rooms of a museum. In a museum layout system a reader may select a room to reveal enlarged detail of that room. For an actual museum this is done by using a diagram of a museum with various subjects in each room, such as art, science, or geography. The user looks at the map and has to move to the relevant place using commands, such as forward, left and right. The user then sees a picture relating to the topic of interest and can select further information by using a mouse on the picture itself. Subsequently, menus may be displayed.

On the hypertext system screen, the user may not be able to readily discern how much information is available or how it is structured. Hierarchical or fisheye views help users get a sense of the overall information landscape. In one *fisheye view,* the reader gets to see a 'table of contents' in one window, and by selecting a heading in one way the user can view the contents associated with that heading in another window. By selecting the heading in another way, the user can cause the 'table of contents' underneath that heading to either unfold or fold (see Figure 3.6). This simple cognitive model makes this fisheye view attractive [172]. The concept of the fisheye view is based upon the analogy to a fisheye camera lens, which distorts the image so that the nearest objects are seen in detail and distant objects are compressed.

Figure 3.5: *Spaghetti Layout.* Plate of spaghetti on left, and museum floor plan on right. The plate of spaghetti suggests the disorder that can be perceived when dealing with hypertext.

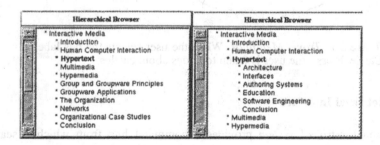

Figure 3.6: *Fold-Unfold*: Two windows are shown from a hypertext system with a fold-unfold feature. In the window on the left the chapter names under the title 'Interactive Media' are shown but no sections within the chapters are shown. After the user has selected the chapter heading 'Hypertext', then the sections within that chapter unfold, as illustrated in the window on the right.

To provide the kinesthetic or tangible feel which people appreciate on paper or in person-person interactions one might exploit space and time metaphors [41]. For instance, a guided tour across a town with the help of a map and a tour company suggests the *travel metaphor.* In an interface that exploits the travel metaphor, guided tours are initiated when the user selects a coach icon labeled with the topic of the tour (see Figure 3.7). The user is then guided round a sequence of presentations on the topic until the tour ends, at which point he is returned to the starting point. In experiments contrasting interfaces with and without travel metaphors [2], guided tours allowed more accurate overviews of the available material and resulted in a higher rate of exposure to new rather than repeated information.

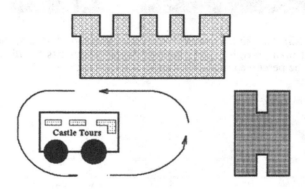

Figure 3.7: *Travel Metaphor.* When the user selects the bus labeled 'Castle Tours', the user is taken to nodes about castles.

3.2.2   Retrieval Interface

The traditional *retrieval system* provides a command line from which a searcher specifies a *query.* The system then retrieves items from the information space that match that query. Hypertext systems offer to augment this facility by helping searchers formulate their query through first browsing semantic networks which characterize the information content of the system.

A fictitious screen is presented in which a user is looking for information about hypertension. The user first has the choice of browsing the *semantic net* or entering a term directly. Say the user enters the term 'hypertension'. Next the conceptual neighborhood around hypertension appears on the screen. That neighborhood includes both the hierarchically related terms for hypertension and a constellation of terms connected by 'etiology', 'prognosis', 'treatment', and other such links that are appropriate for the disease hypertension (see Figure 3.8).

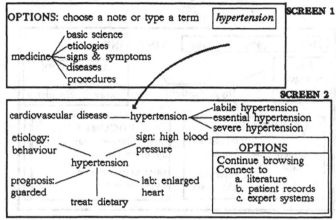

Figure 3.8: *Retrieval Interface for a Richly-Connected Term.* In the top screen, the user requested information about 'hypertension'. In the lower screen the user sees the nodes around 'hypertension'.

If the user now chooses to pursue the 'lab link' of hypertension, there appears another screen which shows both specific 'lab links', namely 'xrays' and 'chemistry', and specific 'enlarged heart' terms (see Figure 3.9). Simultaneously there appears: 1) a time line and 2) the titles of documents. Users can interact with the time line to specify the dates of publication for *retrieved documents.*

The Worldviews system uses a thesaurus as a conceptual map of an information space to support both search and navigation of the information space [57]. The three basic components of *Worldviews* are automatic indexing, an information retrieval system and a user interface, all relying on a thesaurus. Thesaurus entries are assigned to documents as content descriptors by automatic indexing. A document that explicitly refers to the terms 'wasp' and 'bees' but not 'insects' will be indexed under the broader term as well as under the narrower terms.

The Worldviews information retrieval system uses the *thesaurus* to interpret user queries as conjunctions of thesaurus entries and then points to documents containing the terms. Subtopics that are associated with the query topic and are one level below the topic are also displayed. Users can access documents and explore subtopics and further documents online. Subtopics may lead to more specific subtopics at deeper levels which can be similarly explored.

The interface to a retrieval system should make apparent the relevant options to a user [134]. For instance, the interface might make it easy for searchers to request information written across some period of time. However, the most complex part of

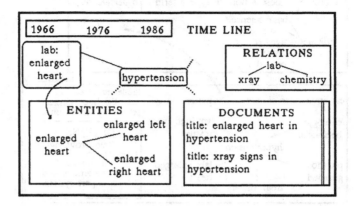

Figure 3.9: *Expansion of Relations.* The user has followed the link from hypertension of laboratory studies and found (via xray) enlarged heart.

the retrieval interface must support access by *content descriptions.* When a very large semantic net is accessed via a computer screen, the user may need to change the contents of the screen many times to find the nodes of interest. This difficulty has been substantiated in experiments on the impact of depth of menu on performance which indicated that performance time and errors increased as the depth of the menu increased [170]. To counteract this problem the user might be allowed parallel modes of presentation of data.

3.3   Authoring Systems

The first *document production* systems began to emerge in the 1960s. These were simple extensions to program editing tools, basically low-level formatters. Formatters are programs that can interpret commands embedded within text. For instance, the command '.ce' may be inserted in a text, and when the text is processed by the document formatter, the '.ce' command causes the next line of text to be centered on the page. In the last thirty years, formatters have evolved and diversified to a high degree of sophistication. The commands were enhanced to take advantage of the possibilities offered by new generations of printing technology and to handle non-text elements in compound documents.

In a document production system based on a formatter, the input and updating of the document description is handled by a separate editor, which can submit the document to the formatter. A development of this process was to combine the functions of the editor and formatter, to produce *editor-formatters* which were the precursors of word processors. Based initially on the use of graphics screens to display an image corresponding to what would be produced on a laser printer, most word processors of today exhibit the 'What You See is What You Get' (WYSIWYG) approach to document production. A command in a WYSIWYG system is interpreted immediately upon being expressed. For instance, a command to center a line immediately centers the line on the screen. The center command is never explicitly visible in the text.

Having followed the path from an interface that presents only plain text to a *WYSIWYG* one which dynamically displays physical layout information, the developers of authoring tools took the next step of offering dynamic links. In a traditional document, a pointer to another part of the document must be manually pursued but in a hypertext system this link is defined by the author and then the reader can point to the link and the computer follows it.

Intermedia was developed in the mid-1980s at Brown University Institute for Research in Information and Scholarship [201]. A document is created with *Intermedia* in a direct manipulation environment. Cutting and pasting can be done from one application to another. Links may be created between any two blocks. A block is defined as any material which the user selects within a document. One selection provides the source of a link and another selection determines the destination block. A bi-directional link is created which can then be followed in either direction by user choice. Intermedia supports the creation of graphics and animation. Paths can also be defined as a sequence of links.

The first popular personal computer hypertext authoring product was HyperCard [61]. *HyperCard* presents information on cards and several cards may appear on the screen at one time [106]. Icons or buttons may be inserted in a card to link the button to another card. A link between two cards in a stack is created by entering link mode, defining a button in the one card, and then pointing at the other card. The meaning of a link can be extended beyond 'goto that card' by adding a procedure to the description of the link. For instance, authors commonly specify that in going from one card to another the reader should see a fade-out from the source card and a fade-in to the destination card (see Figure 3.10).

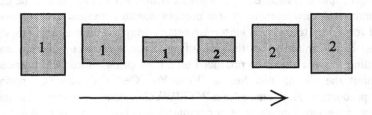

Figure 3.10: *Fading*. The card with a '1' in it is fading from the
screen before the card with a '2' in it fades into the screen.

3.4   The MUCH System

A sequence of hypertext authoring systems have been developed under the name of
MUCH for *Many Using and Creating Hypertext*. Early versions used various software
and hardware platforms, such as relational database management systems on
mainframe computers and HyperCard on Macintoshes [153]. The current version is
based on Unix workstations and has its own database system.

The MUCH system is based on the *Dexter model*.   A network of nodes and links is
defined in a storage layer.   A within-component layer contains the actual media
content to which nodes point. The linked nodes form an extended semantic net with
each node as a semantic unit append to end of existing paragraph. To add a new link
to a document, the user exercises a 'Create link' option (see Figure 3.11). Other
authoring options support the creation of nodes, the deletion of nodes or links, and so
on.

A document view can be generated by traversing the semantic net following a certain
strategy [154]. A document is actually only certain kinds of nodes' contents
connected together with certain relationships. In the information base, different kinds
of material are represented by varying link types. When a user needs to generate a
document, he can set a criteria to specify which type(s) of link the traversal program
will follow. For example, one can generate a document with or without other authors'
annotations by turning on or off the annotation switch for the traversal program from a
dialog box (see Figure 3.12).

When the MUCH system is started, the hypertext information is presented on two
separate windows with the fold-unfold outline in one window and the content of a
selected node in another. When the user selects a node in the *fold-unfold outline,* the

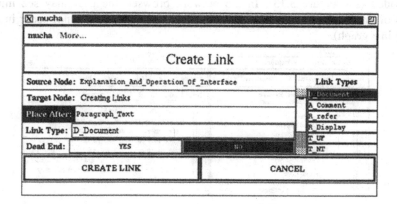

Figure 3.11: *Creating a Link.* The user creates a link within this 'dialog box' by specifying source node and target node. The user may also place the link in an order relative to the other links from the source node with the 'Place After' entry.

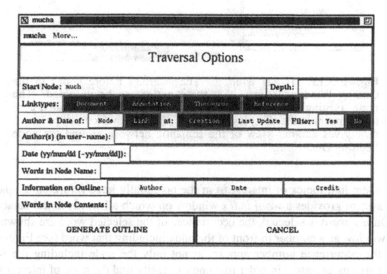

Figure 3.12: *Traversal Dialog Box.* With the traversal option dialog box, the user can specify a start node, link types, and such and then get a new outline of the information space based on this specification.

associated content appears in the content window (see Figure 3.13). Although on the interface, the logical network is presented as a tree, the data in the logical network is truly an unrestricted network rather than a tree. The outline on the hierarchical browser (outline window) is only a specific view of (a part of) the logical network. To enable users to follow the links which are not shown in the outline, a *network browser* is provided (see Figure 3.13). In the network browser, the user may see multiple parents of one node and may discover a cyclical path (a cycle can not occur in a tree but can in a graph).

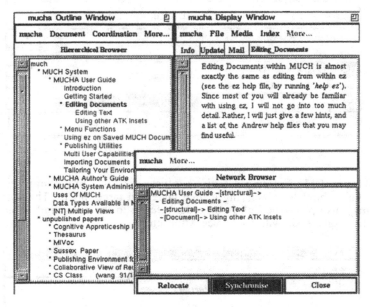

Figure 3.13: *MUCH Window.* The asterisks before nodes in the Outline Window indicate that these nodes can be unfolded. The node 'Editing Documents' has been selected and its associated content appears in the 'Display Window'. The 'Network Browser' window gives another view of the semantic network around the node 'Editing Documents'.

To help users find topics of interest from the potentially huge information space, the MUCH system provides a *word index* window on which all words in the database are listed. Once a word is selected, the occurrences of the selected word are shown on the outline window as a number in front of the node including that word (see Figure 3.14). In fact, the occurrence number appears at not only the node including the selected word but also its ancestors in order that one can easily find the node of interest when it is folded under a high level node. However, the number shown at the ancestor node is the occurrences in the whole sub-tree. This fold-unfold view of word distribution has proven valuable in searching tasks [29][43].

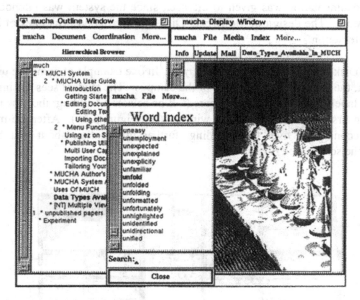

Figure 3.14: *Word Index*. Word index utility in the MUCH system to help users to find a topic in the information base. The word 'unfold' has been selected and is shown to occur 2 times in 'menu function' and 1 time in 'unpublished papers'.

3.5   Education

Education is basically about augmenting a student's model of the world. The teacher needs to present experiences or models to which the student can relate and from which the student draws new insights. Computer systems presenting linked information can convey these richer perspectives and support the necessary interactivity in a way which traditional information could not.

3.5.1   Branching Instructions

Drexel University has for years required all entering freshmen to have access to a personal computer. One need created by this policy was that of introducing students to the capabilities of their computers. To this end the University created a consulting service of which the 'The Drexel Disk' was a part [85]. The *Drexel Disk* was distributed to all Freshmen at Drexel University from 1984 to 1989. One design goal of the Drexel Disk was to create landmarks to orient users. Another goal was to place the burden of communication and organization on the computer rather than on the user. The menu structure was shallow and wide. Multiple paths to each point were provided. Graphics were extensively used to provide information about space and time. No documentation was given to the user, since the system was intended to be self-explanatory. The design of the Drexel Disk followed good principles of human-computer interaction.

The Drexel Disk provides an attractive *interface*. In one example of someone using the Drexel Disk, the user is taken to a map of the campus. The student sees the university with streets labeled and buildings numbered. If he selects a building, then the name of that building first appears in the lower window (see Figure 3.15). After the mouse is clicked a second time over that building, further information about that building appears on the screen (see Figure 3.16).

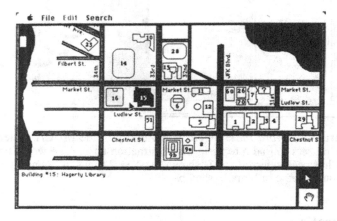

Figure 3.15: *Drexel Map.* The cursor has been placed over Hagerty Library on the map of Drexel University.

The Drexel Disk has been successfully used by students to obtain information about personal computer facilities at Drexel University. However, since the software was developed there and was not widely used elsewhere, Drexel remained responsible for any modifications to the software. Additionally, as with any such directory service, the directory information itself must be regularly updated. For instance, the hours of operation of the Library may change, and the information in the Drexel Disk about the Library would then need also to be changed (see Figure 3.16). Since index maintenance of the Drexel Disk was expensive, the developers decided in 1989 to switch to a standard software system, namely *HyperCard*. Sophisticated users could then take advantage of the well-documented and popular features of HyperCard to themselves implement updates to the information system and propose that the updates become part of the next release of the directory. The university was also no longer responsible for the development of the system software. In the academic year 1989-1990 all Freshmen at Drexel University were given the campus, computer directory in a HyperCard environment [86].

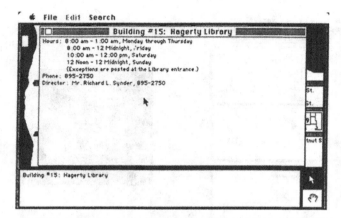

Figure 3.16: *Details of one Building.* After the second click on the map location of Hagerty Library, the library's hours of operation and other details come to the screen.

In *branching computer-assisted instruction,* information is presented to the student followed by questions. On the selection of a response, the program comments on its appropriateness. In this way the student gets specific feedback for specific mistakes. In branching computer-assisted instruction, the extent of learner control and characteristics of the interface can be tailored by the author or teacher to match the requirements of the student. The Drexel Disk includes simple examples of branching computer-assisted instruction. For example, if the user chooses the 'Truth or Consequences' option from the 'Rights and Responsibilities' screen [85], he is then taken to questions which test his knowledge of the subjects offered elsewhere (see Figure 3.17). The next screen is a question about buying a piece of software from another student for very little money (see Figure 3.18). If the user answers 'false', then the computer notes that this answer is incorrect and informs the user accordingly (see Figure 3.19).

3.5.2 Simulation

The *simulation model* is one of the most effective applications of computer-based instruction. For instance, a computer can realistically model a physiological process or a pharmacological experiment, or even a patient. Simulation models can be interactive, and respond to the student with evaluations of decisions taken.

At the Ancona Medical School lessons have been written on arthritis following the hypertext architecture of the program *Guide* [35]. This architecture provides for the multilevelled organization of information using 'notes', 'buttons', and 'cross-

Figure 3.17: *Start with Truth and Consequences*. The user is selecting the 'Truth & Consequences' icon on the screen.

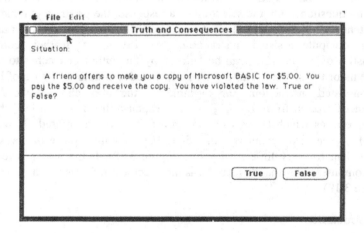

Figure 3.18: *Drexel Question*. The user is posed a question and must choose 'True' or 'False'.

references'. Interactive, high-definition images are included to help the student, particularly to illustrate medical procedures with radiological images. Overall, the lessons were adjudged successful by students.

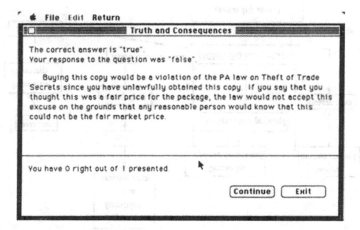

Figure 3.19: *Drexel Answer.* The user is told why 'False' is not the correct answer.

The Guide software was also used to prepare a *questionnaire* about the medical treatment for diseases. At meetings dealing with the care of rheumatic patients, the paper questionnaire was augmented by an opening projection on a screen of the same questions in hypertext form. Keywords within each question acted as buttons that could be selected to display answers and comments. For example, a list of the side-effects induced by a drug could be expanded by clicking on the word 'side-effects'.

Another *simulation* deals with a young man who presented with a severe asthmatic attack after a walk (see Figure 3.20). The season is spring and the walk was in the countryside, both facts suggesting an allergic etiology of the disease. If the student's choice is to perform the case history or the skin tests, the computerized tutor comments that the choice is wrong given that the priority is to relieve the patient's symptoms. An essential physical examination and appropriate treatment should be immediately performed. Once the prescription of the correct medication results in normalization of the respiratory sound and congratulations from the tutor, a case history may be taken. The tutor emphasizes the key questions that should be asked in order to determine the possible allergic origin of a respiratory disease. The student performs the skin tests and evaluates the reactions. Diagnosis of the allergy pollens may be made and a correct treatment planned.

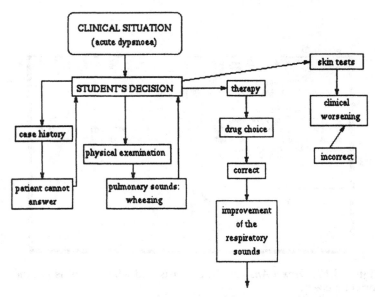

Figure 3.20: *Flow chart.* Flow chart describing all routes that the student may follow managing the simulated patients affected by allergic asthma [35].

The experiences at the *Ancona Medical School* were positive. It was concluded that hypertext was an effective and powerful learning environment that could be used to supplement, but not replace, traditional methods. It was noted that the direct management of a patient in distress evoked sympathy on the part of the student, which indicated that the hypertext could provide a link between theory and bedside practice.

3.5.3 Pathology

In 1985 the *Cornell School of Medicine* began experimenting with the idea of using computers to make the learning process more efficient [40]. As a result, students taking the course Introductory Pathology can enroll in an electronic version of the course. Macintosh computers tied into a database are scattered throughout the campus for student access. Students can study online textbooks, run simulated laboratories, or test their mastery of physiology by viewing online dissections.

Seven *gigabytes* of images and bibliographical material can be searched intelligently, cross-referenced, and printed. Software includes applications written in HyperCard, Guide, and other software tools developed in-house. The opening screen allows students to indicate which course they are taking. A selection of materials is available for biochemistry, anatomy, neuroscience, parasitology, physiology, radiology, and pathology.

One online application is an electronic pathology text called *HyperPath*, which includes large portions of a version of the well-known book *Robbins Pathological Basis of Disease* . This was written in Guide and includes both text and images pulled from the original. Professors can add text and graphics nodes as needed. Terms can be linked to pop-up notes that provide definitions or citations. The textbook is structured in a three-layer system containing the instructor's lectures, the textbook itself, and relevant citations.

A visual archive called *Carousel* includes over 3000 images. Carousel images can be paired with questions. Diseased organs can be shown on the screen and the student asked to make a diagnosis. The images can also be used to study anatomy or to compare images of normal against abnormal tissue cells. Images are brought into Carousel using a scanner and may be retouched with the use of image software.

Another program is used to perform *simulated laboratory experiments* that otherwise would be performed on live cats. The system can be set up to test the response of various drugs on simulated cat muscle. The students choose which drug to inject, in what quantity, and then electrically stimulate the muscle and record the results on a simulated strip chart. Much more control over the results can be achieved than is possible with real live muscle. No two runs of the program produce the same results.

Another program consists of a *patient simulation* system in which students are presented with situations requiring medical intervention. Students are provided with written case histories. Forms are used to request diagnostic tests. Once the tests are done and all the questions answered, the computer compares the students' actions with a recommended course of action and provides suggestions.

3.6 Software Engineering

Software engineering is a natural area for hypertext. This section will first describe hypertext authoring for software documentation which provides a new and more powerful documentation. Then the more general utility of hypertext to link all the information of the software life-cycle is described through two systems that support such linking.

3.6.1 Software Manuals

Because of higher publication costs and growing environmental concern, online documentation has become increasingly attractive as an alternative to conventional printed books within corporate documentation centers. In contrast to hypertext developed for students, which emphasizes browsing for learning purposes, commercial hypertext must have a strong task orientation, emphasizing the quick solution of specific user problems or providing fast access to just the information that is needed. The lack of a strong task orientation results in hypertext that is hard to use. To address this problem, the Computer Systems Operation at Hewlett-Packard has developed a *rule-based methodology* which ensures a high degree of task orientation [28].

Extensive interviews with *Hewlett-Packard managers* revealed that they had particular concerns for *liability*. If manual users make a serious error such as deleting all their critical data while following the instructions in the manual, then the company which produced the manual can be sued. Since hypertext may indicate more explicit paths through a text space than a paper document would, the authors have more power to present important paths but also greater risk of providing a path which mistakenly assumes some previous path taken by the user.

From interviews with users of hypertext systems, a set of general *usability goals* for hypertext volumes has emerged. These goals include the following:

•   Ensuring the user's completion of each task.
•   Ensuring an appropriate time to task completion.
•   Satisfying the user's expectations.
•   Gaining the user's acceptance and trust of the system.
•   Avoiding disorientation.

These goals must be met if users (customers, in the commercial world) are to be satisfied with hypertext volumes. The authoring method, described next, incorporates these usability goals in particular rules, conformity with which can be measured using software tools.

Task analysis is an important method in the development of requirements and designs for software which helps ensure that the software will be usable. At Hewlett-Packard the emphasis on usability leads to a stress on task analysis across many fronts for software development and other kinds of product development as well. In particular, task analysis is the first phase of authoring at Hewlett-Packard.

As the software is being developed, writers, together with product engineers and marketing experts select customers as subjects for a task analysis. Different types of *customers* are chosen, such as system administrators or programmers with a specific level of experience. These customers are observed either on the job using a current product or in a controlled laboratory setting using a prototype of a new product, such as an operating system. Then they are asked which tasks are the most difficult to do, as well as which tasks are the most common and which are the most dangerous or error-prone. For each task, the customer is asked to describe the steps required to carry it out.

In the main task of authoring, technical writers create the hypertext according to a set of rules. One rule states that each *primitive task* (a task which does not contain any other tasks) must be represented as a separate node. Another rule states that for each task node, an associated Examples node, Details node, and Errors node must be defined. Each object from the task analysis must also be represented as a node in the hypertext. As the process of authoring continues, the writer creates each required node and writes the content for it.

A more complex rule defines a *task-specific path* as a sequence of primitive tasks. As an example, the higher level task 'Creating a New Logon' in the operating system might contain several primitive tasks:

- Creating a New Account
- Creating a New User
- Creating a Home Group
- Assigning Access Rights

In coding this example, the author creates a node for the task-specific path 'Creating a New Logon', and separate nodes for each of the primitive tasks. The name of the task-specific path appears in the Table of Contents.

The authoring process should produce hypertext with an improved degree of usability, since it employs rules that are based on usability goals. Validation that a hypertext volume complies with the authoring rules can only provide limited validation of usability. Testing with users is the only means for verifying *usability*.

3.6.2 Neptune

Broadly, system software, ranging from operating systems to various utilities can be thought of as systems that support software development. However, there are systems that are specifically designed to support software development in an integrated way. CASE (*Computer-Aided Software Engineering*) is a generic term that refers to integrated environments for the development of software.

The advantages of using hypertext systems over database systems in CASE tools are the flexibility in handling the diversity of representations of software documents and the linking of these documents [37]. *Neptune* and *Dynamic Design* are hypertext systems whose goal is to support software engineering [13]. The base level of both Neptune and Dynamic Design is a transaction-based server (or hypertext engine), called the *Hypertext Abstract Machine* [24]. The Hypertext Abstract Machine associates attributes with each link and node in order to facilitate identification of the stored data and its relationships to other data stored in the system.

Neptune's user interface supports four browsers: a 'graph browser', a 'document browser', a 'node browser', and a 'node difference browser':

- The *graphic browser* displays a directed graph of node names visible from a starting node.
- The *document browser* supports successive application of a set of candidate nodes whose names are displayed in a series of windows. Each window displays the names of nodes satisfying the specified predicate when applied to previous candidates.
- The node browser displays the content of a node and allows user to edit the content or link the node to another node.
- The *node difference browser* displays the differences between two versions of the same nodes by placing two node browsers side by side and highlighting the discrepancies between the two versions.

A query mechanism directly accesses a set of nodes and their interconnecting links. In Dynamic Design nodes contain all the project components. Links are used to connect these nodes. Related nodes and links are grouped into *contexts*. A link or a node can have any number of attributes. Attributes label the types of nodes and links. The attribute 'projectComponent' is applied to nodes and can have any value from the set of project components such as: {requirements, design, source code, tests, documentation}. The attribute 'relatesTo' is applied to links and can have any value from the set {leadsTo, comments, refersTo, callsProcedure, followsFrom, implements, isDefinedBy}. A node may contain any amount or type of information. A link is not restricted to pointing to an entire node but can point to any place within a node. Contexts are defined by grouping nodes and links with certain values. For instance, nodes with the 'projectComponent' value of code are implicitly grouped into a context and each node gets an attribute called 'System'. Contexts play an important role in both Neptune and Dynamic Design.

3.6.3   HyperCASE

HyperCASE is an architectural framework for integrating a collection of *CASE* tools. It supports software developers in project management, system analysis, design and coding [37]. The system provides a visual, integrated and customizable software-engineering environment consisting of loosely coupled tools for presentations involving both text and diagrams. The reuse of designs and concepts at the earliest possible stages of a project is one of the system's primary goals. The integration of tools for interactively constructing system descriptions into a uniform CASE environment demands that certain fundamental requirements are met:

- There must be different document classes at different development stages.
- Documents must be reusable by the various tools in the environment.
- Navigation must be possible among the various types of document (see Figure 3.21).
- All documents must be coherent and consistent throughout the software's life-cycle.

Software engineers frequently need to see different representations in parallel. For instance, a process symbol in a dataflow diagram could be viewed in conjunction with the code associated with the process, or its representation in a state diagram, or its description in a section of a systems requirement specification or a corresponding paragraph in the feasibility description, or any and all of these simultaneously.

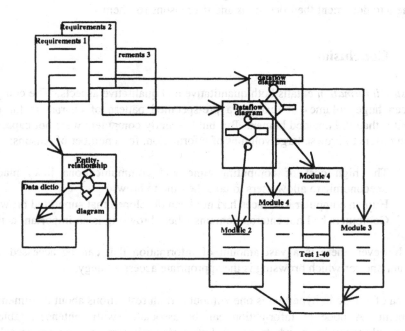

Figure 3.21: *Navigating among software documents* [37]. Rectangles correspond to document components and arrows to links from one component to another.

HyperCASE's architecture contains three subsystems: *HyperDict, HyperEdit,* and *HyperBase.* HyperDict stores all the HyperCASE documents and is a common data dictionary. HyperEdit is an authoring system that provides standard text and diagram editors that support major software development methods. Each editor is an instantiation of HyperEdit's graphical environment, tailored to manipulate specific classes of objects with a range of attributes and behaviors. New object types and their components can be described by authorized users.

HyperBase is a knowledge-based repository of hypertext software documents. It comprises base tools and CASE tools. Base tools accommodate the mechanisms and structures to organize a generic hypertext system, while CASE tools help ensure that a document is consistent and complete and that design components are reusable. The base tools include a document manager, a configuration manager, and design tracker. The *document manager* analyzes, indexes, aggregates, and stores graphics and text attributes to enable interdocument linking and navigation. The *configuration manager* controls the current state of the knowledge-base and determines dependencies in the project's structure. It applies heuristics to ensure that system descriptions, their versions, and the products they define are consistent. Completed software-engineering systems often omit intermediate design documentation. The design tracker forces designers to document their decisions and the reasons for them.

3.7   Conclusion

Accessing information entails both quantitative and qualitative aspects. The computer can scan huge volumes of text for a pre-specified pattern of characters far more efficiently than the unaided human. But until recently computers were not capable of allowing users to browse large volumes of information, for a number of reasons:

- The high cost of computing time and communications links made it uneconomic to allow users to take the time to browse.
- Human computer interfaces had not been developed that supported browsing.
- Computers had not entered domains where browsing is an important activity.

Now, however, there is a vast amount of information that can be accessed via a computer and for which browsing is the appropriate access strategy.

The idea of a *node* in hypertext is one without certain restrictions about its dimensions or content. A node of information can be associated with sentences, tables of numbers, photographs, or whatever. A *link* is also arbitrary as there are no rules to say where it shall be made. But unless some discipline is followed in creating and linking nodes, users will be lost.

A convenient *architectural model* of the implementation of a hypertext system employs three layers. The within component layer, the storage layer, and the interface. The storage layer contains the model of the hypertext as nodes and links. The textual content of nodes are in the 'within component layer'. The interface tailors views of the storage layer to the needs of the user.

The *Many Using and Creating hypertext* (MUCH) system supports structured hypertext authoring and multiple access routes. The architecture of the MUCH system is faithful to the de-facto Dexter standard which includes a user interface layer, a node and link logical layer, and a storage layer. Outlines of the hypertext logical graph can be dynamically generated and presented in fold-unfold form.

The fields of *education* and *software engineering* are significantly different and highlight the range of domains to which hypertext is applicable. In schools people can be exposed to new technology as part of their education, but sophisticated technology may be scarce. Software engineers use machines regularly and are thus in many ways to be expected to be the first to comfortably accept new computer-related support. In both educational and software engineering domains, hypertext offers advantages over traditional information organization.

Within the educational domain, one can see many examples of the ways in which *interactivity* can transform media. A teacher may ask a student whether the day is longer than the night and on the student answering 'day' the teacher might say 'no' and next ask about the relationship between summer and winter as regards the relative lengths of day and night. This kind of interactive teaching is infrequently practiced in the large classroom where hundreds of students take notes from one lecturer. Hypertext systems can support this interactivity.

4
Multimedia

Multimedia may generally mean any mixture of media but in this book the term usually refers to *time-based media,* including video and audio. Of the two perspectives from which multimedia systems can be viewed, the *user-centered perspective* focuses on the possibilities offered to the user for manipulating richer information using natural sensory abilities [3]. The technology perspective addresses the computational and representational requirements of multimedia — this chapter takes the *technological perspective.*

While the popularity of multimedia has grown enormously in the 1990s, the history of multimedia naturally traces to earlier years. One of the first major engineering accomplishments with combining video and computers was the work of Douglas Engelbart in his Augment system in the mid-1960s [48]. Around the same time, *Nicholas Negroponte* started the Architecture Machine Group in the Architecture Department at MIT. This group subsequently developed the Spatial Data Management System which synchronized video screens and other projection devices through joysticks, a touch screen, and stylus. Auditory cues were used to help people navigate in an information space [15].

4.1 Views

When an author prepares a message, the choice of medium provides a view on the message. An initial step in this direction is taken when a photograph is combined with text, or a spreadsheet with a pie chart, and so on. Photographs, text, spreadsheets, and pie charts are not time-based media, while sound and video are. Yet, allowing readers to have different *media views* of the same information is a kind of multimedia particularly when multiple views can be generated dynamically.

The *Andrew Toolkit* supports the development of editors that allow users to edit text, equations, graphs, tables, pictures, and so forth, all in a single program [16]. For example, an Andrew Toolkit document containing both text and a picture appears to be a single object, but the text and the picture are actually separate objects that can be manipulated independently (see Figure 4.1). For example, if one pops-up the menus in the text region, one will see a full set of menus for editing text. If one pops-up the menus over the picture, however, one will see a different set of menus for editing the picture.

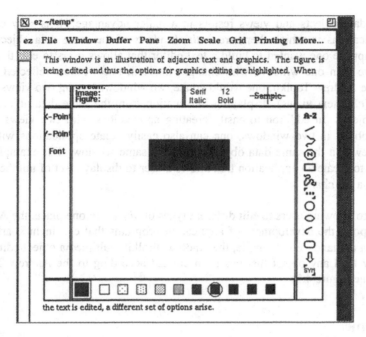

Figure 4.1: *Andrew Text and Graphics.* Andrew Toolkit document with picture-editing menus.

The Andrew Toolkit provides a set of basic objects to use as building blocks for developing applications. Two of the most important of these objects are *data objects* and *views*. A data object contains the information to be displayed; a view contains information about how the data is to be displayed and how the user will be able to interact with the data (e.g., via keyboard, menus, or mouse). A data object/view pair is an inset. In a widow with text and graphics (see Figure 4.1) there are two insets, one for the text (text data object/text view) and one for the picture (picture data object/picture view). The text data object contains the actual characters (e.g., 'This window is an illustration'), style information (e.g., bold, italics) and pointers to any embedded data objects (e.g., the picture data object). The text view contains information such as the currently selected text, the portion of the text that is visible on the screen, and so forth, and also provides methods for drawing the text on the screen and handling various input events (keyboard, menus, mouse). Likewise, the picture data object contains the elements of the drawing, such as lines and shading. The picture view provides methods for drawing the picture on the screen and handling various input events (keyboard, menus, mouse).

Separating data objects and views results in a major advantage: it is very easy to create applications in which there are *multiple views* of the same data object. For example, suppose one wanted to build a text editor that allows users to edit the same data in more than one window, with changes made in one window reflected in the other. In the Andrew Toolkit, one would create two windows having two views of the same type (e.g., text views), displaying information from the same data object (e.g., text data object). In addition to easily creating applications with two views of the same data object in two windows, one can also easily create applications with two different views on the same data object within the same window. For example, one might want to create an application that allows a user to display a set of numbers in a table and in a pie chart.

In addition to allowing users to edit different types of *objects* in one place, the Andrew Toolkit supports the development of application programs that can include arbitrary objects upon demand. For example, the Andrew Toolkit multimedia object editor can dynamically load any object that has been created according to the Andrew Toolkit protocols (see Figure 4.2).

4.2   Time

Time-based media, such as video and audio, may have *synchronization* requirements [121]. A newscast can be used to illustrate the importance of timing in multimedia. Various presentational and representational media produced with various mechanical means all arrive on the television screen with some critical timing considerations. The storyboard for the newscast might usefully distinguish voice, video, graphics, image, and the newsperson (see Figure 4.3). The importance of the speech being synchronized with the newsperson's mouth opening is just one of the more obvious synchronization requirements.

Data can be time-dependent at some times and not at others. For instance, a set of cross-sections of a body is in the first instance related by anatomy or space. If one, however, wanted to present a time-based path through the cross-section, then temporal connections between the components would be required. *Time dependencies* present at the time of data capture are natural, such as the sequence of images in a video, or implied, such as when audio and video are simultaneously recorded. On the other hand, data can have no obvious natural ordering, such as a set of randomly selected photographs of people, and this data is called static. Yet, even on static data some temporal ordering can be imposed.

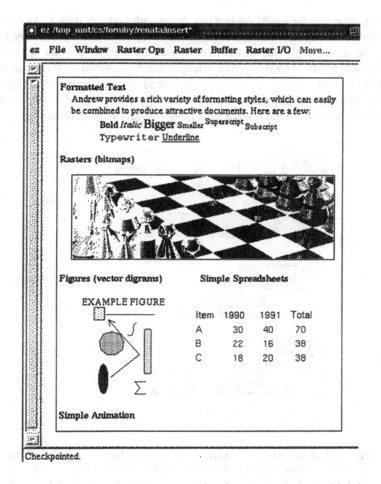

Figure 4.2: *Andrew Inset*. An example of content window which includes various insets.

```
MEDIA               TIME LINE->
voice          |hello ...........read story
video          |city traffic ....show newsman
graphics       |station logo ...............
image          |............sun rising......
newsman        |shuffles papers...read story
```

Figure 4.3: *Newscast and Timing* The different media are in the left-most column and the time-line is on the right. The textual description inside the media-time space shows activity.

Models of time can be based on instants or on intervals. A time instant is a zero-length moment in time, such as 11:00 a.m. A time interval is defined by two time instants, one at the beginning of the interval and the other at the end of the interval. These two endpoints naturally define a length for the interval.   Two *time intervals* may relate to one another in time in numerous distinct ways (see Figure 4.4). Effectively dealing with the richness of relationships in time-based media are apparent to people in everyday life but remain a challenge to information technology.

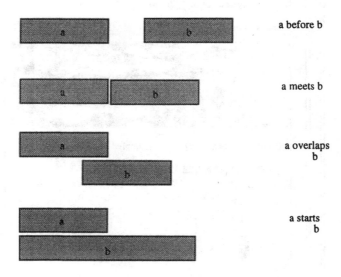

Figure 4.4: *Relationships between Two Time Intervals.* Four of the possible 13 relationships between two time intervals are indicated here.

For authoring of time-based media both graph-based and script-based representations have been developed. Graph-based representations have the advantage over scripting languages of providing a pictorial representation of synchronization. *Petri nets* are special graphs which may be interpreted as having media events at the nodes. Edges go from the media events to synchronizing transitions and from those transitions go other edges to other media events [179]. The Petri net can usefully depict events in parallel as all edges from a transition will be initiated at the same time, and it can also be used to enforce synchronization as a transition will not be crossed unless all media events which are providing incoming edges to the transition have completed (see Figure 4.5).

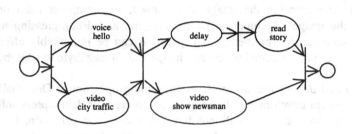

Figure 4.5: *Petri Net*:   This Petri net represents some of the media synchronization in the newscast which was given earlier.   The voice event 'hello' and the video event 'city traffic' occur at the same time at the beginning of the newscast.   After and only after they are both completed, the video event 'show newsman' begins, while a voice 'delay' is in effect.   Then the voice reads the story while the newsman is shown.

4.3   Compression

The *storage space* needed for multimedia may be enormous. A simple photograph can require more storage space than an entire book. One alphanumeric character can be stored in 1 byte of the computer. An average word is 4 characters, and a typical page of text contains about 500 words. If a book is 200 pages long and has only alphanumeric text, then it occupies about 200 x 500 x 4 bytes or 400,000 bytes. The storage space for a photograph is surprisingly large in contrast to that for a book. A photo may contain 1,000 by 1,000 dots or pixels. If representing a dot in color requires a byte, then the storage space for one photo would be about one megabyte. Thus storing one high-resolution photograph may require more space than 100,000 alphanumeric characters require.

Silent video may contain about 30 photos or frames per second. Thus a minute of the video occupies about 60 x 30 megabytes or 1,800 megabytes. Thousands of text books without pictures would occupy no more space than *one minute of video*.

Text is highly symbolic and a description of the operation of a company might be portrayed in a few pages of text, whereas video of the company operation might have difficulty in conveying the same kind of information. People do not yet have a language for abstracting information from images, instead images are stored as zeroes and ones with no semantic significance. Methods do, however, exist to *compress* the information in an image. If a large space in the image is of a constant character, then this constancy can be encoded so that less space is required to store the image. Of course, in later presenting the image to a viewer, the computer must decode or decompress the image. Techniques for compressing and decompressing media are vital to the success of hypermedia. Compression can be remarkably effective and might reduce the space required to store an image from a megabyte to a kilobyte.

Compression and *decompression* are time consuming operations. One challenge for hypermedia system developers is to be able to compress or decompress information quickly enough so that users will not have to wait for information, because the computer is busy compressing or decompressing [8]. Two types of compression-decompression relations are the asymmetric and symmetric. *Asymmetric relations* are those that require frequent use of the decompression process, but for which the compression process is done once and for all at the production of the program. Asymmetric applications include electronic publishing, video games, and delivery of movies. *Symmetric relations* require equal use of the compression and the decompression process. Video telephone and video conferencing are symmetric applications.

4.4   Video

Video is an enormously important aspect of multimedia but also difficult to handle. It makes enormous demands on a typical computer for memory and speed. Hardware and software are developed to cater to video needs. The hardware makes compression or decompression faster and thus allows higher resolution video on the computer screen.

4.4.1   MPEG

The basic functions and motion coding schemes required for video compression can be combined in different ways to obtain various degrees of video quality, data compression, bandwidth, and coding speed. One aspect of video compression is motion compensation. *Predictive interframe coding,* also called 'forward' *motion compensation,* is initiated with one coded frame. Each subsequent frame is compared to its predecessor and only the differences between the two are coded. Because there may be some loss of detail during the process of compressing and decompressing each predicted frame, new frames are periodically recorded.

During the 1980s standards committees worked to establish uniform approaches to video compression. The *Motion Pictures Experts Group* (MPEG) standard addresses the compression of video and exploits the fact that pixels change little from frame to frame in moving video images. The MPEG method first takes a reference frame, and then breaks the frame into blocks of 8-by-8 pixels [137]. Those blocks are then transferred from the spatial domain to the frequency domain by implementing a cosine transform. In the frequency domain, elements that are not visible with the human eye are readily isolated and then removed. Once several sequential frames have been handled in this way, motion estimation is performed to determine whether a block has moved relative to the reference frame. Vectors are chosen to signify what blocks have moved and in what direction. A new reference frame is chosen about four times per second. The MPEG standard can also deal with audio. The premise of *MPEG* is that a video signal and its associated audio can become a form of computer data, i.e., a data type to be integrated with text and graphics; and motion video and its associated audio can be delivered over existing computer and telecommunication networks.

4.4.2 Video Software Support

Microsoft Video For Windows (VFW) is a software digital video solution, and thus on most machines is limited in the motion video it can display. The default video window is just 160x120 pixels. At this size it still requires a powerful personal computer to achieve the 30 frames a second that the system is designed to provide. However part of the design of the system is that it will work with machines of lower specification, to some extent. VFW is fully integrated with Windows 3.1. Clips can be embedded into, for example, Word for Windows documents where the animation is represented as an icon. Clicking on this icon in the document will run the animation. Alternatively a clip can be viewed using the Windows 3.1 Media Player (see Figure 4.6) which offers standard tape transport controls, with the addition of frame-by-frame controls. The playback software is public domain and available to anyone. The image can be resized but playback rate suffers and the blockiness of the images is greatly increased (see Figure 4.7).

QuickTime is a software architecture that has been designed to allow the user to manipulate multimedia information across applications. For example the user is allowed to display, cut, and paste multimedia data specifying compression algorithms or file formats used by different application programs [195]. QuickTime supports two file formats. The first one is the PICT format used for still images. PICT allows image compression and decompression, and the previewing of images whereby the user can store a smaller version of a picture along with the picture itself, permitting the user to browse quickly through still picture libraries. The second format, the Movie format supports time-dependent data such as video, animation, and sound. The Movie Format consists of two types of tracks, one for video and one for digital sound. Data is kept in separate media files. The tracks point to the media files. In addition to supporting start and end times they have their own time scales and screen coordinates. QuickTime consists of three components that handle the Movie Format:

- The *Movie Manager* deals with the sequencing and synchronization of tracks.
- The *Image Compression Manager* is used to turn compressed data into a usable form. It has compression schemes to manage compression/decompression needs of still images, animations, and video.
- The *Component Manager* keeps a record of the capabilities of external multimedia resources attached to the system, such as digitizer cards, videocassette recorders, system software extensions, microphones, video and audio boards, and hardware compression boards. Applications do not need specific drivers for every resource. The Component Manager is able to make decisions based on a set of flags and values that describe attributes of the external resources.

When the user starts a presentation it is QuickTime's responsibility to find the data used by the two types of files and make sure for dynamic data that the tracks point to the data, the data is in a usable form, and the tracks start and end at the proper time.

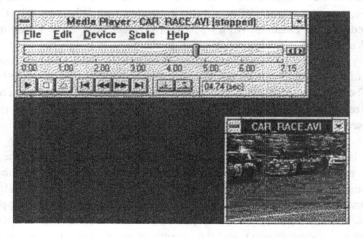

Figure 4.6: *Video for Windows*. VFW at standard size. The CAR_RACE.AVI clip shown on these clips lasts 7.15 seconds and is just over 1 megabyte in size.

4.4.3 Audio Video Kernel

Conceptualizing a digital audio-video system as a conventional audio-video-cassette recorder is limiting. The conventional model works well enough for applications that treat audio-video files like tapes to be viewed by a non-interacting audience, but a more sophisticated model for applications which are essentially interactive, is based on a model of a *digital audio-video production studio* [64]. Typically, a production

Figure 4.7: *VFW2*. Video For Windows with window enlarged.

studio contains mixers, tape decks, monitoring systems, effects processors, plus other items that connect together to record, modify, and play audio or video tracks. These items are analogous to the entities in the audio-video kernel model.

The *Audio-Video Kernel* (AVK) system addresses the needs of both platform and software vendors for a uniform, cross-platform multimedia system able to [94]:

- support motion video in a window with dynamic scaling,
- provide real-time task scheduling for synchronizing audio and video,
- support standard desktops,
- facilitate implementation on various hardware and operating system platforms, and
- integrate with new hardware.

These goals are achieved through a multi-layer architecture. By targeting their applications to the top layer of AVK, software developers are assured of a consistent software environment. In turn, hardware distributors need only modify the lower layers of AVK to port it to their platforms.

At the lowest level of AVK, a microcode engine frees the host system from dealing with real-time scheduling and data compression/decompression. While the microcode engine supports low-level, performance-sensitive operations, the next layer, called the *Audio/Video Device Driver* (AVD), insulates the upper layers from hardware dependencies (see Figure 4.8). The AVD provides a programming interface, which provides logical access to each component at the lower level. Above the AVD layer is another layer called the *Audio/Video Library* (AVL). AVL implements aspects of the digital production studio model. AVL supports the specialized data types, called streams, needed for motion video and audio. Streams are collected into groups, and a group is controlled with functions such as play, pause, stop, and frame advance. AVL also provides control over the attributes of these data types, such as adjusting the volume of an audio stream or the tint on a video stream. Integration of AVK to an operating system environment is accomplished through a layer that:

•   reads and writes data to the host file system, and
•   integrates AVK into the host windowing system.

Thus AVK can support specific high-level interfaces without requiring changes to AVK itself [64].

4.4.4   Video DVI Hardware

Without special hardware a typical personal computer of the mid-1990s presents much weaker video than is found on normal television. Special hardware can give the computer an excellent presentation plus interactivity. The Audio-Video Kernel which was just described was designed with particular hardware in mind. This hardware, called Digital Video Interleaved (DVI), is a board of computer chips which fits into personal computers and is connected to the machines monitor. *DVI* offers a dedicated hardware solution for compressing video and audio information and playing it back in full-color at 30 frames-per-second on a full screen. Users may also capture their own video sequences in real time using an extra capture card to record DVI motion video onto their hard disk.

The DVI programmable chipset supports a wide range of multimedia functions. DVI technology can do both *symmetric* and *asymmetric* motion video compression and decompression [124]. The asymmetric approach produces Production-Level Video and requires large computers with specialized interfaces for compression, but a DVI system can decompress and play back the video. The other DVI approach produces Real-Time Video and does both the compression and decompression with the DVI chipset. The final video is of less high quality with the Real-Time than with the Production-Level approach.

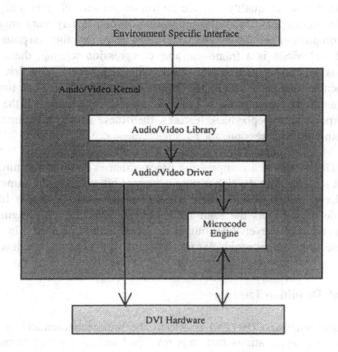

Figure 4.8: *AVK Architecture*: The Envirnoment, such as Microsoft's Multimedia Extensions to Windows, sends information to the AVK. Arrows indicate direction of information flow, and there is bi-directional flow between the Microcode Engine and the DVI Hardware (in this book, the DVI Hardware is described after the description of AVK).

For *Production-Level Video* compression is done by a large computer costing hundreds of thousands of dollars. Special, proprietary interframe compression schemes are employed. The data rates created by the initial digitizing are high, even for large computers. This happens because the initial digitizing must be done in real time. Although quality tape machines can play at slow speeds, they do it by introducing frame storage which would interfere with the quality of the compressed video. The initial storage of the video in digital form requires a data rate of two megabytes per second, which is far higher than the typical storage data rate of a typical personal computer. Nine minutes of this video occupies about one gigabyte of storage space. In non-real time, the video is taken from the digitial disk frame by frame and compressed.

The Production-Level Video compression algorithm must be given goals for the amount of DVI processor chip time per frame which will be devoted to decompression of the video. The application developer may also require processing of audio and be willing to sacrifice video quality. While 30 frames per second gives a higher quality result than 15 frames per second, the application developer may want only 15 frames of video decompressed per second and reserve resources for other purposes. Because Production-Level Video is a frame-to-frame compression scheme, there are special considerations to starting playback in the middle of a scene. The first frame of a motion sequence must be treated as a *reference frame*, and about three times the data of an average motion video frame is required for a reference frame. If the application developer expects special playback features, then these should be communicated to the group doing the compression.

DVI's *Real-Time Video* is a compression process that is done in real time on a DVI development system. The developer may compress his video to the same size as the Production-Level Video would do it but the quality will be much less. If the application developer feels the Real-Time Video results are encouraging, then the expense of Production-Level Video might be subsequently incurred. In some cases, the Real-Time Video might provide as much quality as the end users will need to have.

4.4.5   High Definition Television

High-definition television (HDTV) is one of the most economically and culturally significant of the applications that requires equal use of the *compression* and the *decompression* process. *HDTV* represents the next generation in video technology, with a picture that is wider and twice as sharp as that currently appearing on television sets. This significant improvement in picture clarity and quality is made possible mainly by increasing the number of scanning lines from 525 (the American production standard for over 40 years) to about 1000 lines. In addition, HDTV improves on regular television by its greatly enhanced color and its capability to deliver digital stereo sound. However, a big challenge to the commercial success of HDTV is the currently lack of agreement about its exact format. Numerous groups have proposed HDTV format standards, but they are sometimes widely different. The proposals in the USA use anywhere from 780 to 1,200 scanning lines to produce high-resolution images [147]. Exactly one format will have to be accepted before the economic impact of HDTV will be widely felt.

Much of the interest in *HDTV applications* has centered on potential uses in the television, motion picture, and consumer electronics industries. HDTV may have a significant economic impact on manufacturers of video cassette recorders, video cameras, television sets, and other associated equipment. In addition to entertainment, there are a number of other applications for HDTV — spanning defense, medicine, and more. HDTV can provide instant, high-resolution images for air reconnaissance. For example, the US Air Force may replace 35-millimeter, air reconnaissance cameras with HDTV video cameras, thus eliminating the logistics and time lags involved in processing film. The US Defense Mapping Agency has a large requirement for high-resolution systems to aid in the development, storage, editing, and transmission of maps. The clear, high-resolution images provided by HDTV can assist medical personnel in making diagnoses and in educating medical students. HDTV, with its ability to provide instantaneous pictures of tissue slides, trauma patients, and surgical procedures, is ideally suited to be used as a medium for recording and reviewing medical events.

4.5 Sound

Not until the late 1960s did serious interest in processing *sound* on the computer occur. Sound or audio is, however, for people a fundamental sensory modality. In its raw form, sound is often described in terms of its frequency and amplitude. The *frequency* of the sound corresponds to what the person perceives as the sound's pitch. *Amplitude* corresponds to volume.

Frequency and amplitude for sound are traditionally viewed as continuous or analog phenomenon, but for digital processing this analog sound is sampled. To sample a signal means to examine it at a point in time. From the digital representation which is produced after the sampling, another analog form can be later generated (the same argument applies to video). In principle one computer could communicate with another, if each computer had analog-to-digital and digital-to-analog converters. However, with each of these *conversions* some noise is likely to be introduced. For this and other reasons, ways have been found to encode digital sound so that its storage and transmission from computer to computer can stay in digital form and so that this processing is as economical as possible.

The *format* in which digital sound is stored may vary depending on the hardware and software which one uses and converters may be available that will move from one format to another. The suffix on the digital sound file will often indicate the format in which it was stored; for example, the suffix for Microsoft Corporation's audio format is '.wav' [191]. Software exists for editing sound and playing it in many different ways (see Figure 4.9).

The quality of rendered sound will depend on the resolution of the sampling and on the accuracy of the transformations and compressions/decompressions which have been performed. Sound stored on audio compact disks has been *sampled* at about 44 thousand times per second and 16 bits have been used to represent the amplitude of the sound at each instant of sampling. This high quality encoding will require large

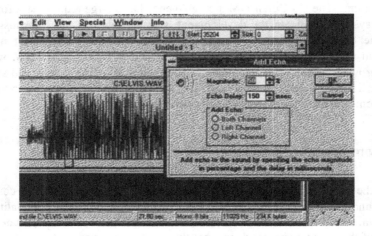

Figure 4.9: *Audio Waveform:* This copy of part of a computer
screen shows software that is being used to display the frequency
and amplitude of sound that is being played on the audio system
connected to the computer. The pop-up window entitled 'Add
Echo' allows the user to choose parameters of an echo to add to the
sound. In this case the sound which is being played is a recording
from Elvis Presley.

amounts of space for storage, as a minute of this quality audio will require well over a
megabyte of storage. Much lower rates of sampling and less accurate measurements
of amplitude may suffice for many purposes and radically reduce the storage
requirements. The study of transformations and compressions for sound is a large
and diverse discipline, and the reader might look elsewhere for further details [180].

For efficiency of converting sounds from musical instruments into digital form and
subsequently presenting that music through digital synthesizers, another
representation was devised that is separate from the simple frequency and amplitude
approach. *Musical Instrument Digital Interface (MIDI)* is a standard digital protocol
developed to facilitate the transmission of musical sounds. MIDI encodes the
sequence of the actions taken by an instrument capable of playing MIDI music.
Messages are defined for musical events, such as note on, velocity with which the note
is produced, and instrument on which the note is played. A melody recorded on one
MIDI synthesizer's clarinet sound, for example, would be played back as a clarinet,
and not a flute, on another MIDI synthesizer.

Part of the MIDI standard is a widely accepted and portable file format for music. As most wordprocessing packages allow for the creation and downloading of plain text files, so much music software allows for the import and export of plain MIDI files. Unfortunately, while the MIDI file standard is a fairly good way of transmitting the note pitches and durations, it's not a very good way to transmit the 'feel' or 'sound', which might include hardware-specific expression controllers, timbres, and effects that only users of identical hardware would be able to reproduce. The *timbre* of instruments is not yet a universally describable phenomenon, and synthesizer-specific features are often exploited which can frustrate users with different hardware. One good way to communicate how a piece actually sounds is via a digital recording or audio sample.

Given that a *library of music* exists, one way to index a musical file is by title, composer, a historical description (if available), by lyrics (if any), and by musical theme. The first items are all free text items, but a theme is usually three or four bars of score. One way to represent music by theme would be to record whether the pitch rises, falls, or stays steady between successive notes. Substitute 'U' for up, 'D' for down, and 'E' for even, and the string 'EEDUEED' might represent the first eight notes of Beethoven's Fifth Symphony (the first note should be discarded, since there is no prior note to which to compare it). A drawback of this alluringly simple scheme is that there are probably other pieces which 'EEDUEED' might match.

For centuries, librarians have been cataloging music based on *incipits* (the term incipit comes from the Latin for beginning), or the first few measures of a piece. A wide number of different ways to represent incipits on the computer have been developed, and no single standard exists. The incipit catalogs form only an index, and do not necessarily include the full scores themselves.

4.6 Compact Disks

Compact Disk-Read Only Memory (CD-ROM) is an important technological development that has supported the spread of multimedia [142]. The salient characteristics of *CD-ROM* are [52]:

- *High information density.* With the density achievable using optical encoding, the disk can contain almost 1 gigabyte of data on a disc less than five inches in diameter.

- Low unit cost. Because disks are manufactured by a well-developed process similar to that used to stamp out long-playing audio records, unit cost in large quantities is less than two dollars.
- *Read only medium.* CD-ROM is read only. It is an electronic publishing, distribution, and access medium; it cannot replace magnetic disks, because magnetic disks can be rewritten arbitrarily many times.
- *Robust medium.* The disk is comprised mostly of, and completely coated by, durable plastic. This fact and the data encoding method allow the disk to be resistant to scratches and other handling damage. Media lifetime is long, well beyond that of magnetic media such as tape.
- *Multimedia storage.* Because all CD-ROM data is stored digitally, it is inherently multimedia in that it can store text, images, graphics, sound, and any other information expressed in digital form. Its major limit in this area is the rate at which data can be read from the disc, about 150 kilobytes per second. This is sufficient for all but uncompressed, full motion, color video.

The technology of the CD-ROM is based on small-holes burnt into a disk by a laser beam (see Figure 4.10).

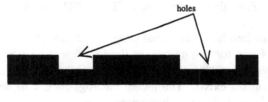

Compact Disk Side View

Figure 4.10: *Compact Disk*: This schematized, side view of a CD shows holes burnt into it. The device which reads the CD interprets the difference between holes (valleys) and non-holes (the high plateau) as a change in binary state. An actual CD is much thinner than the thickness shown in this schema.

Naturally enough, devices must exist to write onto a compact disk. A disk for writing once and reading many times is called *Compact Disk — Write Once Read Many* (CD-WORM). The CD-WORM and its associated drive cost more than the CD-ROM and its associated drive but have greater flexibility. Also available on the market are Rewritable Compact Disks which can be used as one might a traditional computer disk or diskette. In the long run, one might expect an increasing prevalence of rewriteable compact disks. The remainder of this section, however, addresses only CD-ROM.

4.6.1 History

While the CD-ROM was first announced in 1983, its history naturally traces to earlier dates than that [17]. The development of a laser in a light emitting diode in 1962 signified the beginning of work on a storage disc that was based on laser reading of the disc content. In 1978 the videodisc was commercially launched. Modern *videodiscs* are 12 inches in diameter and can store about 2 hours of video. Information is encoded in analogue form and interactive video and audio are supported by devices that access the videodisc.

In 1982 Compact Disc Digital Audio (CD-DA) was launched. The Philips and Sony Corporations developed standards for storing information on these discs and by 1990 the *CD-DA* had virtually eliminated production of the vinyl disc record. The mass production of CD-DA has considerably influenced the development of CD-ROM.

CD-ROM was announced as an information storage medium by *Philips* and *Sony* in 1983. But a draft standard for encoding of information was not agreed till 1985, and an international approved standard appeared in 1987. The standard stimulated the development of both materials to store on CD-ROM and also drives for reading CD-ROMs.

4.6.2 Encoding Standards

Storing data on a CD may be thought of as occurring through a *data encoding hierarchy* with each level build upon the previous one. At the lowest level, data is physically stored as pits on the disc. It is actually encoded by several low-level mechanisms to provide high storage density and reliable data recovery. At the next level, it is organized into tracks and then a file system is built on the tracks. Finally, end-user applications specify a content format for files.

There are many different standards for CD data encoding. These are called 'books' in their documentation:

- *Red Book:* This is the standard for Audio compact discs.
- *Yellow Book:* This is the standard for CD-ROM data discs.
- *Orange Book:* This is for writable compact discs.
- *Green Book:* This is the standard for CD-i discs.

CD-ROM/XA (eXtended Architecture) is an extension to Yellow Book, it extends Yellow Book to add some of the features of Green Book (CD-i). Yellow Book is thus now described as having two modes, Mode 1 is for computer data (and is heavily error checked) and Mode 2 is for compressed audio or video data (which is not error checked so heavily).

4.6.3   Compact Disk Specialist Systems

The *Compact Disk-Interactive* (CD-i) Specification was announced by Philips and Sony Corporation in 1987. CD-i is a self-contained system aimed at the consumer market. The system consists of a 'player' hooked to standard, domestic television and stereo equipment. The CD-i [17] player includes a central processor, one megabyte of integrated circuit memory, audio processor, and joystick.

A *CD-i picture* may be generated using four image planes. CD-i accommodates numerous effects familiar to the video industry, such as cuts. Technically, a cut can be achieved by switching from one image plane to another. Scrolling provides a means to move a window in an X-Y motion and is popular in graphical adventure games.

Kodak Photo CD is a subset of CD-i. The actual Photo-CD players are very similar to CD-i players and are manufactured by Philips for Kodak. *Photo-CD* is designed to allow home users to store their 'photo-album' on compact disc and to view the images using their TV. 35mm negatives of pictures are scanned at a bureau by specialist and expensive hardware and then written to a special CD by the same machine. The owner of the negatives can then take the disc home and view the images. The system aims to provide several benefits over conventional prints: preservation of the images for greater periods of time, allowing people 'to see themselves on television', and easy functions for a gallery of pictures. Each picture can be rotated, panned, or magnified.

Each Photo-CD image is stored on the disc in five levels, each containing a varying quantity of information, from a small thumbnail sketch size, which is used for previewing purposes, to a very high quality version which is stored at greater resolution and quality than any current display system can achieve, to ensure *future-proofing* in the system, and to allow users to zoom into the image without a loss of quality. A system displays an image of the desired quality, e.g. low (for quick retrieval) when browsing, by only decoding the levels necessary for the image required. The more levels that are accessed the better the quality of the image achieved,but the longer it will take to decode. The quantity of data required for each image is high (compression rate is only 4:1) and each disc can only hold 100 images.

Tiny computers called *Electronic Books* from Sony and Panasonic use 3-inch CDs, rather than the usual 5-inch CDs used by most systems. They have a keyboard, a joypad device, and two buttons, much like CD-i. These Electronic Books have a small screen, typically 3.5 inches, which is bit-mapped and will allow the use of graphics. The machines can be linked to personal computer monitors.

4.7　Multimedia Personal Computers

The technology in a *multimedia system* (hardware and software) may have been available before the advent of the multimedia system. However these individual technologies may not easily integrate into a multimedia system. They may have been designed individually without the designers having in mind their integration. Various hardware and software products are often incompatible to each other [131]. In addition to compatibility needs, multimedia systems require authoring tools and multimedia information filing tools, and both of these tools underdeveloped [12].

Creating multimedia environments requires accepting tradeoffs, such as:

- using the standard operating environment but with specialized, hardwired support for real-time multimedia,
- augmenting the operating environment with specialized, real-time software, and
- using stand-alone, dedicated multimedia units.

With the hardwired, environment-specific approach, the software which is used must also be developed just for that environment. The approach of tailoring the *software* to exploit the current hardware is, however, generally insufficient because the current *hardware* can not deal adequately with multimedia.

When a user purchases a multimedia personal computer, they typically get hardware for audio and large data storage, and software for the rest. Few vendors offer the entire multimedia package [196], and the *competition* among vendors is stiff. Machines running Microsoft Windows or the Macintosh operating system come prominently to mind.

To overcome compatibility problems, several vendors jointly created the *Multimedia Personal Computer Marketing Council.* In 1991 this council consisted of 15 computer-related vendors (including, AT&T, NEC, Philips and Tandy) and was sponsored by Microsoft. The resultant Multimedia Personal Computer (MPC) standard set the minimum standards for multimedia hardware in order to run a set of common, multimedia applications.

To the extent that the *MPC standard* survives, it can be expected to undergo continual evolution. In broad strokes, the 1991 standard required:

-      a mid-range microprocessor.
-      several megabytes of random access core memory,
-      a large hard-disk,
-      a CD-ROM drive,
-      audio facilities including microphone input and speaker output,
-      high resolution, color graphics, and
-      the Microsoft Windows operating system.

Microsoft Windows made the standard workable. For example, any compatible additional hardware for handling sound can be used in a MPC, as long as the vendor writes appropriate Windows software to control the hardware, and all software run under Windows can access that hardware. This situation is also true for the CD-ROM drive and so forth.

Multimedia on *Macintoshs* is well integrated and any Macintosh application can make use of multimedia to some extent. Sound capability (speakers and a microphone), for example, are built into every machine, and thus it is unnecessary to add to a Macintosh (except for the addition of a CD-ROM player) for multimedia, unless high quality motion video is needed. Multimedia resources exist in the Macintosh's user interface which allow for the interchange of motion video, still images, and sound easily between applications using a clipboard or directly. Motion video support is software only but includes sound.

Numerous multimedia devices have been launched on the market and sunk. *CDTV* was launched by *Commodore Business Machines* in early 1991, as a device to be used in the home like a video-cassette recorder. It was launched over a year before the similar, in concept, Philips CD-i system. Commodore hoped to use this fact and that it had a large easily converted software base available to it to get a headstart and to build a user-base. However this also meant that software which was simply converted to the machine was in the majority and this did not utilize the power of the CD-ROM technology. The CD-ROM element of the system was simply used to provide real music during games and similar applications. This left the CDTV with simply an unsuccessful games-based image.

4.8   Conclusion

Multimedia computing places stringent *performance demands* on the operating environment. Unlike traditional graphics processing, a single multimedia presentation combines multiple streams of different types of data, each with its own unique demands for special processing and presentation (see Figure 4.11). The system must decompress stored data or compress recorded data to deal with the massive amount of data in multimedia.   Information must be synchronized, so that for instance the voice appears at the same time that the lips start to move. The synchronization of related video and audio data streams requires a careful orchestration of the processing tasks required to manage the individual data streams.

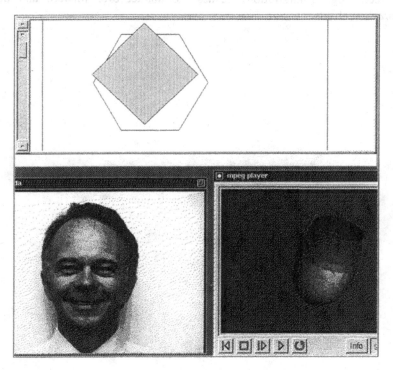

Figure 4.11: *Multiple Streams.* Each window on the Computer Screen is presenting a different view of the same topic. The top window is an abstraction drawing of a heart, the lower left window is a photo of a person, and the lower right window is an animation of that person's heart beating.

The *Compact Disk-Read-Only Memory* (CD-ROM) is a storage device whose principles of operation are straightforward but whose impacts remain diverse. Numerous new consumer devices, such as 'Compact-Disk Interactive' and 'Electronic Books', access CD-ROMs. A CD-ROM stores as much information as 600 diskettes but mass production costs for CD-ROMs are basically the same as for diskettes.

Technology to implement multimedia is so varied in its character and the vendors of technology are so competitive in their practices that the consumer is often confused. Microsoft Corporation made a major effort to harmonize the efforts of vendors when it supported the unofficial *Multimedia Personal Computer* standard. Yet, the rapid pace of new technological innovations pushes the market ever forward and thwarts standardization efforts.

5
Hypermedia

Hypertext has links, and multimedia has timing. *Hypermedia* properly has both *links* and *timing*. The Dexter model of linking is extended in this chapter to handle timing. Linking in video is presented as a simple example of hypermedia. Finally, problems of compatibility among different formats are discussed.

5.1 Links and Timing

A *hypertext* may be modeled as a graph. The basic support provided by a hypertext access system is visiting nodes by traversing links. The user determines how much time to spend at a node and what node to visit next. The way the node contents is presented to the user on the screen is normally a function of the internal specifications of the node. *Multimedia* on the other hand is time-based. Components are meant to be presented in some author-defined order. The user can control part of the presentation. The interface may be similar to that on an audiocassette or compact disc player. The user can stop, start, fast-forward, or rewind.

The combination of the linking facility associated with hypertext and the synchronization facility of multimedia constitutes hypermedia (see Figure 5.1). To model hypermedia the *Dexter model* (which was presented earlier) for linking is extended to include synchronization capabilities [79]. *Temporal relationships* may be viewed as those which determine which components are presented together and the relative order in which components are presented — these may be called collection and synchronization relations, respectively. The Dexter model provides some support for the collection relation via composite nodes. However, the definition of a composite does not provide a mechanisms for specifying relative timing relationships among the entities of a composite.

For conventional hypertext, blocks of text can be broken into arbitrarily small sizes. A block could be a book, a chapter, a section, a paragraph, a sentence, a clause, a word, or a letter. In this way a new link can be created to many different units of textual information. The relationship between any two of these blocks of text is also not fixed by a timing relationship. For time-based media this kind of *decomposition of the content* is not as straightforward. Methods for describing hierarchical levels of video and audio have been developed but are not widely accepted or used.

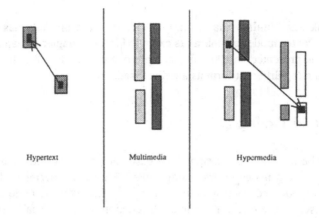

Hypertext   Multimedia   Hypermedia

Figure 5.1: *Hypertext, Multimedia, and Hypermedia*: The leftmost column shows a link from an anchor within one hypertext node to another anchor in another hypertext node. The middle column shows two media types that should begin presentation at the same time with time going from top to bottom. Each media type experiences a delay before resuming but the delays are not at the same time. The rightmost, hypermedia column indicates two multimedia composites and a link from one composite to another.

Another problem with the hypertext link is that it does not say what happens to the *screen* when the user activates an anchor within a text block. Most systems present a single hypertext node which is either replaced by the destination information or is left on the screen, while another window is provided for the destination information. This is not usually problematic in hypertext because the reader typically will only read one block of text at a time anyhow. For multimedia, however, the presentation of multiple media 'blocks' at the same time may be crucial to the intended meaning and the author must be able to determine what does or does not remain on the screen. For instance, an audio track may begin to refer to a video sequence and while this video sequence is being shown the author requries that the commenting audio component occur simultaneously.

5.2 Hypermedia Model

A hypermedia model can be derived from the Dexter hypertext model. The *Amsterdam Hypermedia Model* (AHM) uses atomic and composite nodes and extends their Dexter model representation. The atomic component contains metainformation that refers to a particular media component or 'blob', while the composite component defines such information for a collection of atomic or composite components. A blob is only directly referenced by an atomic component [79].

The *atomic components* of the AHM contain presentation information, component attributes, link anchor information, and more. The presentation information is expanded from that in the Dexter model to model time-related aspects of the blob. The *composite component* in the AHM is used to build a presentation structure rather than to simply collect related components for navigation purposes. The composite contains synchronization arcs and timing offsets among the children.

The *synchronization arc* allows an author to specify fine-grained synchronization information among components by specifying constraints which the run-time system should support. A synchronization type includes indication of whether the constraint must be met or might be met. If a 'must' relation can not be met, the hypermedia system must abort its execution, but for a 'might' relation the hypermedia system will keep running whether or not the relation is satisfied. By example, a synchronization arc might say that an audio blob 'must' finish before a video blob finishes.

The AHM uses source and target link contexts to help the author specify what should happen on the *screen*. The source (destination) context for a link is that part of the hypermedia presentation affected by initiating (traversing) a link. For example, the source context can be specified as being retained or replaced when a link is followed.

Another level of presentation specification concerns channels, and the AHM adds a channel presentation specification. *Channels* are abstract output devices for playing a blob. Associated with each channel are default presentation characteristics for the media type displayed via that channel. For example, an audio channel may have a default volume. The use of channels has several advantages, such as allowing the specification of speech to be in one language or another.

5.3 An Authoring System

CMIFed is an authoring and presentation environment for hypermedia documents based on the Amsterdam Hypermedia Model [165]. CMIFed was implemented with an object-oriented prototyping language on Silicon Graphics Indigo machines as a research and development prototype and to demonstrate the utility of the Amsterdam Hypermedia Model. In general any authoring or viewing system for hypermedia should include an interactive, What-You-See-Is-What-You-Get interface. Since CMIFed allows an author to specify presentations that might not be supported on some platforms, the system must also provide a facility to map a presentation to a particular platform. To provide these needs, CMIFed supports three views on a presentation: a hierarchy view, a channel view, and a player view. The author can open or close each view independently of the other.

The *hierarchy view* is for displaying and manipulating the structure of the hypermedia presentation. The view is presented as embedded nodes in a tree-like fashion. The outermost node is the root of the tree. Nodes next to each other are started in parallel unless synchronization arcs specify otherwise. Nodes higher in the tree are activated before those lower in the tree (see Figure 5.2). There are three groups of commands: to insert new nodes; to cut and paste nodes; and to display and edit information about nodes, such as the attributes. There is also a generic editor command which invokes an external editor for modifying a node's blob. The choice of editor can be determined by the author so as to conform to the media type of the blob. CMIFed does not have native editors because users are assumed to already have their favorite editors for individual media types.

The *channel view* shows a transformation of the hierarchy in terms of abstract media channels. This view is presented as a time line, with placement determined automatically by CMIFed. The atomic components are displayed in their own channel along with their precise durations and timing relationships. If the author changes the timing in any part of the presentation, this is immediately reflected in the channel view (see Figure 5.3).

The CMIFed *player view* interprets a hypermedia document and plays the presentation on the available hardware. The player also allows the author to edit the layout-oriented aspects of a presentation, such as the geometry of the windows. The player displays a control panel and additional windows for screen-oriented channels. From the control window the viewer can select a channel and whether to go forward, backward, or stop in that channel. While the player's control panel is the main preview interface, it is also possible to start the player by selecting a portion of the hierarchy or channel views.

5.4   Linking in Video

Hypertext authors often take advantage of existing structure in text. The Table of Contents of a document provides a ready indicator of *logical structure* and immediately provides levels of abstraction of the document content. Headings in the Table of Contents can become node names for the hypertext and links between the

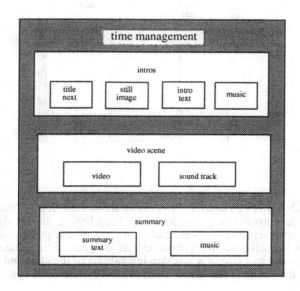

Figure 5.2: *Hierarchy View of CMIFed*: This illustration of how a window of CMIFed appears in the hierarchy view shows the embedded nodes of a presentation about 'time management' that includes text, image, music, video, and sound. Time goes from top to bottom and the composite node 'summary' comes last with its two atomic nodes of text and music.

nodes reflect the hierarchical structure of the Table of Contents. For video and audio this kind of pre-existent structure may be lacking. Thus the challenge of adding links to time-based media begins with the need to identify some logical structure in the media.

5.4.1 Film Indexing

In a film, the production of a single frame often costs hundreds of dollars. Amazingly this expensive footage is not catalogued per se and is only used once. The million dollar scene has its place in the movie, and that is the only place it will be seen. Several efforts have been made to build video libraries in which each video would have labeled components. Efforts to *label video components* for purposes of reuse have been, however, largely unsuccessful [38].

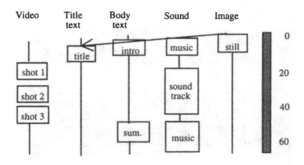

Figure 5.3: *CMIFed Parallel View:* Time flows from top to bottom through the diagram as indicated in the time line at the far right. Columns represent the different channels used by the presentation, and boxes in each column represent events assigned to that channel. The placement and size of a box are indications of the start and duration of the event. The arrow from 'still' to 'title' is a synchronization arc.

The MIT Media Laboratory has a toolset for *indexing video databases.* The toolset includes a database browsing tool, a story generation tool, and a visual editing tool. The editing tool allows descriptions to be attached to any group of contiguous frames of video and also allows for layered descriptions. This allows the video to be described at different granularities and in different contexts [59].

5.4.2 Automatically Generated Reference Frames

Browsing video sequences is critical in many domains in which the user is required to choose a few video sequence from many [5]. Such situations exist for remote access of video, video editing, video-based training, video electronic mail, and so on. The user must view the contents of the video sequences in order to choose the most relevant. Given that several videos have been identified from some database as potentially relevant to the user's interests, the user is stuck with the task of retrieving those videos and examining each of them. One solution to this is similar to that of browsing the abstracts of journal papers or the Table of Contents of books. Namely, *abstractions* of each of the video sequences is pre-computed and only the abstractions are retrieved and initially viewed. The abstractions are many orders of magnitude smaller in size, and therefore reduce the system's response time and the user's viewing time.

Content-based video browsing is achieved by pre-processing steps which are performed off-line and a few steps during the browsing process. The pre-processing steps take advantage of long developed methods of scene analysis and are similar in some ways to methods used to compress videos. Namely, changes in the frames are detected and the existence of these changes is used to guide the detection of frames which are prime indicators of major content shifts in the video. A motion analysis is performed in producing a *representative frame* (Rframe). Rframes are displayed to the user while maintaining their temporal sequence. In one approach the Rframe is every 10th frame of a video but includes associated information which indicates what kinds of changes have occurred in the 9 frames since the previous Rframe was presented. Various shape and color-based attributes may also be made available to the user as a way to organize or filter Rframes.

This kind of content-based browsing is advantageous over fast forward or rewind operations. Using *fast forward* or *rewind* the user must view every frame at rapid speeds and may miss critical short shots and be forced to view long lasting and irrelevant shots. In addition, users must repeatedly go forward and backward in trying to focus on the points of interest. In content-based browsing, the effort required of the viewer is much less.

When the user decides that a given Rframe is of interest, the user can then request to see the entire video in full detail around the time of that Rframe. In this sense the Rframe is like an *outline of the video* and has a link between itself and the associated body of the video. This is a kind of hypermedia, namely linked and time-based media.

5.5 Formats, Converters, and Containers

As long as hypermedia platforms continue to be distinguished by differing abilities to process various media there will continue to be good technical reasons for having native *media formats* that are closely matched to platform-dependent interfaces. This has led to the definition of different media formats and will continue to lead to the definition of new formats in areas where technology is rapidly progressing [156]. The market place supports the development of new technologies which in turn require the tailoring of formats to suit the technology. This is behind the proliferation of different and sometimes incompatible formats and sometimes standards in the hypermedia arena.

5.5.1   SGML

To make electronic information more exchangeable, standards of logical document structure are useful. The Standard Generalized Markup Language (SGML) is a language for logical document structure and is an international standard for publishing [95]. *SGML* is based on the generic markup of the structural elements of a document without regard to their presentation, which is regarded as a separate issue. SGML contrasts to typographic markup, since font and style are not considered during logical markup. Each SGML document uses a document type definition (DTD) which declares what element types can exist in a document, what attributes each of these element types can have, and how instances of these element types are hierarchically related. Typically, a DTD defines a whole class of documents, and many document instances share a common DTD.

The syntax of SGML is based on *tags* that mark the beginning of logical components of the document. For example, the first tag to be entered in a document would signify that what follows is a general document. Security for the document could be set through the 'security' attribute and might, for instance, be useful for a confidential report. A heading at level 1 is specified with <h1>. Cross-reference may be made in the text to a heading via the <hr> marker.

The appeal of SGML is that a document prepared with SGML should be immediately useful to many other groups because they will be prepared to deal with it. SGML applies to computer-assisted publishing where the final product is a typeset document (hard copy), electronic publishing where the document appears on the screen (soft copy), and database publishing where document elements are retrieved in combination with other elements. Many *publications,* be they books, manuals, reports, directories, or messages may be represented in SGML. Graphics and scanned images may be included in a SGML-marked document.

5.5.2   HyTime and MHEG

HyTime is a standard called precisely Hypermedia/Time-based Document Structuring Language [138]. HyTime is an extension to SGML so that markup and DTDs can be used to describe the structure of hypermedia documents. The standard defines a set of *architectural forms* for the definition of hypermedia DTDs. These architectural forms constitute a meta-DTD which governs how a HyTime-conforming DTD can be constructed.

The HyTime architectural forms are grouped into six modules, called the base, measurement, location address, hyperlinks, scheduling, and rendition modules. The *base module* is required by all the other modules and specifies the properties which are global to the document. The measurement module gives a document the ability to represent concepts involving dimension, measurement, and counting. The *location address module* provides various means of specifying locations in a document which could not be specified by SGML alone. If the measurement module is used, then locations can be specified which are indices along particular dimensions. The *hyperlinks module* supports the defining of links betwen portions of a document and can invoke the location address module. The scheduling module places document objects in finite coordinate spaces that are defined in the measurement module. The *rendition module* expands the scheduling module to specify how events in generic coordinate spaces can be mapped to presentation coordinate spaces.

HyTime allows hypermedia *document interoperability* to the maximum extent possible without standardizing multimedia objects, and without requiring existing documents to be recast to make their contents linkable by HyTime documents. HyTime documents can allow HyTime software to browse, render, format, and query them even if that software is not able to understand or render its multimedia objects. If the notation of an object is uninterpretable because no interpreting system is locally available for it, the rendering can still incorporate some form of blankness so that the space and time relationships of the rendered and unrenderable objects is preserved.

The U.S. Department of Defense has developed technology and document architectures for revisable databases in support of Interactive Electronic Technical Manuals as replacements for paper technical manuals for logistic support of military equipment. To constrain costs, to immunize hypermedia document databases from obsolescence of presentation and querying systems, and to allow the information to be available on a wide range of different types of machines, the Department of Defense needs a standard way to represent its technical data and has chosen to base its approach on HyTime.

MHEG standardizes descriptions at a level between low-level representations, such as for a photograph, and high-level structured languages and scripts, such as HyTime. The MHEG object is only defined at the interchange point [149]. The MHEG standard relates to classes of objects which are specified in three steps:

1   an informal description of the object's structure and its behavior,
2   a precise object-oriented definition of the object structure and behavior, and
3   the coded representation of the object using the coding rules specified by various interchange standards, such as SGML.

MHEG *objects* have structures in time and space and are related to other objects through links. The link objects may be triggered by actions and interactions such as user selection and are therefore conditional links. The MHEG engine will trigger a link when it detects the appropriate change in the state of an object. The behavior of objects is specified by actions, such as 'make modifiable', and by the effects of the actions on the state of the objects, such as 'ready/not ready'. Whereas a HyTime program sees the whole of a document or script before it is executed, a MHEG program will typically see the small part of a document a user is using during an interaction. The MHEG standard supports the interactive, real-time interchange of hypermedia objects between diverse applications and services across multiple platforms.

5.5.3   Converters

Standards can make *conversions* easier. If converters can go from a non-standard to a standard format or from a standard to a non-standard format, then the standard plays an important role. If a *converter* exists between each non-standard format and the standard format, then going from any non-standard format to any other non-standard format can be accomplished by going first to the standard format. For instance, if one had four different hypermedia logical markups and wanted to convert between any two, then one way is with twelve converters that go pairwise between each two. Alternately, one intermediate format, such as HyTime, can be used, and then only four conversion programs are needed (see Figure 5.4).

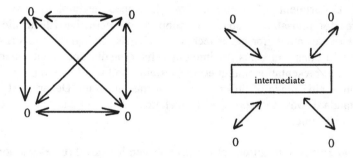

Figure 5.4: *Converters.* With 4 different end-user formats and no intermediate format, 12 converters might be needed. With an intermediate format, converters are only needed between the intermediate format and each end-user format - in this case a total of 8 converters. As the number of end-user formats increases, so does the advantage to using one intermediate format.

There are many different types of formats. In converting documents between hypermedia systems, one has to convert more than the logical format, which might be represented in an intermediate markup language such as HyTime. Each hypermedia system will support its own preferred *monomedia formats*. To convert a document from one hypermedia system to another each monomedia component within the document may have to be separately converted [132].

With the *conversion utilities* in a hypermedia authoring system, the user who is examining a particular monomedia unit chooses some unit (see Figure 5.5). Then he selects any of many available formats in which the unit should be stored. The system will then retrieve the monomedia unit, automatically convert it into the desired format, and then store it with the proper *format.*

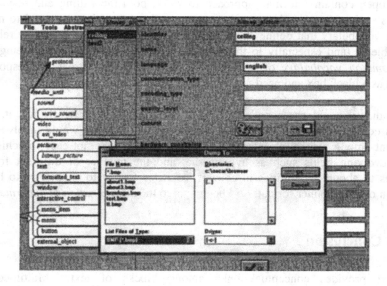

Figure 5.5: *Converter.* Screen dump from a system which presents information about a particular bitmap and gives the user an option to convert that bitmap into a variety of formats.

5.5.4 Containers

To completely convert documents between two different hypermedia systems, the systems must support the same hypermedia features. This is not the case and as long as products continue to have different feature sets, conversions from one to another will be less than 100% effective. *Feature-based product differentiation* is a characteristic of growing markets, such as computer software.

The need for converters may be lessened by new generation interchange formats, such as OpenDoc, which allow private objects and structure to be described on an equal footing with public ones. In time, this may allow all applications to 'interpret' those parts of each others formats that they can understand. OpenDoc uses open, object-based, *container formats.* Such open object formats are combined either with platform facilities that can locate applications or with other code objects that can process a given type of data object. Thus one program can use the facilities of another program to process those objects that it does not handle itself. Thus, someone using a word processor can incorporate in her document a spreadsheet prepared in another package which can communicate via OpenDoc with the word processor. Whenever someone wants to edit the spreadsheet, the spreadsheet program is invoked without terminating the word processing application. Of course, the user must have a copy of the spreadsheet program on her system.

For the open container format approach to work, both the calling and responding programs — in this example a word processor and a spreadsheet — need to have a common vocabulary that defines the embeddable data objects and how they relate to active objects (and especially to the methods on those objects.) By agreeing on a fixed, *common vocabulary* of methods, the application may treat the responding program as a black box and need not know details of its implementation.

If the industry could agree on one standard format and consistently use it, then products could be created and distributed more easily. But this would involve some agreement among competing interests. Such agreements are not easy to achieve in rapidly evolving fields such as hypermedia, and the number of different formats continues to abound. Abilities to convert from one format to another or to handle objects in open container formats will be crucial to the *dissemination of hypermedia.*

5.6   Conclusion

Hypertext provides conceptual links among blocks of text. Multimedia is synchronized media streams, such as a voice with a moving image. Hypermedia is the combination of the two, namely *synchronized media* that additionally have *conceptual links* between their components. For instance, the presentation of a hypermedia audiovideo sequence might allow the user to point to an object in the video and to then see an additional window appear on the screen in which an animation and associated descriptive text about the object appear.

The Dexter model of hypertext can be extended to account for synchronization of media. Individual nodes are associated with blobs that may contain several media which will start and stop at prescribed times relative to one another. Composite nodes specify timing relationships or 'synchronization arcs' among multimedia blobs of different nodes. The conceptual linking structure of the Dexter model remains viable for the hypermedia case, and thus one has both conceptual linking and time-based synchronization in this *extended Dexter model.*

One person's way of encoding media may be different from another person's way. The abundance of media formats means that when one person sends an image to another person that other person may well not be able to understand the format of the media because the two people use different methods for representing the media. This dilemma of *incompatible formats* gives rise to the need for standards. In order to take advantage of the new opportunities for information-sharing offered by hypermedia it is imperative that standard formats should be followed.

Hypermedia appeals to the senses of people, but has such vast storage and computing requirements that its diffusion in the world is tightly connected to the advance of technology. The *hypermedia market,* be it of the hypermedia content or platform, should increase dramatically over the next decades [190]. The direction of the market depends in part on the match between the hypermedia, such as an interactive multimedia training course on driving, and the hypermedia systems, such as the Multimedia Personal Computer.

Part II:

The Group and Groupware

Hypermedia has in this book been categorized as a tool for individuals not because it applies only to individuals but because other technological developments, such as groupware and computer networks, build on hypermedia and then more directly address the concerns of groups and organizations. The next two chapters particularly address *groups* and *groupware*. First, the principles are described, including a theory of coordination and an extended hypertext model for groupware. Then groupware applications or experiences are described particularly in the domains of education and software engineering.

6
Group and Groupware Principles

This chapter explores the characteristics of groups and how these are germane to *technology for groups*. Each member of a group is normally responsible for one or more distinct activities such that the sum of the activities accomplishes some group objective. Tools may be designed to support this group work by being a natural extension of the group process. To be effective the technology of a work group must fit the structure of its tasks [73]. This chapter develops a framework from which the relationships between groups and their groupware is understandable.

6.1   Definitions of Group and Groupware

A group is a set of people that function as a unit, communicate directly, and have some or all of the following characteristics:

- *Communication.* The members of a group must be able to communicate directly with each other about the group itself and their activities.
- *Identification.* The members of a group must identify themselves as members of the group. This sense of 'groupness' affects individual actions.
- *Long Life.* The life of a group may be longer than even the life of the longest living individual member of the group because groups have the ability to replace members that retire.
- *Motivation.* The members of a group must have a motive to join the group and to continue to be members. Individual reward or benefit must accrue from being a member.

The term *groupware* means:

> intentional *group* processes and procedures to achieve specific purposes + *software* tools designed to support and facilitate the group's work [103].

This definition of groupware emphasizes the union of group activities and its software support. Groupware is effective when it is designed to match the group needs.

The discipline of *Computer-Supported Cooperative Work* (CSCW) is interdisciplinary and focuses on exploiting groupware to augment team work. The first CSCW conference occurred in 1984 and included people from a variety of disciplines, such as office information systems, hypertext, and computer mediated-communication. The topics included experiences in introducing computer conferencing systems and design and use of electronic mail filtering tools. When the term *CSCW* was coined it simply designated multiple people working together and using computers to support and augment their work. However, designing such systems requires a thorough understanding of the nature of cooperative work [30] [65] [108] [168].

CSCW and groupware refer to the same body of scientific and engineering work. Two main streams characterize research efforts within this domain. *Engineers* form one stream and develop decision support systems, collaborative writing systems, and such. *Social scientists* form another stream and investigate how people employ the technology.

People from a wide range of fields are interested in CSCW and groupware. Vendor companies are interested because they see the market for products that support groups [71]. Telecommunication and network companies are interested because they realize the need for connectivity, concurrent processing, and high bandwidth. Organizations are interested because they want to use technology to support teams and projects [197].

6.2   Coordination and Communication in Groups

Communication is a *cyclical process* (see Figure 6.1). The individual accesses information in order to create new information which he then communicates in a form that he hopes will be comprehensible to his intended audience. When people work together, the communication serves decision-making which is, in turn, necessary for coordination of individual efforts toward the group objective.

6.2.1   Coordination

The term *cooperative work* is vague. Usually the common-sense notion of two or more people working together to accomplish some activity is used to connotate cooperative work [175]. The term cooperative work was used in social sciences in the first half of the 19th century by economists to designate work involving multiple actors [6]. *Marx* formally defined cooperative work as:

> multiple individuals working together in a planned way in the same production process or in different but connected production processes.

The term 'cooperative work' may not reflect real work situations where conflict, competition, and politics may be mingled within activities that seem cooperative on the surface. *Coordination* in a cooperative setting is needed to deal with contingencies that arise, such as a change of goals.

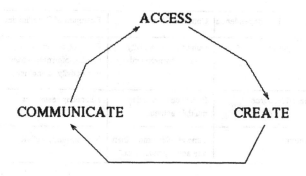

Figure 6.1: *Communication Cycle.* People access information in order to create what they then communicate.

Coordination theory is the body of principles describing how [127]:

- activities can be coordinated, or
- actors can work together harmoniously.

There must be one or more actors, performing some activities which are directed towards some ends or goals. The goal-relevant relationships between the activities are interdependencies (see Figure 6.2).

Components	Processes
Goals	Identify
Activities	Map to goals
Actors	Map to activities
Interdependencies	Manage

Figure 6.2: *Components of Coordination.* Components of coordination and associated processes.

If there is no *interdependence*, there is nothing to coordinate. Interdependence between activities can be analyzed in terms of common objects that are involved in both activities. These common objects constrain how each activity is performed. For example, software can not be properly designed until the requirements for the software have been defined. This pattern of interdependence is called a prerequisite, and other patterns include 'shared resource' and 'simultaneity' (see Figure 6.3). One way in which technology can help manage these interdependencies is simply by helping to detect them in the first instance.

Kinds of Interdependence	Common Object	Examples of Coordinating
Prerequisite	Output of one activity required by next activity	Ordering activities; moving information from one activity to another
Shared resource	Resource required by multiple activities	Allocating resources
Simultaneity	Time at which more than one activity must occur	Synchronizing activities

Figure 6.3: *Interdependencies.* Interdependencies can be essentially categorized as prerequisite, shared resource, and simultaneity.

Coordination may be described in terms of successively deeper levels of underlying processes. For instance, many coordination processes require that some *decision* has been made and accepted by a group. Group decisions, in turn, require members of the group to communicate in some form [110]. This *communication* requires that some messages be transported in a language that is understandable to both. Finally, the establishment of this language depends on the ability of actors to perceive *common objects.* The strongest dependencies are downward through these layers (see Figure 6.4).

The identification of generic coordination processes should *inform the design* of groupware systems. Humans may have problems coordinating their work because of their inherent cognitive and physical limitations. Groupware could aid humans by assuming actions that humans find difficult to perform.

6.2.2   Communication

The *communication process* consists of two alternating dimensions: the perceptual or receptive, and the communicating or control dimension [56] (see Figure 6.5). The process begins with event E which is perceived by M. M's perception of E is a precept E1. The relationship between E and E1 may involve *selection,* in that M cannot possibly perceive the whole complexity of E. M might in fact be a machine, and its selective perception is determined by its engineering. Complexity arises where M is human. In the latter case, meaning derives from the matching of external stimuli with internal concepts. Matching is determined by culture, and peoples of different cultures perceive reality differently.

The precept E1 is converted into a signal about E, or SE. This is a *message.* The circle representing this message is divided into two; S refers to form, and E refers to content. The relationship between form and content is dynamic and interactive. In both the horizontal (perceptual) and the vertical (communicating) dimensions, selection is of

Process level	Components	Examples of Generic Process
Coordination	goals, activities, actors	identifying goals, ordering activities, assigning activities to actors, allocating resources, synchronizing activities
Group decision making	goals, actors, alternatives, evaluations, choices	proposing alternatives, evaluating alternatives, making choices
Communication	senders, receivers, messages, languages	establishing common language, selecting receiver, transporting messages
Perception of common objects	actors, objects	seeing same physical objects, accessing shared database

Figure 6.4: *Processes Underlying Coordination.* Levels of coordination and correspondent representations are identified, particularly in terms of generic processes.

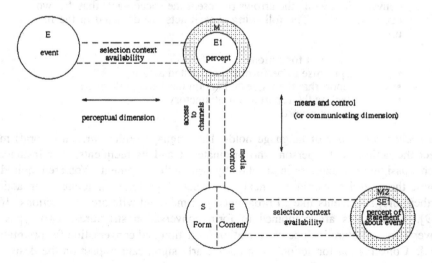

Figure 6.5: *Two Dimensions of Communication.* E is an event. M is the communicator, M2 is the receiver.

vital importance. Perception occurs through the filter of the mind; communication occurs via certain external channels and not others.

Anything that is transmitted via a channel of communication is a *selective interpretation* of reality. This distorted view of reality (SE) is then perceived in turn by the receiver (M2), who makes his own conscious or unconscious selection of what to attend to and what to ignore in the relayed message. The meaning of the message, then, is the result of an interaction or negotiation between the receiver and the message. In the transmission of SE to M2, the concept of availability becomes significant in determining what is actually perceived. Availability is determined by the communicator, who selects how and to whom the message is to be sent.

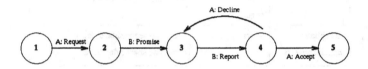

Figure 6.6: *Conversation for action structure.* Two agents A and B are involved in a conversation. The circles represent states of the conversation, while the arrows represent the speech-acts that the two agents perform. The following speech-acts are depicted in the figure:

- a request for action
- a promise to perform the requested action
- report that the requested action has been performed
- decline the report as unsatisfactory
- accept report

The *speech-act theory* of language holds that language (either written or oral) may affect the action of the person who originates it and its recipients. For instance a teacher assigning an exercise in his class by issuing the statement "You are required to submit the exercise within the next two weeks" performs a request for action. Furthermore, statements like "I pronounce you man and wife are" are actions [163] [169]. Speech-acts are combined to form conversation structures. Two types of conversation structure include conversation for action and conversation for orientation [198]. Conversation for action has a particularly significant impact on the design of groupware systems (see Figure 6.6).

Beyond communication processes and speech-act theory one can study specific channels of communication. For example differences between face-to-face and written communication include [88] [192]:

- *Expression:* The visual channels of face-to-face communication are capable of conveying emotional information about the participants' feelings.
- *Precision:* Written communication has the advantage that it allows the participants to take their time in constructing their messages. This allows them to check the information for correctness and precision.
- *Participation:* Written communication flattens existing status and eliminates discrimination among people based on physical appearance.
- *Turn-taking:* In face-to-face communication people use both audio and visual channels (voice intonation, vocalizations, gestures, facial expression) to regulate turn-taking. In synchronous written communication, turn-taking mechanisms are difficult to establish and require additional effort [18].

From such observations one might suggest guidelines for the choice of a channel based on the user's task.

Another perspective on communication looks at the network of communication between members of a group. There are three basic networks: the *wheel,* the *circle,* or *all channel* (see Figure 6.7). The wheel is always the quickest to reach a solution or conclusion, the circle is the slowest. In complex open-ended problems the all-channel is most likely to reach the best solution. The level of satisfaction for individuals is lowest in the circle, and highest in the all-channel. Of course, the kind of technology that would support these human-human networks is paralleled in the kinds of computer networks.

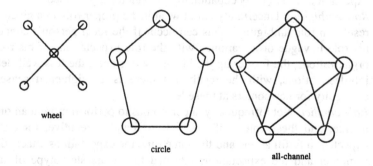

Figure 6.7: *Three basic patterns.* The wheel, circle, and all-channel are three basic communication patterns within a group.

6.3   Roles and Processes in Groups

Groups may be usefully viewed from several different perspectives. The need to coordinate provides one such perspective. Another perspective focuses on the identities or *roles* which individuals assume. Yet, another perspective is based on observation of *group processes* and generalizations about changes that tend to occur across time and in different settings.

6.3.1   Roles

One theoretical perspective on interactions between people that has endured is *role theory*. Role theory addresses the roles which people play in groups and attempts to understand the group behavior in terms of the roles which are enacted in the group. The theory is useful in linking individuals to groups [105] and in making general predictions, e.g., in ill-defined situations individuals may experience role ambiguity.

Role theory has a number of specific concepts:

*   *Role set:* An individual who is the subject of analysis is termed the focal person. The role set includes all those with whom the individual has more than trivial interactions.
*   *Role definition:* The focal person's role definition is not given by his own view of his position within the role set, but is the combination of the role expectations that others in the role set have of the focal person. Role expectations are often occupationally or even legally defined.
*   *Role ambiguity:* Uncertainty about what is the proper role in a given situation results in role ambiguity. This can occur if the focal person's conception of his role is vague or at variance with the role expectations of his role set. In organizations, the further up the hierarchy one goes, the less well-defined are job-descriptions, with the result that there is a heightened sense of role ambiguity for newcomers at these levels.
*   *Role conflict:* Not infrequently, a person has to perform more than one role at a time, and these roles will conflict. A female executive, for example, is expected to fulfill at one and the same time the expectations attached to being a mother and the expectations attached to a male stereotype of successful executive.

For individuals, the group is necessary for a feeling of identity and security. Egocentric individuals can cause much conflict in groups and organizations, but to submerge oneself totally in the group identity is also a danger. Groups tend to impose norms of behavior on individuals. By complying with these norms the individual maintains his group membership. These norms can be equated with role expectations.

Group members must have the requisite skills and abilities to do the job for which the group was formed. People who are similar in their attitudes, values, and beliefs tend to form stable enduring groups. *Heterogeneous groups* tend to exhibit more conflict, but most studies show them to be more productive than homogeneous groups. Those groups where there is the greatest differentiation of influence among members are high in morale and group performance.

A study of the optimum mix of characteristics in a team [9] discovered the so-called *Apollo syndrome;* that is, a team composed of the brightest did not turn out to be the best. The same study formulated a list of eight roles that are needed for a fully effective group:

- The *Chairman:* Presides over the team and co-ordinates its efforts.
- The *Shaper:* The task leader who deputies for the chairman and is a spur to action.
- The *Plant:* The source of original ideas and proposals.
- The *Monitor-Evaluator:* Carefully dissects ideas and sees the flaw in arguments.
- The *Resource-Investigator:* Brings new contacts, ideas and developments to the group.
- The *Company Worker:* Turns ideas into manageable tasks.
- The *Team Worker:* Holds the team together by being supportive to others.
- The *Finisher:* Without the finisher the team might never meet its deadlines.

One person may combine more than one role, especially in a small team. Stable groups can often get by without the full set of roles, but for any group to be effective there is a set of functions, corresponding to these eight roles, that have to be carried out by someone in the group. A trade-off has to be made between a large group with a diversity of talent, skills, and knowledge, or a small group with fewer of these attributes but more opportunities for individuals to make a worthwhile contribution. In practice, a *group size* of between five and seven seems to be optimum.

6.3.2 Processes

In the sociology of small groups a basic distinction is made between so-called primary and secondary groups:

Members of *primary groups* have mutually strong emotional attachments and a unique subculture which includes an informal normative system which serves to control the actions of members in relation to the group.

Secondary groups are organized chiefly to get a job done; performance is measured in terms of effectiveness or excellence and is a more important variable in determining group membership than personal feelings or attachments.

Primary and secondary groups will differ in the extent to which they have these characteristics, and furthermore across time a secondary (primary) group may change into a primary (secondary) group.

Groups can be seen as having four successive stages of growth. The initial stage is that of *forming* when the group is as yet incoherent. Preliminary activities involve talk about the group's purpose, composition, leadership pattern, and life-span. The second stage is that of *storming* when agreements are challenged and re-agreed and personal agendas are revealed. The third stage of group growth is that of *norming* where the group establishes norms about when and how it should work. The fourth and final stage of group growth is that of *performing* and shows the group at full maturity and greatest productivity (see Figure 6.8).

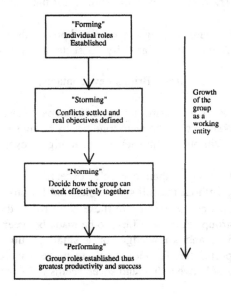

Figure 6.8: *Stages of group development.*

The term *groupthink* [99] describes a syndrome that involves a group's loss of its capacity for critical thinking. A cause of the lapse of critical thinking may be excessive cohesiveness among members of the group: their overriding goal is to continue to be together. In line with the suggestion that loosely joined, heterogeneous groups facilitate idea-generation [123], longevity has been found to be negatively related to performance in research and development groups [107].

6.4   Groupware Principles

To match groups to groupware technology depends not only on an understanding of groups but also on an understanding of groupware. This section describes *groupware principles*. Groupware systems are composed of a large number of interacting components (people, workstations, information) and must process information concurrently [87]. This involves not only computer database and interface concerns but also other technologies for sharing information.

6.4.1   Distributed Information

As a group manipulates information, various *distribution* or data sharing issues become prominent. How can information be stored so that users can both quickly get what they need and yet rest assured that information is safe and widely accessible? If two people try to modify simultaneously the same block of text, are they allowed to do so, and if yes, how are conflicting changes resolved?

There are three *architectural alternatives* for constructing software that might support distributed information: the centralized, replicated, and hybrid approaches [66]. The centralized architecture contains a single central program that controls the distributed work of all users, while a replicated architecture executes a copy of the program at every workstation. A hybrid approach combines features of both.

In the *centralized approach,* a single program which resides on one machine controls all input and output to the users (see Figure 6.9). Server processes residing on each person's workstation are responsible only for passing user input events to the central program, such as mouse movements, and for displaying output sent to the workstation from the central program. The advantage of a centralized scheme is that synchronization among users is easy, as information about user activity is located in one place. The disadvantage is that the distributed system is vulnerable to problems with the possibly overworked central server.

In the replicated approach, each application program is replicated on every machine and the replicated programs are synchronized by communicating directly with each other (see Figure 6.10). Each *replicated program* is totally responsible for its local user and for exchanging any needed information with other workstations. The system is no longer vulnerable to overwork of a central server but may have difficulties in adequately coordinating the work across the workstations.

Many *hybrid architectures* are possible. For instance, the individual workstations may use the central machine only for synchronization matters. All other activities would be performed only within and between the participating workstations. In a

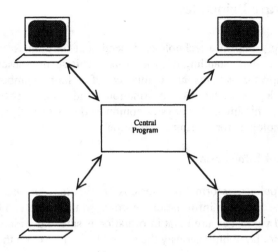

Figure 6.9: *Centralized Server:* Coordination among the four workstations is controlled by the central program.

hybrid example, a handful of users may be simultaneously changing a large information space. Each user has a full copy of the information, and each is connected to a central server [115]. Each user views and modifies his own copy of the information. Each editing change is checked locally, to see if any constraints are violated, and then the change is broadcast to the central server. At the central server, checks are again made because now the interaction with the changes of other users can be determined. If, once more, no constraints are violated, the update is broadcast to all users.

In one use of the replicated architecture approach, sometimes called the cooperative database approach, each machine has a copy of the database, and changes are installed by broadcasting the change without any synchronization. While this approach allows inconsistencies to occur, social factors in the collaborative setting may mitigate against the likelihood of these inconsistencies. Of the various information management models, a *cooperative database* model is one of the best for the needs of groups [176].

To implement a cooperative database, one may have unfortunately also to create one's own *operating system.* In many operating systems, the right of users to perform a read or write operation on a file depends on how attributes of the user match the access rights associated with the file. This is, however, not sufficient for an application that has a more abstract model than reading and writing files [68]. This

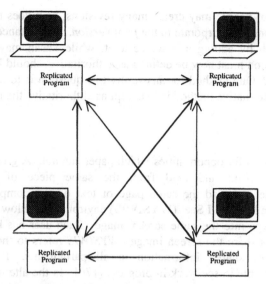

Figure 6.10: *Replicated Architecture*: Each workstation has all the software and other information which it needs to support the user. Coordination with other users is done through communication with each and every other user workstation.

limitation implies that the cooperative database's access control must be implemented by the cooperative database itself. If the operating system is not changed, files must be left unprotected at the operating system level and are vulnerable to accidental or malicious modification by users who bypass the cooperative database program.

6.4.2 Version History

An information block can undergo a number of changes in its lifetime. The contents may be totally changed, or one word may be spelled differently. Each time a block is revised, a new version of the block is created. A *version management* tool provides a useful means for distinguishing between versions of a block and facilitates the retrieval of different versions.

In one version management model, revisions are traced in a *tree structure*. The method may save space because, instead of storing copies of files, the differences between files are stored [184]. Only the original version has the full contents of the file. Each revision is stored as the editing commands which caused the change. To go from the original to a first revision, the editing commands are applied to the 'full file'. For example, if one had a file called 'A', which had the contents [a b c] and after revision became [a b c d], the method would hold the revision as 'add [d]' and the original as [a b c].

Given that a group of people may create many revisions, how does the group finally decide which revisions to incorporate in the *final version*. For instance, Pete may have changed a paragraph by adding a sentence to it, while Susan may have deleted a sentence. If one version must now be defined as authoritative, should Pete's or Susan's change be accepted? One method for answering this question is to have a discussion and then vote. An alternative method is to accept as authoritative the latest revision.

6.4.3   Interface

Groupware interfaces offer opportunities which paper can not. A group of people can not simultaneously write and read from the same piece of paper but can simultaneously write and read the same page of text on the computer (see Figure 6.11).'What You See Is What I See' (WYSIWIS) environments allow multiple authors to simultaneously type into the same screen image. Each user has his own physical screen, but the users share the screen image. *WYSIWIS* refers to the presentation of consistent images of shared information to all participants. It recognizes the importance of being able to see work in progress [176]. In the alternative of relaxed-WYSIWIS a change on one workstation, such as adding an entry, is not immediately broadcast to all others. Instead, new information is automatically retrieved and the screen updated on the next user action.

Allowing *private windows* and control of placement of windows on an individual screen seems advantageous for the *flexibility* it gives the user. Yet, in practice the users may be frustrated by not being able to see what others are doing in their private windows and needing to manage screen layout options. In trials of one WYSIWIS system, the researchers who developed the system liked its flexibility, but other users thought the technology was too complicated [176]. The proper trade-off between simplicity and flexibility depends in part on the class of users.

6.4.4   Extended Dexter Model

In one hybrid architecture a central server does consistency checks and updates, but the user workstations run their own editors and browsers. The interface is a partial-WYSIWIS interface in that updates may or may not be broadcast to all users and those updates may or may not occur in real-time. End-user editing and a run-time process that connects this end-user editing and the storage layer are fundamental to the architecture [69]. This *groupware architecture* provides several types of server and client processes that correspond to layers in the Dexter model (see Figure 6.12).

The *end-user editors* may include text editors, video players, hypermedia browsers or other such tools to operate directly on objects. The data objects may be stored by the editors in the OODB or in separate files. The data objects manipulated by these

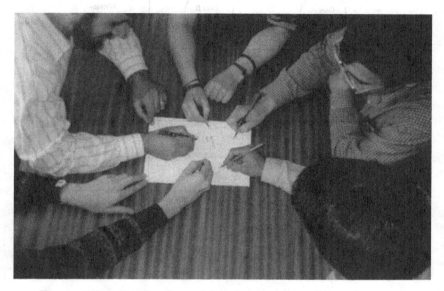

Figure 6.11: *Hands.* Several hands can not easily work on one piece of paper.

editors belong to the *Dexter within-component layer* which is now extended to include this editor functionality. The editor's hypermedia functionality only exists through communication with the run-time instantiation of the object on which the editor is operating.

A *run-time process* provides the hypermedia service for a set of active editor processes of one user by handling links, anchors, and components. This run-time process also defines a conceptual schema which is consonant with the storage-layer of the Dexter model. The 'physical storage layer' provides permanent physical storage for the hypermedia objects as instances of the conceptual schemas defined in the run-time process. The run-time processes also distribute event notifications from the 'physical storage layer' to the editors.

Nodes and *links* possess *attributes,* such as who was the creator, who was the last modifier, and who are the owners. These attributes allow a session to selectively present only the objects the current user would like to use and has the right to. In one scenario of usage, Tony and Judy both start a session on a component. Tony obtains a write lock on the component. Judy opens the component with read access and subscribes to immediate updates when it is changed by other users. Tony makes changes and commits them to the database, and immediate updates appear on Judy's screen.

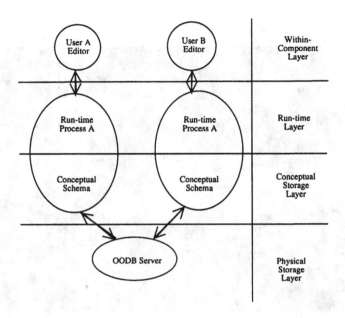

Figure 6.12: *Groupware Dexter*: This groupware architecture is presented in a different order than it would be in the Dexter model. The within-component layer is given at the top and connects directly with the run-time layer. The storage layer is divided into conceptual and physical parts. Explanations of these changes are included in the body of the text.

The 'physical storage layer' provides support for *locking of objects*. With a create operation on an object, the client gets a write lock on the created object. If an object is changed, and those changes are to be stored in the database, an update operation occurs. If an update operation is invoked on an object which is only open with read access, an exception is raised.

6.4.5   Real time Shared Workspaces

Sharing information on the computer is a key aspect of groupware but this approach must not exclude the complementing of computer support with other technological aids to collaboration. Experience has shown that simply being able to see another's workspace can be helpful in collaboration and that *television* may provide this kind of information sharing without necessarily being connected directly to the computer.

In a *real-time shared workspace*, a key idea is the overlay of individual workspaces. Each co-worker can continue to work in the same mode he was working individually so that the cognitive discontinuity between the individual and shared workspaces is minimized. A simple camera and powerful *video overlay* functions may be added to a system to increase the effectiveness of cooperative working.

The experimental 'Shared Alternate Reality Kit' provides a shared workspace. The system is equipped with an audio link as well as a video link (see Figure 6.13). The video link consists of a camera and a monitor that enables users to establish eye contact. The video link device is called a *video tunnel*. The video tunnel includes a television camera, a television monitor, a mirror, and a beam splitter. The *beam splitter* is essentially a one-way mirror which reflects the image of the viewer onto the mirror from whence it goes into the camera, while the projection from the monitor goes through this one way mirror and is seen by the viewer. To achieve the eye contact effect the camera is placed on top of the monitor. With the proper arrangement of the mirror and the beam splitter the camera's point of view is transferred from the camera's actual position at the center of the monitor. The effect of this arrangement is that users can have eye contact by aligning their sight at the center of the monitor instead of looking at the camera (see Figure 6.14). The video tunnel is an attempt to draw a real world analogy by allowing users to employ 'everyday physical and social intuitions'.

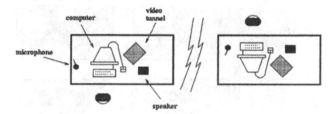

Figure 6.13: *Shared setting.* Each user has a computer, a video tunnel, and audio equipment.

6.4.6 Types of Groupware

Groupware may support either synchronous or asynchronous coordination [102]. Some tasks (e.g. brainstorming) require synchronous interaction where all the collaborators are present throughout the task. On the other hand, in some tasks, like group writing, collaborators often work in an asynchronous manner. In addition to time considerations, groupware is characterized by the support it provides for the geographical distribution of its users. Group members may work in the same place (e.g. face-to-face meetings) or in different remote places (e.g. software development teams). Groupware systems could be designed to support groups across both *time and*

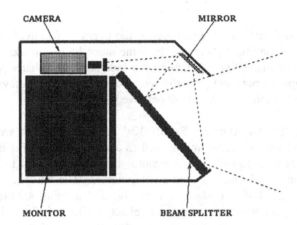

Figure 6.14: *Video Tunnel.* The video tunnel allows the user to look into the television monitor and see eye-to-eye the other person with whom a communication is occurring. The beam splitter or one-way mirror reflects the image of the user to the camera, while allowing the image of the other person to pass directly.

space boundaries (see Figure 6.15) [164].

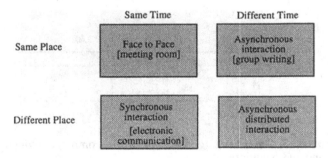

Figure 6.15: *Time and space dimensions of group work.* The type of interaction is indicated in the shaded boxes with possible elaboration in brackets.

A conference may be viewed as a universal paradigm for collaboration [158], representing both the mechanism and the process of collaborative communication. Recent advances in computer and communication technology are enhancing support for rich multimedia communication and interaction in the *conferencing paradigm.* Audio and video services are integrated through distributed computing and real-time transmission of digital multimedia to support conferencing.

A taxonomy for the conferencing paradigm has been proposed which can support many types of multimedia collaborative interaction. The taxonomy is based on the following conference attributes:

- *Static versus Dynamic:* Dynamic conferences permit changes in conference or participant attributes after initiation - static conferences do not. Most conferences are a mixture, but, for example, examinations do not permit a change of participants after the start of the examination.
- *Simple versus Super:* A Super conference contains at least one super participant, a participant that itself represents another conference; simple conferences contain only simple participants - individual users.
- *Unrelated versus Hierarchically Related:* Hierarchically-related conferences share semantic contexts, allowing for inheritance of conference and participant attributes from a parent to a child conference.
- *Transient versus Persistent:* Transient conferences last only as long as there are at least two active participants (e.g. a telephone conversation). Persistent conferences consist of a series of active and inactive sessions among participants.
- *Symmetric versus Asymmetric:* Symmetric conferences require all participants to use the same set of media for communication, whereas asymmetric conferences allow each participant to use media of his choice for communication.
- *Homogeneous versus Heterogeneous:* Homogeneous conferences do not allow conversion between different media during communication between the participants, whereas heterogeneous conferences allow media conversions such as speech-to-text recognition and text-to-speech synthesis.
- *Sequential versus Concurrent:* Sequential conferencing allows a user to participate in exactly one conference at any given time, although participation in a conference may be put on hold while the user participates in another conference. Concurrent conferencing allows users to participate in multiple conferences simultaneously. For example, while participating in a telephone conversation, a user might be also monitoring a television screen for news updates.

Various collaborative situations can be modeled within this taxonomy.

Groupware is a multidimensional concept. For example, of significance for the characterization and evaluation of a groupware system in addition to the already described parameters [193] are:

- human or machine allocation: the extent of the automation of the tasks to be performed; and
- artifact or process focus: groupware support to the product of a work processes (e.g. document production) or to the process itself (e.g. management).

Along another dimension two *approaches to groupware* are:

- groupware as mechanism, that is the system imposes and constrains people to work through explicit forms and procedures;
- groupware as context, that is the system allows groups to self-organize and adapt their procedures to the requirements of their environment.

The mechanistic approach to groupware is based on the social theory that human interaction is deterministic and can be modeled in terms of certain procedures. Under this assumption the groupware product should provide well-defined mechanisms for interaction [103].

The *Coordinator* [198] system is an example of *mechanistic groupware*. It imposes and constrains group communication to a predefined set of actions and commitments. Communication is mediated through electronic mail. Several message types are defined, and the recipient of each message has to commit to taking an action. People's reaction to The Coordinator are extreme and contradictory. Employees at the World Bank found the system very supportive, on the other hand employees at Hewlett-Packard resisted the use of the system and called it 'Naziware' [83]. Mechanistic groupware suits only certain situations. Mechanistic groupware might be successful in organizations which already base group work on strict rules and procedures. In more flexible organizational cultures such systems may reduce effectiveness and creativity.

Groupware as context reflects the opposite approach to mechanistic groupware. It is based on the social theory that human systems are self-organizing and encourages open, unrestricted interaction [103]. Freedom of choice and individual autonomy are particularly valued. Many conference systems follow this approach. Systems in this category do not focus on group dynamics. Their main focus is on user interface tools and tools that allow the structuring and the browsing of social knowledge.

6.4.7   Informal Information Sharing

Much cooperative work takes place using *informal means of communication*. But much groupware relies on formal protocols. Formal protocols for cooperative work may be particularly inappropriate in the context of loosely-coupled, socially-organized systems, lacking institutional computer networks. Information may be transmitted as a byproduct of interpersonal communication and takes advantage of chance encounters in terms of exchanging information [200].

People could carry diskettes and employ software which would allow their diskette to be updated by information on a colleague's diskette. Trials with such a method of informal information exchange showed some useful effects in certain circumstances. The spread of computer viruses is further testimony to the power of social networks to support *information distribution.*

Informal information sharing occurs in numerous circumstances in the workplace. A spreadsheet is a cognitive artifact that can be understood and shared by a group of people, providing a point of cognitive contact that mediates cooperative work [136]. Although *spreadsheets* constitute a certain class of traditional computer applications, and that means they lack the technological support that groupware provides for cooperative work, they function as actual cooperative work environments. Cooperation among spreadsheet users is informal and has a spontaneous and self-directed character.

The cooperative use of spreadsheets is obvious when describing how its users:

- share programming expertise through exchanging of code;
- transfer domain knowledge via spreadsheet templates and the direct editing of spreadsheets;
- debug spreadsheets cooperatively;
- use spreadsheets for cooperative work in meetings and other group settings; and
- train each other in new spreadsheet techniques.

The problem of *sharing domain knowledge* can be overcome by the introduction of software systems which provide a strong visual format exposing the structure and data of user's problem-solving models. Spreadsheets achieve the distribution of cognitive tasks across different kinds of users in a highly congenial way. They support an informal but effective interchange of programming expertise and domain knowledge.

6.5   The New Media and Groups

The term *new media* refers to technologies of telecommunication and computing, user devices, and their applications. The telephone which was developed in 1876 is an early example of an electrical aid to communication. The use of telephone connections between computers supports electronic mail. The combination of telephone links with television links allows people to hear and see one another at the same time. However, the combination of technologies to support electronic communication does not always lead to the beneficial effects that might be predicted.

6.5.1   Historical Lessons

The first commercial application of the telephone plus television was called the PicturePhone. When AT&T introduced the *PicturePhone* at the 1964 World's Fair the product was expected to sell very well. Julius Molnar, executive vice-president of Bell Laboratories wrote in the Bell Laboratories Record in 1969:

> Rarely does an individual or an organization have an opportunity to create something of broad utility that will enrich the daily lives of everybody. Alexander Graham Bell with his invention of the telephone in 1876, and the various people who subsequently developed it for general use, perceived such an opportunity and exploited it for the great benefit of society. Today there stands before us an opportunity of equal magnitudePicturePhone service.

Regular users of PicturePhone over the network between Bell Laboratories and AT&T's headquarters agreed that conversations over PicturePhone conveyed important information over and above that carried by voice alone.

The enthusiasm for PicturePhone from its creators at AT&T was not, however, shared by other users. These new users felt self-conscious about being on television and didn't feel that the value gained by the extra information outweighed the equipment or social costs. In one assessment use of the PicturePhone was described as 'talking to a mentally defective foreigner' [44]. The PicturePhone was a *commercial failure* and highlights the difficulty of predicting how high technology will work.

The history of videoconferencing provides a good lesson for developers of groupware (similar to the lessons from the 'PicturePhone'). By the 1970's the enthusiasm misplaced for the PicturePhone had been replaced by a somewhat similar enthusiasm for videoconferencing, which was to allow groups of people to see and hear each other through electronic media and thus avoid large travel costs. *Videoconferencing* has not become as popular as many predicted it would become. The reason for this is partly that people prefer the informal, face-to-face contact that meetings in person support. In two studies of the early 1970's, it was concluded that 85 per cent of physical meetings could be replaced with videoconferencing, while a very similar study concluded that only 20 per cent of the meetings could be thus substituted. The latter study had taken the extra step of asking people whether they would choose to use videoconferencing as a substitute for a face-to-face meeting [44].

6.5.2 Audio

Audio links can provide a useful means of communicating when face-to-face communication is not feasible. Today a large percentage of business meetings are held via *audio facilities*. However, these meetings are focused on *simple tasks,* such as simple problem solving, information gathering, information exchange, and discussion of ideas. For complex tasks, such as conflict resolution, people often prefer face-to-face meetings.

One of the reported advantages of *audio communication* is that of reducing the need of people to travel in order to conduct a meeting. Although this is important for reducing costs, it is countered by the requirement that all parties involved in the meeting should be available at the *same time*. Given the different schedules and differences in time in remote locations, conducting audio meetings may be particularly problematic. Also initiating audio meetings with people who never met is difficult. Previous acquaintance could greatly affect smooth communication.

6.5.3 Video

Research results indicate that video conferencing could be adequate in situations involving giving or receiving information, asking questions, exchanging opinions, solving problems, and generating ideas. It could also support coordination of committee-like teams. In situations where the team faces a complex task, the *visual channel* is quite useful since it is capable of conveying cues such as body movements, facial expressions, and gestures. In addition the video may allow users to have a sense of presence of other people. The sense of presence is an important factor that may affect individual performance within the group. The sense of presence depends on the size of the video screen. The feeling of 'presence' is low for normal television screens. A large projection display increases the feeling of presence.

Video's ability to support group formation is questionable. People who have not known each other previously prefer face-to-face meetings over video meetings. It is also perceived as lacking a sense of personal contact with other participants. Sometimes video may inhibit communication because participants might unconsciously use film or television as models for how they are to behave ('Hollywood syndrome'). *Inhibited communication* might affect performance. In a seminar taught by video, students at locations remote from the professor felt inhibited, had more negative attitudes toward the course, and earned lower grades than those in the same room with him.

Video use in a business context is diverse, as well as the opinions about the necessity of video. The diversity of opinions seem to suggest that rules that govern video use depend on the particular *organizational context*. The Bell Labs' video system has been used for talking to several people at once, communicating with people of the same rank, and communicating within the company. High-status persons may use video telephones to call subordinates, while subordinates would be more likely to use the telephone when communicating with someone of higher rank.

Desktop video conferencing has the advantage that participants can see and hear each other and can also make use of the facilities provided by the computer to share objects such as documents and drawings [27]. The most common use of the visual channel is to express understanding through, for example, nodding the head, which is non-intrusive in an interaction. Other facial expressions and postures also convey understanding or lack of understanding and gestures emphasize verbal descriptions. Continuous visual feedback assists the participants to create a fluid interaction. Desktop video conference participants can see what the others are doing during silent phases - such as taking notes, searching for material in the office, thinking about suggestions made - whereas extended pauses on the telephone generally need to be explained. Nevertheless, compared with face-to-face interaction, video has limitations, mainly affecting the coordination of interaction [96]. Interacting remotely through video makes it difficult for participants to control the floor through body position and eye gaze (it is not possible to ascertain exactly who other participants are looking at when all the other participants appear on each participant's screen). By the same token users have difficulty pointing at things in each other's space.

6.5.4   Virtual Reality

Virtual reality (*VR*) enables the real world to be simulated and manipulated in realistic ways without, necessarily, the danger, inconvenience, or cost consequences of action in the real world. An early example of artificially representing the world is flight simulation used for training pilots. Computer-generated graphics rather than actual video often provide the visual aspect of the VR world. The VR user knows that the VR world is *simulated* but can accept its objects such as landscapes, rooms and corridors as representations of the real world. Some tactile sensation is also being offered in VR by the use of touch sensitive pressure pads. Hand gloves may be used to manipulate VR objects in this way. Movement in the VR world is commonly synchronized with the user's actual bodily movements of walking, jumping, and running [21]. The virtual environment can be defined as a multi-dimensional experience which is totally or partially computer-generated and can be accepted as cognitively valid [100].

In *virtual reality* group applications, individuals directly interact and collaborate within a simulated world. The virtual office gives teleworkers an impression of being in a familiar place in the presence of co-workers and with access to the usual office equipment. Trainee surgeons may acquire many of the skills required to perform keyhole surgery by practicing on virtual patients. Keyhole surgery is already performed remotely, by means of microscopic cameras which can be connected to monitors displaying close-up images of the patient's tissue. The keyhole method of surgery is beneficial to patients in terms of minimizing surgical intervention and improving recovery rates but it is difficult to teach. Real patients may not be used for practice. A virtual reality patient displayed on the monitor can, however, provide a good simulation, enabling the surgeon to learn the required techniques by doing surgery. Nevertheless, at present, the direct tactile sensation of using keyhole surgical instruments is missing, there is no tactile connection between the instruments and the virtual patient. As a result, surgeons trained in this way have to initially make delicate adjustments consciously in order to compensate for tissue resistance when performing real operations.

6.6   Conclusion

The relationship between *technology* and the *social environment* is a reciprocal one. Therefore, a new technology does not exert a singular force on the people who adopt it, nor is its meaning shared equally by all. Pre-existing social patterns alter responses to the use of such technologies. New computer tools are affecting the ways in which work is accomplished, and in turn, existing patterns of social interaction are shaping the evolution of these highly malleable tools.

Computer-supported cooperative work (CSCW) is the study of groups and their information technology. The key phrase in CSCW is *computer-supported;* this suggests that the computer has a subservient role as the provider of tools, called groupware, with which certain types of work are made possible. The computer should have the same relationship to the user that the craftsman or artist has to his tools. Rather than limiting the scope for the exercise of human capacities, these tools extend this scope. Computers have for decades been used to replace human components in production systems CSCW as practiced is not concerned with how computers can be used to replace humans, but with how they can augment human capacities [101].

Groupware was influenced by a number of developments in different fields. Traditional views of *office automation* led to the design of systems that could automate the office work and replace human activities. These models were not capable of capturing what actually happened in an office environment. The office automation view was too ambitious and a shift occurred towards understanding what actually happens in the office. The understanding led to the design of systems that support office activities rather than automate them.

A groupware system supports a *transparent information space* and deals with the problems of information ownership and dissemination of that information. In addition to transparency, groupware allows users to evaluate information in its context. Non-task related information such as the identity of the originator of the information is represented. The difference in group members' goals and motives raises the need for participants to share information about the originator of the information as well the situational context in order to be able to interpret it properly.

With the availability of interactive multimedia, the sharing of information among members of a group can include moving images and sound. The fit of this kind of technology to the tasks of the group is not always as one might predict. The PicturePhone of the 1960s allowed communicators to both see and talk with one another across great distance. Consumers, however, found the poor quality of the video more troublesome than helpful.

The richest communication occurs when people are physically face-to-face, and the most sophisticated technology for connecting people with audio and video has not been able to substitute for *face-to-face communication*. Groupware development must consider *human and computer components*. It has been limited by the lack of knowledge of how people cooperate using computers as mediating technology. One must understand both the principles of groups and of technology to develop good groupware.

7
Groupware Applications

To fully appreciate the relationship between groups and groupware one must look at the *practice*. This chapter first describes the experiences of several university classes and a software engineering house with largely text-based groupware. Then experiences with several real-time, audio-video groupware systems that support meetings are described.

7.1   Collaboration in Education

In the traditional *classroom* the teacher lectures and the student takes notes. Ideally, however, interaction between the teacher and the students and among students is encouraged. Groupware can facilitate such interactions [166].

7.1.1   Hypermedia Linking

Systems whose databases are shared and updated by multiple users become immediately opportunities for students to work together. *Intermedia* is the networked hypermedia system developed at Brown University in the mid-1980s and considered a landmark for its sophisticated use of hypermedia. Hypermedia is integrated into the curricula of courses in English, Biology, Anthropology, Political Science, and Medicine at Brown University [113]. 'Context32' and 'In Memoriam' are two applications of Intermedia for education.

Students in English at Brown use *Context32,* as part of the Intermedia corpus, to supplement assigned readings. The full Intermedia corpus contains thousands of electronically linked documents in various forms, and Context32 itself contains over 2,000 documents. Context32 is a mixture of materials, study guides, summaries of state-of-the-art scholarship, introductions to basic critical concepts, and original scholarly and critical contributions. The development of Context32 was undertaken by five individuals, who each wrote documents on a set of authors and topics, and gathered graphic materials. Some materials created by others were modified and linked to the original contributions.

The student made contributions to Context32 by:

- creating links among documents present on the system;
- creating text documents (and linking them to others); and
- creating graphics documents (and linking them to others).

Graphics documents were produced by adding digitized images, such as maps or reproductions of pictures, and by creating concept maps. Student users created new *concept maps* in the form of overview or literary relation files, and used earlier ones as templates, making minor modifications and changing the texts.

The In Memoriam project at Brown University took advantage of the capacities of Intermedia to do things virtually impossible with book technology. Tennyson's *In Memoriam* is a complex, experimental Victorian *poem,* that was an attempt to create new versions of traditional major poetic forms from 133 separate sections. Each section is a poem that can stand on its own. It is particularly appropriate for hypertext representation as it makes extensive use of echoing, allusion, and repetition. The entire poem was placed in Intermedia and linked to:

- variant readings from manuscripts;
- published critical commentary; and
- passages from works by other authors.

Between January and April 1988, links and documents were added to the corpus of material already online. In the subsequent few months, members of a graduate seminar added more than a hundred documents, each commenting specifically on one or more sections of the poem and on one another's work. The first assignment for the project required them to create five documents to append to individual sections of the poem. Each week members of the seminar read the contributions of others, added more documents and then made links. The final assignment of the project involved students putting online the texts of poems by another poet that had obvious relevance to individual sections of Tennyson's work. The In Memoriam project was successful in promoting a style of *collaboration* that is foreign to much work in the humanities, where the notion of individual responsibility and authorship is firmly established, in contrast to the sciences, where collective authorship of papers and books is the norm.

7.1.2   Telephone Conferencing

The Department of Geography at Boston University has experimented with several *phone-based, undergraduate courses* since 1990 [4]. The novel, phone-based elements for the classes are telephone conferencing, asynchronous and real-time computer conferencing, electronic mail within and beyond campus, and the use of data bases and external networks for research.

The *Department of Geography* offered a new course in 1991 which explored the relationship between poverty and environmental degradation in Central America. It examined the causes and consequences of environmental deterioration, current debates among scholars and policy makers, and the range of policy and institutional responses that are being attempted in the region. The course was designed to be half 'traditional' and half 'phone-based'. In the 'traditional' mode, readings were assigned, lectures were given, and seminar-like discussions were held one day a week. Students viewed the phone-based tools as complementary and enriching, not as a substitute for more familiar classroom instruction.

Telephone conferences are simpler and initially more engaging than computer conferences. For most students, the most successful and popular element of these classes is the part that is technologically simplest: the use of a speakerphone to enliven class sessions with outside guests. This is done by plugging a speakerphone into a regular phone jack and making a pre-arranged, long-distance call.

Guests are selected on the basis of *real-world experience*. Despite some initial awkwardness, most guests express pleasure at the opportunity to interact with college students. Presentations and discussion with the guest usually lasts about an hour. When the call is completed, the class then usually discusses the presentation for another 20 minutes.

Most of these talks were planned and arranged beforehand in accordance with the structure of the course syllabus. However, some themes developed a life of their own. For example, after a lecture and readings on rainforest issues, the class interviewed a distinguished tropical ecologist who was helping to develop an international Biosphere between Costa Rica and Panama. This discussion in turn raised a new set of issues about the politics of conservation. The class then spoke with a leader in Costa Rica, who articulately explained why he bitterly opposes the formation of an international Biosphere. Such *dynamics* would be difficult to achieve without the telephone conference.

7.1.3 Computer Conferencing

The Geography course at Boston University, which was described in the previous section for its use of telephone conferencing, also extensively used *computer conferencing*. The management of the course, assignment-giving, and considerable interaction between instructor and students was conducted through a semester-long computer conference. Class members exchanged information in an organized fashion through the campus computer system and personal computers that are connected to the campus through modems and outside phone lines.

The course was structured so that major syllabus topics were introduced by lectures, class discussions, and the long-distance speakerphone presentations. Topics such as deforestation, coastal resource management, and sustainable agriculture were then set up as subconferences. Students kept individual *subconferences* running by adding comments to the particular subconferences, raising questions and carrying on student-to-student debate, and writing short critiques of assigned readings and of each other's work. As students became more skillful network users, they would reinforce some subconferences by importing relevant material from the hundreds of other conferences on the electronic highways. Often, vast amounts of highly up-to-date, technical material could be found that would carry the discussion far beyond the initial class presentation.

At the outset of the semester, students tend to participate in these conferences somewhat passively. They relate to them as if they were books — reading messages, taking notes, and sometimes importing ('downloading') information for general use within the class-only conference. Gradually, however, they learn that they can 'talk back' from their keyboards; and they begin to engage more aggressively in two-way communication. For more mature students — in particular, the graduate students in environmental studies — the course structure fades into the backdrop as they begin to relate more directly to their self-discovered communities of common interest. Typically, their energies are captured by *conference participation* and the requirement to produce an original research paper.

A *virtual reality* was created by a graduate student who applied her background in tropical ecology and computer programming to construct the shell and initial biological population for a 'virtual rainforest'. This is a text-based simulation of a rainforest environment, something like the popular adventure games on personal computers. In this case, a 'player' receives messages something like, "You hear a fluttering screech and look up through the green canopy where you see a troupe of howler monkeys . . ." Though kinetically less dramatic to students than the competition in video arcades, such 'games' are intriguing for several reasons. They can be freely accessed through the Internet from virtually any networked campus computer, they can accommodate hundreds of players in real time who are working interactively within the created environment. Their educational content could be developed in highly sophisticated ways by succeeding generations of players and rainforest-makers. For example, the plant and animal population of the 'virtual rainforest' could be biologically expanded; the forest could be populated by slash-and-burn farmers, cattle ranchers, and ecotourism operators; and so on.

The applications of technology described here ranged from simple long-distance telephone calls from a speakerphone to the creation of imaginary rainforests in a computer conference. These relatively simple technological tools can be applied to many different kinds of classroom and disciplinary settings, not just geography and environmental studies. Several broader trends on campuses encourage continuing *innovation* in this direction.

7.2   Authoring and Publishing

Work with documents, be they traditional paper documents or hypermedia documents, is often done in groups. Groupware systems to support the work of *authoring* and *publishing* are numerous. Both authoring and publishing systems allow users to work either asynchronously or at the same time. They offer mechanisms for separating comments from text, defining roles, and notifying group members of one another's actions.

7.2.1   Collaborative Authoring

In one complex collaborative writing project computer-mediated groups had to work harder and communicate for longer periods of time, facing greater difficulty in coordinating their work, than groups who met face-to-face. On the other hand, contributors in the computer-mediated groups said that such a form of communication is a satisfactory means of handling independently completed interim products [54]. So, this technology is believed to be valuable in conditions where the work could not be done *face-to-face* for geographical or other reasons.

A shared editor system, called ShrEdit, was developed at the University of Michigan and tested with interesting results. The *ShrEdit system* supports a set of coauthors with read or write access to a document. Authors may work independently on separate sections of the document. If two or more authors try to write in the same section at the same time, one of them will be granted a lock and the others will be informed of who holds the lock. The lock is obtained implicitly when an author starts editing. A user may read text that is being modified. If someone else is writing a section, the reader's view will be refreshed periodically as the section is updated. Although the system does not explicitly support real-time conferencing, a degraded form of real-time interaction (with longer delays in propagating changes) is achieved by having multiple users view the same section and taking turns updating.

In experiments with the use of ShrEdit, design teams of a few people each were asked to work together for several hours to prepare an initial design for an automated system. One set of teams worked together with ShrEdit, while another set did not. What had been anticipated was that the teams using ShrEdit would explore more ideas. Surprisingly, the opposite was found to be true. The teams using ShrEdit did a less extensive *exploration of the design space* than the other teams but produced a higher quality result which focused more clearly on the core issues. Although the computer-based tool had no explicit support for collaborative design, the teams using the tool were better able 1) to simultaneously talk and write and 2) to organize their thoughts and prepare their design [141].

7.2.2   Issue Based Information

An *Issue-Based Information System* (IBIS) [34] supports design and planning discourse. An IBIS typically uses three types of nodes (Issues, Positions, and Arguments).   An issue represents a problem, concern, or question which needs discussion. Each issue is a root for a subtree and can have one or more positions linked to it. A position is a statement or assertion which attempts to resolve an issue. It can have one or more arguments, but not more than one issue, linked to it. An argument responds to a position through either a support or refute link (see Figure 7.1).

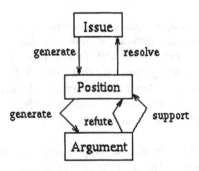

Figure 7.1: *Node and Link Types in a Discussion.* The node is the box and the link is the arrow.

One prototypical graphical IBIS [34] provides various views of its information (see Figure 7.2). This graphical IBIS was used in the research laboratories at *MCC Corporation* and several observations about its use were made.   The non-computerized IBIS method is cumbersome, and would have not reached the popularity that it has at MCC without the IBIS support tool.   Furthermore, the IBIS system was only one of many collaborative hypertext systems available at MCC but the IBIS system proved the most *popular.*   This is speculated to be so because of the good match between the IBIS method and the IBIS tool.

On the other hand, there were also problems with the use of the IBIS tool.   For instance, where several users worked cooperatively in a shared issue group, problems arose with *understanding context.* The readers found that while they had a sense of

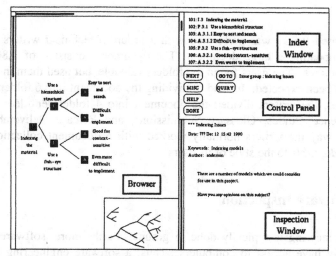

Figure 7.2: *The IBIS Interface.* This illustrative screen dump uses 4 windows to provide different views on the IBIS nodes and links:

1   a graphical browser to provide a visual presentation of the IBIS graph structure;

2   a node index window to provide an ordered, hierarchical view of the nodes;

3   a control panel which is composed of a set of buttons which extend the tool's functionality beyond simple node and link creation; and

4   an inspection window in which the attributes and contents of nodes and links can be viewed.

understanding the individual nodes, they might have difficulty following the thread of the writer's thoughts as they wound through several dozen nodes. The IBIS tool may have forced the user to express ideas in such a fine-grained and separated manner that this obscured the larger idea that was being developed.

7.2.3 Publication Management

Many publishing houses are extensively automated. Documents are created, stored, printed, and communicated electronically. One experimental publishing system from Xerox, called *Shared Books,* explicitly supports collaboration and is modeled on the folders view of publishing [116]. Folders contain the items needed to produce a publication, such as drafts of text and production schedules, and are passed from one worker to another as each job step is finished. An icon on the Shared Books screen represents a folder. Upon opening the icon, the user sees a window that displays the status of all items. Operations such as Open, Copy, and Paginate may be applied to items in the folder.

A test of Shared Books was performed with a group of technical writers who were writing and updating a large document. The document consisted of 1,800 printed pages in 6 volumes. The users found the folders valuable, but used them in a different way than had been expected. Instead of dividing the document into 6 folders based on the 6 volumes, the writers divided the document into 4 folders entitled: Chapters, Quick Reference Guides, Glossary Submissions, and Release Deliverables. This reflected the way the writers normally worked with a document collection. Shared Books was *adaptable* to the style of its users.

7.3   Software Inspection

Software engineering is typically done in groups. Furthermore, software engineers most certainly have access to computers. Thus, a software engineering house is a natural environment for sophisticated groupware tools. The Intelligent Code Inspection Environment in a C Language Environment (*ICICLE*) system was developed as an experimental tool by one software engineering house and is intended to augment the process of formal code inspection. Many of the tasks performed during code inspection are performed during a group session [20].

7.3.1   Code Inspection in the Software Lifecycle

In the *software life-cycle*, code inspection is a phase intermediate between implementation and testing. Code inspection is the review and analysis of source code modules by developers who are knowledgeable in the application domain and programming environment. It has been demonstrated that formal code inspections save time and money in the detection of certain types of coding errors before testing. Code inspection involves a complex set of tasks, many of which are performed in group sessions called code inspection meetings. It is these meetings that ICICLE has been designed to facilitate.

Code inspection meetings involve highly structured procedures which lend themselves to computer support. ICICLE is intended to reduce the transaction costs associated with code inspection by standardizing the interface between subtasks, facilitating the generation of statistical data relating to defects found in the code, and improving the structured communication within and between the subtasks.

Code inspection comprises several distinct phases. Of these, the most difficult and time consuming are comment preparation and code inspection:

- In *comment preparation* the module to be inspected is analyzed by code inspectors who look for coding errors, portability problems, and infractions of coding standards.
- In a *code inspection* meeting comments prepared by the inspectors are discussed with the author of the code. It is determined whether the code needs revision. Various metrics and statistics are recorded.

The standard code inspection procedure requires several participants [49]:

- The *moderator* makes sure the meeting goes according to schedule and productively. The moderator also records statistics relating to coding defects discovered during code inspection.
- The *reader* actually reads aloud the text of the modules being inspected, and directs the attention of other inspectors to areas of interest in the source code.
- The *scribe* records comments that are agreed on by committee. Not only is the text of the comments recorded, but they are classified according to several dimensions.
- The *author* of the code being inspected is present at the meeting in order to answer the questions of the inspectors about the module.
- *Additional inspectors,* if any, have no assigned roles, beyond the responsibility to follow the reader, and propose and discuss comments.

ICICLE augments the above roles electronically.

7.3.2   Code Inspection Meeting

The ICICLE human interface is *multi-windowed*. A central display window of the ICICLE interface displays actual source code, in addition to line numbers, annotations, and feedback from user activity. The majority of user actions concern this window. The presence of comments or annotations associated with the source code is indicated by the presence of symbols to the left of the lines of code.

Comment windows are invoked by clicking on the comment or annotation symbols. The window contains a description of the comment and a set of controls for manipulation of the status of the comment. Users may also enter their own comments through this window.

The *comment preparation process* is as follows. From a given entry point, the user traverses the source code of the module in an attempt to understand the code. When the user notices a bug, standard violation, or other item of interest, the user annotates the code via the comment window. The user may encounter a comment made by ICICLE itself, which the user may change by editing it or changing its status. All comments made by the user during this phase of operation are private to the user, and are completely owned by the user.

An ICICLE code inspection meeting is intended to occur in one room with all the inspectors close enough for easy conversation. ICICLE's groupware utilizes a number of forms of structured communication among the inspectors present at the code inspection meeting. Each *communication mode* relieves a particular secretarial burden from the inspectors.

Communication is first through the *code window*. The reader guides inspectors through the module being analyzed; to facilitate this process, ICICLE locks all code windows synchronously with the reader's so that the inspectors are always viewing the same piece of code as the reader. However, inspectors do have the option to view sections of code other than that currently being narrated by the reader, by splitting their code window in two.

A second major instance of communication concerns the propagation of annotations from one user's screen to the screens of other inspectors, and the ability of the scribe to record these annotations. When an inspector wants to make a comment on a section of code, he does it through the *comment window*, and a small window with the text of the comment pops up onto every inspectors' screen, giving the source and text of the comment.

The status of a proposed comment is recorded by the scribe. The *scribe* controls a proposal window, allowing a comment to be rejected or accepted. Rejection or acceptance of a comment by the scribe clears the proposal window from all inspectors' screens and the floor is free once again for the reader to proceed, or for another inspector to propose a comment. Accepted comments are stored in a file which constitutes a record of the meeting. All inspectors gain read-write access to proposed comments and may store them in their personal files. But only the scribe can modify a proposed comment in the merged comment file which is the output of the code inspection meeting. ICICLE is similar to a number of other real-time meeting support systems in that it requires a voice coordination channel outside the functionality supported by the interface.

Users continued to request *paper copies* of the code. The presence of a paper copy enabled an inspector to gain an overview of the code under inspection. A second reason for wanting paper copies of code modules was that inspector's liked to take the copies home where they could work without interruption.

ICICLE has elevated the role of the scribe from that of mere secretary to that of *unilateral decision-maker.* In a manual inspection meeting, the decision to accept or reject a comment is made jointly, usually through the moderator, who has final say. Likewise, the moderator usually decides on metrics such as error type and error class.

The scribe's role is required because of the labor involved in manually transcribing comments and statistics, and is strictly secretarial, without any decision-making capability superior to that of the other inspectors, or the moderator. But using ICICLE there is no labor for the scribe beyond an average of three button clicks per proposed comment. The scribe's actions signal acceptance or rejection, and the error metrics. This functionality tends to devolve the decision-making task on the scribe, and it seems artificial for the moderator to have to tell the scribe to have to accept or reject a comment, and which metrics to choose, considering that these verbal directions will probably take longer than the scribe's mouse actions in response.

7.4   MUCH System

The Many Using and Creating Hypertext (MUCH) system has features of a hypertext system, as described in an earlier chapter. The collaborative features are, however, also multiple. The *MUCH system* has been used not only to create teaching material, but also to teach students [157]. The MUCH system supports interactive working and learning practices, and emphasis is placed on group work rather than individual work [133].

7.4.1   Group Information

The MUCH database in which the nodes and links are housed also carries information about *user types* and actions. Users are divided into two types of 'managers' and 'others'. Any users can update information. Only managers can arbitrarily delete information.

The MUCH system records details of who created a particular node, who has updated that node, and how many times that node has been selected for viewing (see Figure 7.3). The smallest update upon the work of another will merit a mention in a node's information window. All of the information placed upon the *MUCH database* is marked with the name of the person who created the node containing the information and the time and date of the creation. One quick view of this information is available by asking the outline generation facility to display the name of the author and the date of creation for a node next to the node name (see Figure 7.4).

7.4.2   Peer Assessment

Each time a particular node is selected, and the associated text is displayed, not only is the person who created that node awarded a *selection credit* but also anyone who updated it is. The 'Credit Table' gives details of all of the authors and how many times each author's particular node has been selected (see Figure 7.5). Thus, if the assessment of a piece of work is based purely upon how often someone views the work, MUCH has a ready made environment to support this. Selection credits alone

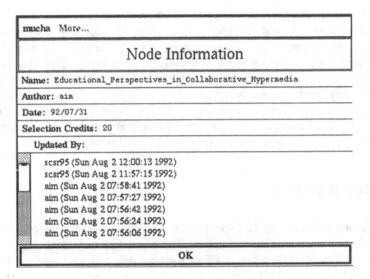

Figure 7.3: *Node Information Window.* The author of a node, the date of the node's authoring, and other information is available from a 'node information' window.

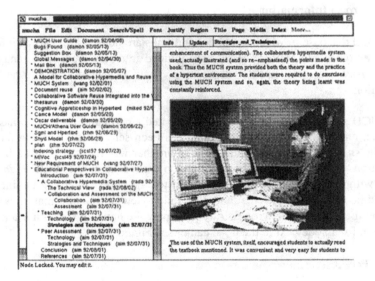

Figure 7.4: *Name and Date.* The author and date of authoring of nodes is listed next to the node name in the left window.

are, however, not a fair method of assessment as a very poor piece of work with an attractive node title may be selected often but actually read or appreciated very little. Also, the selection credit system is very much open to abuse because people can continuously select each others work to obtain a high selection credit total [155].

```
┌────────────────────────────────────────────────────────┐
│ mucha  More...                                         │
│ ┌──────────────────────────────────────────────────┐   │
│ │         Table of Authors and Select Credits      │   │
│ │    damon          (Damon Chaplin)  959           │   │
│ │    david           (David Reid)     36           │   │
│ │    hypbook       (Roy Rada et al)  126           │   │
│ │    iwc      (Dan Diaper (journal))   6           │   │
│ │    kathryn     (Miss. K.J. Coles)    1           │   │
│ │    mdb           (Martin Beer)       3           │   │
│ │    mhashi                           33           │   │
│ │    miked       (Mr. M.W. Dobson)    69           │   │
│ │    norge45     (Mr. J. Russell)     98           │   │
│ │    oscar8                            9           │   │
│ │    perena      (Miss. P.I. Gouma)  183           │   │
│ │    rada         (Prof. Roy Rada)  1266           │   │
│ │    scsr95      (Mr. P.H. Ramsey)    62           │   │
│ │    scst18     (Miss. S.A. Acquah)    7           │   │
│ │    scst49     (Mr. M.R. Anderson)  121           │   │
│ │    scst52    (Mr. A.M. Blanchard)   27           │   │
│ └──────────────────────────────────────────────────┘   │
│ ┌──────────────────────────────────────────────────┐   │
│ │                       OK                         │   │
│ └──────────────────────────────────────────────────┘   │
└────────────────────────────────────────────────────────┘
```

Figure 7.5: *Credit Selection Table.* Authors are on the left, and selection credits on the right.

In response to the student dissatisfaction another feature of the MUCH system was specifically developed for student *peer assessment*. Through a new Assessment Window students could grade the work of their peers. Students were able to assess another student's essay on a scale from one to ten, along each of five different criteria, namely content, clarity, creativity, grammar and spelling (see Figure 7.6). The system allowed each student to mark another student's essay no more than once and also maintained an average score of each essay. Using this method, each student was required to assess the work of each of the other student in the class. Subsequent feedback from the students indicated that they found this method of peer-peer assessment to be useful.

7.4.3 Writing Student Text Books

About ten authors used the MUCH system to write several *hypertext books*. The team used formal meetings to set goals and partition the work. In addition to these formal weekly meetings, the collaborators had numerous informal discussions among themselves about the book. To facilitate the collaborative process, the written records of meetings were input to the MUCH system. In this way everyone would be able to refer back to them.

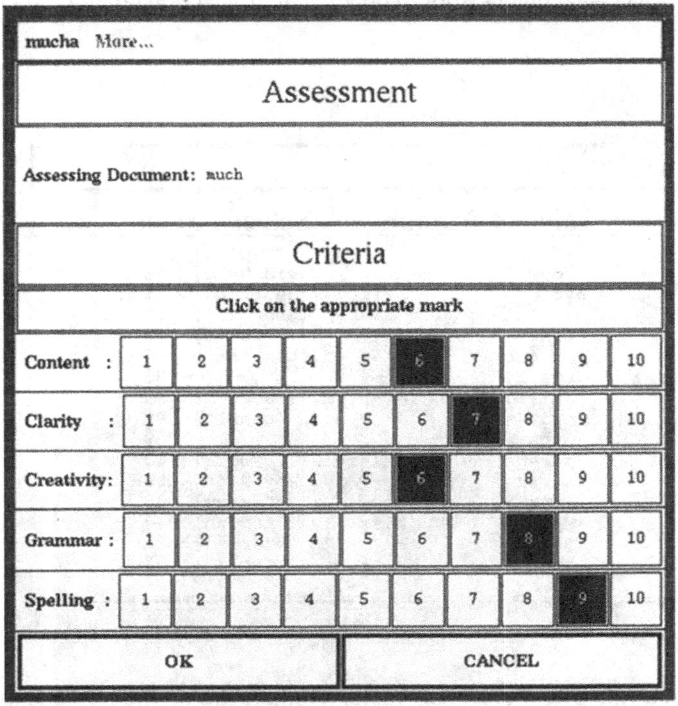

mucha More...									

Assessment

Assessing Document: much

Criteria

Click on the appropriate mark

Content :	1	2	3	4	5	6	7	8	9	10
Clarity :	1	2	3	4	5	6	7	8	9	10
Creativity:	1	2	3	4	5	6	7	8	9	10
Grammar :	1	2	3	4	5	6	7	8	9	10
Spelling :	1	2	3	4	5	6	7	8	9	10

OK	CANCEL

Figure 7.6: *Assessment Window.* The Assessment window used to help students to grade the work of their peers. After allocating a mark, for each of the criteria, the student could then click on the OK button. The Assessment window would disappear and the marks would be written to a database.

Evaluation occurred both at the individual and team level. At the individual level each person read the document and made comments on the system. This was encouraged by the availability of *comment links* that allow comments to be added readily to any node in the outline. At the team level, the members reviewed their work at the beginning of each formal meeting.

Taking the collaboration as a whole, it is interesting to observe to what extent the *collaborative process* was supported by the system and hence try to establish a minimum level of support for collaboration that the system must provide in order for it to be seen as useful by its users [130]. The system was used to aid in the collaborative writing of the book mainly through contributions being immediately viewable by all collaborators. It was not used to any appreciable extent as a medium of interaction between collaborators, though it has this facility. This may be because the system is too cumbersome or because the collaborators actually preferred the mechanisms of the formal weekly meeting round a table, and the informal chats. In addition to face-to-face meetings, electronic mail was frequently used as a medium of communication.

7.5   Real-time Interaction Technology

With real-time groupware users interact through the shared information space in real-time using various types of information such as text, audio, and video [164]. To realize *real-time groupware*, multi-user software running on networked workstations, and video and audio work spaces are needed [97]. This section describes first shared workspaces that emphasize a video link between participants, second conferencing systems which support multiple people in a discussion, and finally systems that add decision-support capability to the conference systems.

7.5.1   Shared Workspace Systems

The experimental *VideoWindow system* developed at Bellcore integrates powerful video and audio into a unique meeting room. One research group that had been divided across two buildings had the VideoWindow installed in the mail room of each building. Traditionally people came to the mail room often to check their mail and also to informally meet with colleagues. In the VideoWindow system, a specially fabricated camera produces an approximately life-size image that is displayed on a 3-foot by 8-foot screen. The microphones are arranged in a way that spatial localization of speakers and other sounds is maintained. The audio channels are duplex so that people at both ends of the connection can speak simultaneously.

The designers of the VideoWindow system expected that the system's configuration could provide a sense of shared space and presence at very low behavioral cost to the user. The system has been tested and results can be summarized as follows:

- Although people used the VideoWindow system and thus had communication that they might not have otherwise had, they did better *face-to-face*.
- In some cases the system was transparent to the users. However, people tended to speak louder in the VideoWindow setting than in face-to-face and often involved in discussions about the system itself. The percentage of conversion from opportunities for discussion to actual discussion was substantially lower in the VideoWindow setting.
- The arrangement of video cameras and monitors in the workplace might inhibit the initiation and maintenance of informal communications. For instance, in a case when people at both ends might be close to the screen this should increase the opportunity for interaction in a physical situation. In the VideoWindow setting it is possible that heads are cut (because of the location of the camera) with people being unaware of that. In such a case possible interactions are inhibited because of the violation of the face-to-face

assumption that if you can see someone else, they can see you and if you can hear someone, they can hear you.
• People in the VideoWindow setting were not able to establish the private conversations that they needed [51].

Many challenges remain in creating artificial, shared workspaces that people comfortably use.

7.5.2   Computer Conferencing

In text-based conferencing a group focuses on a particular topic and shares a sequence of messages. Users can subscribe to one or more groups and can post messages or reply to messages [33]. *Real-time conferencing systems* allow a group of co-located or distributed users to interact synchronously through their terminals.

In real-time, computer-supported conferencing there may be several participants transmitting continuous video and voice streams simultaneously [1]. These streams have to be mixed so that a composite image and audio stream is obtained. The mixing requirement particularly applies to *time-critical applications* such as real-time, computer-supported teleorchestrating. The musicians and the audience need to receive a coherent composition at each multimedia workstation. In addition, each musician has to receive the audible ensemble minus his/her own contribution, since inclusion of the musician's own output in the mixed composition would cause feedback problems. The video images may be juxtaposed rather than mixed on the display.

An experimental desktop conferencing system called *MERMAID* provides an environment that enables geographically dispersed workers to hold real-time conferences by interchanging information through the use of video, voice, and multimedia documents. The system supports input via electronic writing pads, image scanners, video cameras, and microphone-installed loudspeakers [194]. MERMAID's architecture supports synchronous and asynchronous collaboration.

The MERMAID architecture provides five *server functionalities*. The MERMAID Conference Management Server manages conferencing protocols. The Conference Information Server acts as a librarian by recording conference proceedings and making them available to participants for later reference. The Document File Server stores the actual documents produced by conferences; these are referenced from the Conference Information Server. The Local Communication Server guarantees to a group of servers and clients, collectively referred to as a domain, the sending and receiving of information from the multi-domain communication server. The Multi-domain Communication Server supports efficient and accurate communication among clients by controlling transmission routing and information flow among domains. The client provides group members with interfaces for optimum interaction with servers and other clients.

The interface to MERMAID is made up of five kinds of windows.

- A *conference window* shows menus for preparing multimedia documents before and after conferences, convening participants before a conference, requesting to join a conference, editing minutes, and setting options.
- A *shared window* (or electronic whiteboard) presents shared documents. All modifications made by a floor-holder are transmitted to all the participants at the same time. The documents can include text, graphics, still images, and hand-drawn figures.
- A *personal window* (or electronic notebook) presents personal documents.
- A *video window* can display four parties simultaneously. The current floor-holder can select which participants to display. The video window can also be used to view objects. It can be expanded to full-screen if desired.
- A *status window* shows who has the floor duration of the conference; present time; chairperson's name and floor-passing protocol selected.

Experiences with MERMAID led to numerous observations. Voice was the most commonly used medium. But if more than four persons join a conference and participants are not familiar with each other, there is difficulty in determining who is speaking. The quality of the microphones is important. Hand-drawing has been used effectively for supplementary explanations and glosses on documents shown on the shared window.

Where persons of nearly equal rank met, the baton mode (the current floor-holder designates the next floor-holder) and the first-come-first-served mode (the floor is passed in the order of the floor-request queue) were the most popular. In meetings between superiors and subordinates the designation mode was most frequently used (here the chairperson chooses who will be the next floor-holder). In brainstorming sessions, the free mode (all participants can simultaneously manipulate the shared window) was chosen. Users were able to *adapt the functionality* of MERMAID to suit these different group circumstances.

7.5.3 Adding Decision Support

Group Decision Support Systems support a group of people making decisions. CSCW systems are a more general class of systems that provide support for communication and coordination in working groups. Insights from work in both the decision-support and collaborative work arenas should inform the development of groupware products that support decision making.

GroupSystems, which was developed at the University of Arizona, adds decision-support facilities to a groupware environment for meetings. It was installed at more than 22 universities and 12 companies and has been used by more than 30,000 people. The GroupSystems architecture consist of three major components, an electronic meeting room, a meeting facilitator, and a software toolkit [139]. Several variations of the *meeting room* have been designed and used. The minimum configuration includes a network of color graphics workstations. An additional one or two workstations constitute the facilitators console. A large-screen video display, connected with the workstations, is provided along with additional audio-visual equipment (e.g. overhead projectors).

Although *GroupSystems* is designed to support a variety of tasks by different groups, a *common pattern of use* emerged through its use in universities and corporations (see Figure 7.7). Usually the leader of the group wishing to use the system meets the GroupSystems facilitator and determines the tools to be used in the meeting and develops the meetings agenda. The meeting starts with a brainstorming phase. Participants type in their ideas or comments in the workstation and the system collects and displays the data on large screens in front of the participants as well as in their workstation displays. This idea generation occurs in anonymous mode so that people can freely modify, augment, comment, and discard ideas unbiased by who created them. At the end of this phase the ideas are organized into a set of key ideas followed by a prioritization process which results in a short list of ideas. Then the participants make plans of how to realize the ideas. The process is repeated until consensus is reached. Usually at the end of the meeting a large volume of ideas and plans for actions is produced.

The *Colab system* is an experimental meeting room designed at the Xerox Palo Alto Research Center for use by about five people who want a discussion supported by a network of workstations [177]. Besides the workstations, the room is equipped with a touch-sensitive computer screen that is several meters wide (see Figure 7.8).

One subsystem of the Colab system helps users to organize ideas and plan a presentation. The output of this 'idea organizing' mode is an annotated outline of ideas. Outline generators have similar output but Colab supports collective use. The Colab 'idea organizer' divides a meeting into three phases, brainstorming, organizing, and evaluating, among which users may move in any order they like:

1   In the *brainstorming* phase a participant selects a free space in a public window and types a phrase.

2   In the *organizing* phase the group attempts to establish an order for the ideas generated in the brainstorming phase. The basic operation is to assert that one idea comes before another and to indicate this visually by directed links between ideas.

3   In the *evaluating* phase, participants review the structure of the linked ideas and eliminate peripheral ideas.

In sessions with a prototype 'idea organizer', even before moving to the organize phase, members began using *spatial groupings*. Even after items were explicitly linked, the spatial cues helped to display the relationships. The creators of Colab assumed that the outliner would be used after the evaluation phase. In practice, participants found the outlining tool useful for displaying states of the emerging structure.

One premise behind a meeting system is that serial access to problem-solving technology obstructs the kind of equal participation that ideally characterizes collaboration. However, experience with Colab demonstrates that the constraints imposed by current technologies are not just a limitation on collaboration, but in some ways a resource as well. When a technology allows only one person to enter information at a time, a kind of *shared focus* is enforced. Users tend to agree socially on what the focus of activity needs to be each step of the way.

7.6   Conclusion

This chapter describes several *groupware systems* and the *experiences of groups* with that groupware. The role of groupware in supporting group activity is a complex one. Both time and space factors interact with the human and technology factors to determine what technological systems are good for what people performing which tasks.

Hypertext systems in the classroom that allow students to *collaboratively add information* are a kind of groupware. Some experiences with such tools in classrooms suggest that students learn effectively to create and share information. The students both add interesting new information from diverse sources and comment on the additions of others.

Both telephone conversations and traditional computer conferencing have been employed in classrooms to help students learn about a topic by interacting with one another and with other people around the world whose expertise is germane to the course. Such *technologically supported human-human communication* has enlivened classrooms and motivated students to explore topics they might have otherwise ignored.

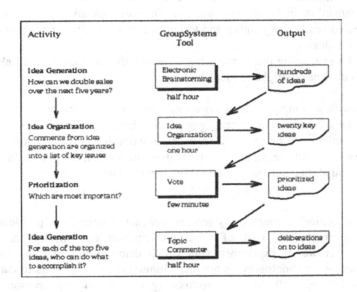

Figure 7.7: *GroupSystems pattern of use.* The activity, the tool, and the output for electronic meetings with GroupSystems are mapped in this figure [139].

Figure 7.8: *The Colab System.* Colab is shown in this photograph with each user having a workstation and the electronic whiteboard connected to the workstations.

Software engineers typically fulfill well-defined roles in groups. One such group performs code inspections. At a code inspection meeting the role of scribe is to take minutes, while the chair guides the meetings to its conclusions. Groupware has been developed to support the code inspection meetings and led to changes in the roles of people. With the groupware, individuals at the meeting entered their own comments directly into the official computerized minutes of the meeting. The scribe then took the role of modifying these entries by the participants so as to make a cohesive record of the conclusions of the group. In this way the scribe assumed functions otherwise specific to the chair. Such impacts of groupware on the group are not unusual and highlight the importance of paying careful attention to the relationship between people and technology.

The Many Using and Creating Hypertext (MUCH) system was introduced in the chapter on hypertext. In this chapter its technical features and usage are explained as they pertain to groupware and groups. The *MUCH system* has various database-like functions which permit tracking of who is using the MUCH system, when they use it, and on what part of the database they operate. This kind of information combined with editable hypertext have supported novel applications in *student-student learning* and in *collaborative authoring*.

The preceding examples of groupware usage have focused on natural language communication either vocally or in written form and on links among blocks of natural language. The new technologies, however, support rich *visual communication* too. Not only can the documents on a desktop be shared but television cameras can capture all the details of the desktop plus the people around the desktop and share the visual information with other participants at other desktops. The technical challenges behind high-fidelity communication of this sort are manifold.

Despite the impressive capability of groupware to support video and audio real-time interactivity, people remain often less satisfied with groupware-mediated communication than with *face-to-face communication*. People are less able to appreciate the focus of attention of a group when only television cameras and audio phones are carrying information about the different members of the group. The boundary between public and private exchange may be difficult to establish in a groupware-based dialog. On the other hand, when physical separation will not permit face-to-face meetings, groupware may allow for better coordination than would be possible without the groupware.

When the computer is involved in the coordination, it can do more than manipulate audio, video, and text. The computer can be programmed to support *decision-making*. It can watch the exchanges among people, and based on how it was programmed, the computer can contribute to the interactions so that the group more easily makes good decisions.　Experiences with such systems have indicated that people tend to prefer the technology to play a supportive rather than decision-making role.

Part III:

The Organization and Networks

Hypermedia is linked and synchronized media and was presented in this book as particularly germane to individuals. *Groupware* takes special care for the communication, decision-making, and coordination needs of groups. Neither individuals nor groups operate in isolation and without the larger fabric of organizations no hypermedia or groupware would exist. Furthermore, the needs of organizations transcend those of the groups or individuals which compose the organizations. These new needs call for new technology.

This Part III contains three chapters entitled 'The Organization', 'Networks and their Applications', and 'Organizational Case Studies'. 'The Organization' chapter examines the communication channels unique to organizations and the models of organizational behavior which can support the development of relevant information technology to support the *organization*. Networks are the subject of an entire chapter because networks are particularly vital to communication and control in organizations. 'The Organizational Case Studies' chapter reviews the experiences of some organizations with networks and, more generally, with information technology.

Networks are also important in groupware and the subject of networks could have been, at least, partly placed in Part II 'Groups and Groupware' of this book. That placement would have deprived the book of the clear delineation of topics which is afforded by focusing on networks in one context. The context for networks is more appropriately the organization than the group or the individual.

8
The Organization

Organizations consist of groups which work together to reach the organization's goals. Each group is expected to have for its members stable roles and defined tasks. Organizations have differing atmospheres, ways of doing things, differing levels of energy, of individual freedom, and kinds of personality - in short, they have different cultures. Cultures are made of interlocking sets of values, norms, and beliefs. Organizations are molded by history and present circumstances, by technology, by the people that work in them, and by their objectives. Following an information processing approach to the study of *organizations,* they can be defined as the "social structures constituted to gather and interpret information about the environment and use it to convert other resources into outputs such as products and actions" [159].

The phenomenon of the globalization of businesses is at one and the same time a result of developments in information technology and a spur to further developments. There is a need for improved coordination within and between organizations. Managers foresee that increased *coordination* can be achieved through the proper use of information systems.

Despite huge financial investments, information system implementations sometimes result in *failure* [161]. Two apparently contradictory assertions have been made:

- Some claim that in order for organizations to realize the benefits of information technology, they have to restructure around the capabilities of the technology [145].
- Others say that the failure of some information systems implementations has been due to their being developed from a partial understanding of the realities of organizational life.

The import of this situation is that organizations need to be very clear about what they are trying to achieve with information technology, and systems designers need to understand how the organization works.

Computer networking and *hi-fidelity interfaces* transform the conventional information-processing tasks performed by employees. Because the pattern of relationships among individuals is defined by the information processing tasks they perform, the adoption of these technologies can shift organizational structures. With computers joining networks and interfaces gaining fidelity, a new opportunity for organizational information systems appears.

8.1   Organizational Environments

The social, economic, religious and political surroundings in which an organization finds itself can have significant effects on its whole orientation. *Environments* exhibit different characteristics, and while some may severely influence the actions of an organization, others may exert relatively little effect. Three types of environmental conditions are [46]: the randomized environment, the clustered environment, and the turbulent environment.

The *randomized environment* is the least complex environment and so presents the organization with few challenges to its survival. Goals and noxiants ('goods' and 'bads') are relatively unchanging in themselves and randomly distributed [173]. A critical property of organizational response under random conditions is that there is no distinction between tactics and strategy.

In the *clustered environment* goals and noxiants are not randomly distributed but hang together in certain ways. In clustered environments strategy emerges as distinct from tactics. Survival is critically linked with the information the organization has about the environment. In the clustered environment the relevant objective is that of 'optimal location'. To reach these locations requires concentration of resources, subordination to the main plan, and the development of a certain level of competence. Organizations under these conditions tend to grow in size and also become hierarchical, with a tendency towards centralized control and coordination. The first two centuries of the industrial revolution constituted such an environment.

In the *turbulent environment* the existence of other organizations is the most significant feature of the environment in terms of survival. To survive, the organization has to have information about the other organizations. In military terms, organizational response to a turbulent environment involves both strategy and tactics, and an intermediate level of the operation. An operation consists of a planned series of tactical initiatives, calculated reactions by others, and counter-actions. The flexibility required encourages a certain decentralization and also puts a premium on quality and speed of decision at various peripheral points. The organizational objective in a turbulent environment is not so much one of determining one's location as of ensuring the capacity to move more or less at will, to be able to make and meet competitive challenge. In certain circumstances, it may only be possible to achieve stability by entering into partnerships with other organizations.

8.2   Organizational Structure

In the 1960s, it was argued that computerized information systems would transform organizations by decentralizing them and substantially reducing the numbers of middle managers [10]. Various writers have sought to categorize the new *organizational structures* that have or will evolve to cope with a rapidly changing environment [188]. The web structure is centralized and informal. The hierarchy structure is centralized and formal. The matrix is decentralized and formal, while the federation is decentralized and informal.

8.2.1   Web

Small entrepreneurial organizations tend to exhibit a *power culture*, and their structure can be pictured as a *web*. This culture depends on a central power source, with rays of power and influence spreading from the center. Effectiveness is maintained through trust and empathy; communication is by 'telepathy' and personal conversation. There are few explicit rules and procedures, and a minimum of bureaucracy. Control is exercised from the center through key individuals. It is a political organization in that decisions are taken very largely on the outcome of a balance of influence rather than on procedural or purely logical grounds.

Organizations with *power cultures* exhibit a high degree of flexibility They can move quickly and respond positively to threat or danger. To be successful in this type of organization, an individual must be politically-minded and rate security as a minor element in their employment contract.

But *size* is a problem for power cultures. The web can break if it seeks to link too many activities. The only way a web organization can grow and remain a web is by spawning other organization. Organizations which have done this continue to grow but are careful to give maximum independence to the individual heads of the linked organizations, usually keeping finance as the one string that binds them to the central web.

8.2.2   Hierarchy

The features of an ideal or pure hierarchy are [144]:

•   *Specialization.* The work of individuals and departments is broken down into distinct, routine, and well-defined tasks.

- *Formalization.* Formal rules and procedures are followed to standardize and control the actions of the organization's members.
- *Control hierarchy.* A multi-level pyramid of authority clearly defines how each level supervises the other (see Figure 8.1) [120].
- *Promotion by merit.* The selection and promotion of staff are based on well-known criteria rather than the unexplained preferences of superiors.

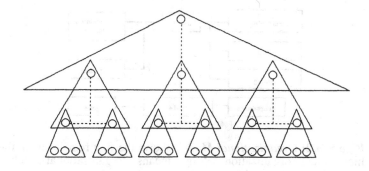

Figure 8.1: *The hierarchical organization.* The vertical and horizontal lines represent formal channels of communication.

A *hierarchical organization* may be seen as having five levels of activities [183]:

- Level 1: an articulated global objective which the organization attempts to achieve.
- Level 2: critical areas which have to be successful for the organization to achieve its global objectives.
- Level 3: particular independent operations which have predetermined and specific inputs and outputs, e.g. accounting, marketing, personnel, and administrative services (see Figure 8.2).
- Level 4: procedures and jobs. 'Procedures' are the work performed to achieve a specific purpose, such as procedures for invoicing, writing programs, and collective bargaining. 'Jobs' reflect the way the work is aggregated into divisible units (see Figure 8.3).
- Level 5: physical and mental tasks actually undertaken such as typing, phoning, traveling, and reading.

The hierarchy will succeed where the market is stable or predictable or controllable, or where the product-life is a long one. Many large organizations with this culture foundered in the changing conditions of the 1960s.

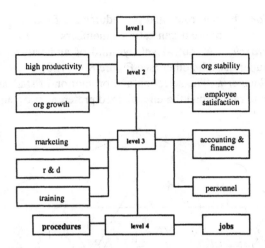

Figure 8.2: *Organizational Model*: shows the first four levels in the hierarchical organization. 'org' means 'organizational', 'r&d' means 'research and development'.

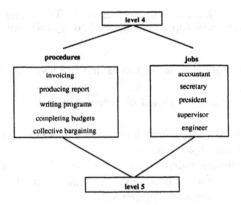

Figure 8.3: *Organizational Model Level 4*: shows the fourth level of the hierarchical organization.

8.2.3   Matrix and Federation

The *task culture* is job or project oriented and its structure is best represented as a net or *matrix* (see Figure 8.4). Some of the strands of the net are thicker and stronger than others. Much of the power and influence lies at the intersections of the net. The so-called 'matrix organization' is one structural form of the task culture.

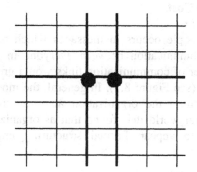

Figure 8.4: *Task Culture Net.* Lines of communication meet at the intersections which is where the power rests.

The emphasis in the task culture is on getting the job done. The culture seeks to bring together the appropriate resources, the right people at the right level of the organization, and to let them get on with it. *Influence* is based more on expert power than on position or personal power. Influence is also more widely dispersed than in other cultures, and each individual tends to think he has more of it.

The task culture is appropriate where flexibility and sensitivity to the market or environment are important. It is found where the market is competitive, where the product life is short, and where *speed of reaction* is important (such as the computer industry). But the task culture finds it hard to produce economies of scale or great depth of expertise.

Federalism takes decentralization further than the matrix does and implies groups allied together with some shared identity [77]. The members of the federation control the center. A *federation* comes into being when a number of sovereign entities perceive that they can do something better in collaboration than they can separately.

8.3 Communication

Organizational communication models attempt to model the communication links that tie the organization together and connect it to the outside world. As an organization grows in size, the number of possible *communication links* grows very quickly. Communication costs can become overwhelming, and control is needed to dampen these costs.

8.3.1   Communication Costs

Communication among people occurs in messages which reflect the enactment of work activities. Full communication between everyone in an organization would mean that the total number of communication links would grow exponentially as the organization grew in size (see Figure 8.5). In general, the more communication links there are, the less structured the organization and the higher the *overheads of communication*. In the real world it is found that as organizations increase in size, formal structures begin to appear. Formal structuring implies the existence of specialisms and hierarchies.

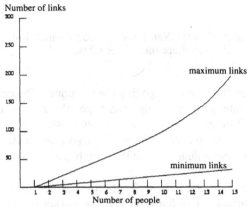

Figure 8.5: *Communication links in the organization*: Number of communication links is along the vertical axis, while number of people is on the horizontal axis. The curve for maximum number of links follows (number of people) times (number of people minus one)! The minimum number of links occurs when each person communicates to just one other person.

By introducing *specialisms* the number of communication links in an organization can be reduced. The division of labor means that the individual will only have the information required for the job to hand. Thus, for a clerk in one specialist department to communicate via formal channels with another clerk in a separate specialist department requires a considerable number of upward, transverse, and downward links. If this type of communication becomes a regular requirement, then, rather than just redividing the existing resources in a different way, the organization of work can be changed so that the work to be done is allocated to project teams. This approach leads to the matrix organizational structure. Matrix organizations are appropriate where customer service is of paramount importance as it avoids exposing customers to a number of different functional sections.

Anything that affects the structuring of communication will have an impact at the organizational level. The development of networked information technology can give rise to further communication channels (see Figure 8.6). An organization must be careful to prevent the increased availability of *communication channels* from interfering with the orderly flow of information.

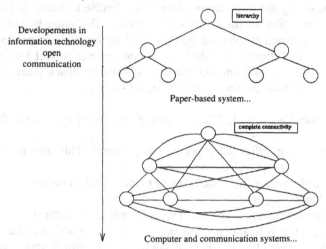

Developements in
information technology
open
communication

Paper-based system...

Computer and communication systems...

Figure 8.6: *Impact of technology upon communication channels.* In the hierarchy each individual communicates principally with his superior and subordinates (if any). At the other extreme is a situation in which everyone communicates with everyone.

The simple assumption about effort is that it is proportional to the product of the number of people working on a project and the amount of time they spend on the project. Thus, if each of 10 people works 5 days on a project, then the project has had 50 person-days invested into it. Assessing projects as to the number of person-days required to complete them implies that assigning more people to a task would shorten the number of days required to complete the project. For instance, 50 people working one day might be able to solve the 50 person-day problem. In reality, however, this assumption about *productivity* is misleading.

Each new person brought into a project needs instructions about what he or she is to do, which takes time from those who give the instructions. The new person can do work but also needs guidance which *costs* the work time of others. In the worst case the communication needs are such that a new person must communicate with every person already on the project. If the communication costs are considered, then adding people to the team may increase the cost of getting the job done.

8.3.2   Control

Feedback is the transmission of the receiver's reaction to the sender. The concept derives from the field of *cybernetics* or *control*. For instance, the thermostat in a central heating system sends messages to the boiler, and receives messages from the thermometer measuring the room temperature. This feedback enables it to adjust the performance of the boiler to the needs of the room. The same is true in human communication. Feedback enables the speaker to adjust his performance to the needs and responses of the audience. Feedback helps the receiver to feel involved in the communication. In complex human information systems feedback takes many forms due to its importance in the continued functioning of society.

The process of control is cyclical. The elements of the control cycle are as follows:

1   An objective specifies the expected performance. This may be a budget, a
        procedure, a stock level, or some other target.
2   Actual performance, e.g. time taken or money spent, is measured.
3   1. and 2. are compared.
4   Variations are red to a manager. This is 'single-loop feedback'.
5   The manager acts to alter performance in accordance with the plan.
6   Feedback is given to a higher level control unit regarding variations between
        overall performance and plan. This is 'double-loop feedback'.

Single-loop feedback is the conventional feedback of relatively small variations between what actually happens and the plan in order that corrective action can be taken to bring performance in line with the plan. This feedback is at operational and tactical levels of management — stock control, production control, budgetary control, and standard costings are examples. These systems are the first to be computerized and may include automatic decision making. *Double-loop feedback* ensures that plans, budgets, organizational structures, and control systems are revised to meet changes in conditions.

The *Law of Requisite Variety* states that for full control, the control system should contain variety at least equal to the system it is designed to control. Therefore, relatively simple control systems cannot be expected to control the multi-faceted activities of a complex organization. Closed feedback systems will only be suitable for simple, structured applications because only in these circumstances will it be possible for there to be enough predetermined control actions to match all possible control conditions. In more complex and uncertain circumstances effective control will only be achieved by open-loop feedback, systems where managerial intervention is needed to generate enough control variety to meet the unexpected conditions which will inevitably arise.

8.4 Models

A *model* is a conceptual structure which provides the apparatus for describing some particular situation [89]. The model is then used to derive properties and predict the behavior of the system. Petri nets are a formalism based on graphs with tokens where the tokens move under certain conditions in parallel through the graph. Petri nets have been used to model organizations [45]. Many other modeling languages have been applied to organizations. The remainder of this chapter describes the Activity Model Environment which incorporates a model within an environment for applying that model to organizations.

8.4.1   An Object Oriented Model

The *Activity Model Environment* (AME) is an object-oriented system for exploring models of organizations [174]. The AME includes a database and an associated rule-based formalism for representing activities and organizational states. Users interact with the model by creating and playing roles. Activity-related communication proceeds via the exchange of messages between roles.

Eight components of the AME framework can be identified (see Figure 8.7):

1   *Activities* are sets of tasks for achieving a goal.
2   *People* are placeholders for actual individuals.
3   *Roles* specify the responsibilities and duties of people.
4   *Workspaces* contain resources associated with roles.
5   *Messages* are objects that flow between the role instances associated with an activity.
6   *Information Units* are used in building messages.
7   *Rules* constrain the behavior of components.
8   *Functions* are performed by roles and messages as part of an activity.

In AME, roles, people, workspaces, information units and messages are represented as objects and are stored in the Organizational Manual which is a database acting as reference both for users of the AME, and for the AME itself. Activities are sets of tasks that are performed by groups of role instances to achieve a set goal.

People have object entries in the *Organizational Manual* associated with them. Each entry specifies the roles that each person is authorized to play. A person interacts with AME through specified role instances. Each person may hold several role instances at any one time. Roles define responsibilities that are taken by one or more people. A role instance consists of the person instance undertaking the role, the set of role rules, and a role agent. The role agent is executed by the system and might undertake some

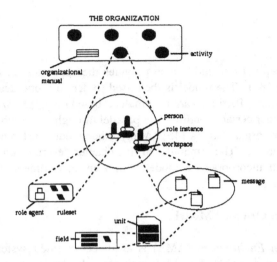

Figure 8.7: *AME components.*

of the person's responsibilities. The role agent uses the role rules in the performance
of the role.

A *workspace* is a conceptual work area that contains resources associated with a
particular role. Multiple role instances may be associated with a workspace. The
workspace also contains message handling resources. Messages are used for role
instances communication.

Messages collect and transfer information associated with activities between roles.
They exist for the lifetime of an activity. There are different types of messages (e.g.
memos, notices, and forms). *Information units* (iunits) are atomic information objects.
Messages are composed of groups of iunits. An iunit has a name, fields, and a set of
completion rules associated with it.

Rules define and constrain the behavior of roles, messages, and iunits under specified
conditions. *Functions* are atomic operations performed within group communication
(e.g. instantiate-message, fill-field). They must be executed entirely by one role
instance or role agent.

8.4.2   An Example

A company that makes interactive media for training purposes could benefit from
information technology support in many aspects of its work. Interactive media for
training may be called *courseware,* for short. In a model of courseware development
several forms are manipulated by several people playing particular roles — this may
be represented in the AME environment. In AME all intermediate products can be

treated as messages. The first phase of the courseware development cycle is the 'Learner Needs Analysis'; another critical phase is the 'Evaluation'; and both of these will be illustrated here.

The objective of the *learner needs* activity is to analyze the actual learning needs in order to define the general educational aims and the prerequisites to enter the course. A 'Customer Information' message is created using a template from the organizational manual. The message's constituent parts, information units, and rules are invoked as well. The message records information about the person who created it (person X), the role the creator was playing (Instructional Designer), and the time it was created. The message is then routed to the workspace associated with the role that created it (see Figure 8.8).

When a *message* arrives in the workspace, the *workspace* tries to determine which person should deal with it based on attributes of the message. The workspace then informs the Instructional Designer role instance that person X is associated with the message and that a message is awaiting attention. If person X does not play the relevant role anymore, then the workspace will notify all other instances of the role. The rules within the Instructional Designer role instance determine whether the message can be processed. If the message can be processed, the role instance locks it until the process finishes.

By default, the person performing the role (person X) would fill-in the details in the current *information unit*. However, some of the fields within the unit may be filled-in automatically by the role agent. After person X or the role agent fills-in the fields in the information unit, the workspace unlocks the message and informs the current information unit that it is complete. At this stage, the information unit triggers its rules which check the validity of the field values and determine which will be the new 'current' unit and which role will process it. The message then routes itself to the appropriate workspace. This circuit is repeated until all the information units are completed. At this point the message is considered complete and the next message is activated and routed to the appropriate workspace.

Another critical phase in the courseware development life cycle is the *evaluation of the storyboard*. This evaluation is critical to improving the educational effectiveness of courseware (see Figure 8.9). Three messages are involved in this activity:

1   Storyboarding Production Forms,
2   Partially Revised Storyboarding Production Forms, and
3   Definitive Revised Storyboarding Production Forms.

The Subject Matter Expert, the Instructional Designer, the Communication Expert, and the Media Expert are the four roles which process the three messages as they conduct a quality review and do a pilot test.

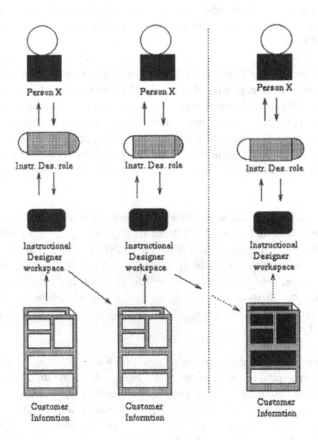

Figure 8.8: *Context Analysis.* The Customer Information (CI) message contains information about its creator (Person X), their role (Instructional Designer), and the time it was created. This Figure shows how the message is routed to the Instructional Designer workspace.

8.4.3   Coordination Services

The AME can be used on the computer to help manage the interdependencies between activities performed by multiple actors (see Figure 8.10). This *coordination service* may provide to the users:

- setup functionalities and

- runtime functionalities.

The setup functionalities are related to the startup phase of the project, while the runtime functionalities support people while working on the project. The process of setting up and running a project, as far as the coordination services are concerned, begins when the project manager or someone that has an equivalent role creates a new project template and enters all the needed values for the attributes of the new Project Template. A set of quality standards must be chosen from the available ones, eventually modified, or created from scratch.

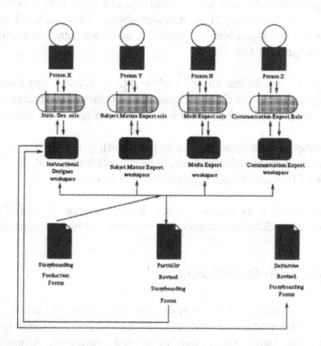

Figure 8.9: *Evaluation.* The story-board is evaluated by several roles.

After these two preliminary steps, the project can be 'officially' started by launching a module called the *Context Sensitive Module.* The Context Sensitive Module (CSM) is able to read the Project Template in order to deduce from it the state of the project, that's to say which message objects have been produced and which message object(s) can be produced at the moment (i.e. the input they need is ready). The CSM puts in action the person(s) that must work to produce the message object(s) by looking into the Project Template, finding the email address(es) of the person(s), and sending:

- the Message Object Template,
- the Message Object(s) needed as input, and
- the list of the persons collaborating on that task, if the task is performed by a team.

At this moment the work of the Coordination services is suspended, and the CSM 'goes to sleep' and waits until the message object is completed. The task of making people interact among themselves is the responsibility of other modules. When the message object is completed, someone 'wakes up' the CSM by passing to it the prepared message object (the completed template), and eventually a rationale of the process that led to the production of the message object. Then the CSM marks in the Project Template the message object as produced, and starts again its cycle to deduce the new state of the project, and so on.

A Project manager or anyone that has been allowed to do it, can at any moment during the project life-cycle, ask of the CSM the *state of the project* to the present date or to a date somewhere in the future. The view that the CSM can give to the user can be on:

- the message objects (produced, to be produced),
- the Phases / Activities (carried out, to be started), and
- the Roles / Persons (being engaged, that will be engaged).

The CSM is just one of many modules which together support the coordination of a project, but the other modules are analogous in fundamental ways to the CSM module.

8.5   Innovation in Organizations

It is useful to make a distinction between the process of creativity and the process of developing the creative idea to the point where it can be communicated to the rest of the organization. The latter process may be termed *innovation*. Organizations are critical to the process of innovations, and can also foster creativity.

8.5.1   Linear Versus Interactive Models

The traditional model of technological innovation is *linear*, involving a chain of successive, interrelated activities [128]. It begins with basic scientific research and continues through applied research, the development of new product ideas, the development of prototypes, to commercial production and finally diffusion (see Figure 8.11). The national industrial success of Germany in the nineteenth century is attributed to its combination of high investment in innovation, the development of a wide range of technical skills in industry, and the close relationship between the

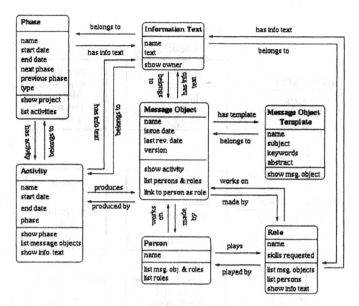

Figure 8.10: *The Coordination Data Model.* A project has phases which are turn decomposed into activities. People play roles as manifested by their exchange of messages. The boxes indicate entities in the system. The first subbox inside a box specifies static attributes of the entity. The second subbox gives the functions which the entity performs.

universities and industry. From 1870, large German companies set up in-house research and development laboratories, and United States corporations followed suit [135].

The growth of information has, however, meant that much university research knowledge is now either too general or too fundamental and long-term, to be easily usable by *commercial organizations* [146]. Assimilating knowledge and technologies from outside the organization is costly. In fact, firms tend to innovate mainly in areas from which they have learned by doing. There is a need for highly interactive models to capture the complexity of the innovation processes where ideas can be developed at all points (see Figure 8.12).

8.5.2   The Xerox Case

Xerox Corporation develops information systems that build on the innovation within the company. Work environments are created where people can legitimately improvise, and where those improvisations can be made part of the organization's collective knowledge base.

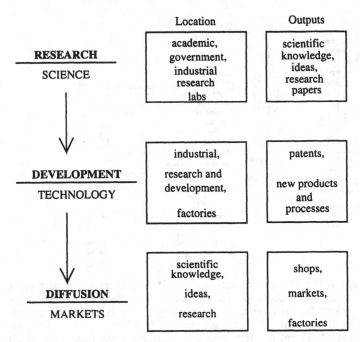

Figure 8.11: *The linear innovation model.* A chain of successive interrelated activities, from research, development, to diffusion makes new applications.

In 1984, Xerox's service organization wanted to improve the effectiveness of its training programs. The original idea was that traditional classroom training could be made to happen faster, perhaps by means of an expert system. But based on Xerox's developing theory of work and innovation, it was eventually decided to send an *anthropologist* (who had in the past been a repair technician) to find how repair people actually do their jobs. It was found that they learn most not from formal training courses but in the field by working on real problems and discussing them informally with their colleagues. These informal discussions are crucial to the learning process. For instance, people could pass around annotated videoclips of useful stories, much like scientists distribute their scientific papers, to sites all over the world. By commenting on each others experiences, employees could define and disseminate new knowledge.

The approach taken at Xerox is to make research relevant to the company's most pressing business problems. Xerox has called their approach 'pioneering research', and it has led them to redefine what they mean by technology, innovation, and research:

- Research on new work practices is as important as research on new products.
- *Innovation* is everywhere, the problem is learning from it.
- *Research* cannot just produce innovation, it must 'co-produce' it. 'Co-producing' new technologies entails a shared understanding with partners throughout the organization and with customers as to why these innovations are important.

The research department's ultimate innovation partner is the *customer.* Prototyping technology in use, harvesting local innovation, and co-producing new mental models of the organization are techniques that are applicable to external as well as internal customers. Xerox feels that future competitive advantage will be gained from co-producing products with customers. Thus there is a need for methods and tools that can help customers identify their 'latent' needs and improve their own capacity for continuous innovation.

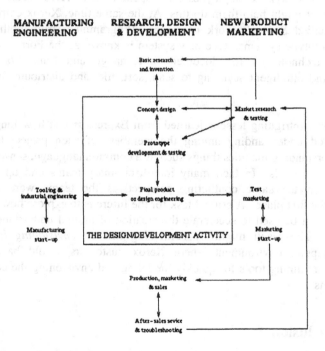

Figure 8.12: *Interactive Innovation.* Manufacturing, research, and marketing are intimately linked in the new model for innovation [128].

8.5.3   Technology Transfer

Another challenge of 'pioneering research' is presented by the problem of communicating fresh insights about familiar problems so that others can grasp their significance. It is not just a simple process of 'transferring information', which is the conventional approach to technology transfer. People need to *experience* the benefits of the innovation for themselves.

An initiative of Xerox's Corporate Research Group known as the *Express Project* is an experiment in product delivery management designed to commercialize technologies more rapidly by directly involving customers in the innovation process. Express involves employees from a client organization, Syntex. *Syntex* is a pharmaceutical company with more than 1000 researchers developing new drugs awaiting approval from the government. Express helps the company manage the more than 300,000 'case report' forms (forms that report on tests of new drugs on human volunteers) it collects each year. Syntex employees have spent time at Xerox learning the new technologies that might help them do this. At the same time, Xerox employees have intensively studied Syntex's work processes. Programmers from both companies worked on prototype systems. One new system is known as the Forms Receptionist. It combines technologies for document interchange and translation, document recognition, and intelligent scanning to scan, sort, file, and distribute Syntex's case reports.

One of the most intriguing lessons learned from Express is just how long it takes to create a shared understanding among the members of such project teams. This common understanding includes things such as a common language, sense of purpose, and definition of goals. In fact, many interdisciplinary teams end up reproducing inside the team the same conflicting perspectives the teams were designed to overcome in the first place. A critical task for the future is to explore how information technology might be used to accelerate the creation of mutual understandings within work groups. The result might by something like an *envisioning laboratory*, a powerful computer environment where Xerox customers would have access to advanced programming tools for quickly modeling and envisioning the consequences of new systems.

8.6   Conclusion

An organization coordinates numerous groups towards common objectives. The organizational patchwork of society has become increasingly complex. The growing complexity of organizations has created for one organization relative to another the need to anticipate actions. Successful *anticipation* depends on information about one's own organization and about the other organizations.

The classic organizational structure is the hierarchy. Here roles and activities are rigorously defined and communication flows in well-specified fashion between supervisor and supervisee. The *hierarchical organization* is particularly well-suited to large, industrial organizations that have relative monopolies. By contrast, in the *matrix structure,* groups within an organization form or dissolve in response to the changing environment. This flexible organizational structure works well when communication channels are flexible and information is easily accessed.

While easy exchange of information among individuals within an organization allows for some flexibility, *communication* also has its costs. In the extreme case, people could spend all their time communicating and no time getting the actual work done. The myth of the 'mythical person month' is that the assignment of an additional person to a project will reduce the time by which the project is completed. It may instead cause such coordination overhead costs that the project completion date is delayed rather than advanced.

To avoid the inefficiencies of excessive communication, an organization must, at least, understand itself. One way to represent this understanding is in the form of an *object-oriented organizational model.* The Activity Model Environment provides an object-oriented language for describing organizations and provides a way to rigorously talk about messages as composed of information units on which functions operate. These functions are associated with roles and people are assigned to roles. While detailing an organization's activities in these precise terms may be difficult, successful descriptions not only provide people with a useful reference but can empower computers to participate as role players in the organization. Once the description of the expected content of a message and the steps by which this content are massaged are precise, the computer can monitor the flow of messages that are exchanged on the computer and under certain circumstances do its part in processing messages.

The ability to rigorously characterize an organization's activities may be particularly difficult for the most innovative activities. An innovation is a creation made practical, and in challenging environments *innovation* is necessary for survival. In some cases research results move easily from the university to industry. Often, however, innovation requires close collaboration among customers, commercial developers, and academic researchers. Such collaboration may be supported by information technology and may produce new technology.

9
Networks and their Applications

Computer networks increase interconnectivity at the organizational level and are advancing rapidly in terms of their technological speed and capacity. Computer networks provide to users *resource sharing* and *computer mediated communication*. Computer-mediated communication systems include computer conferencing and electronic mail. Resource sharing allows users to access and use resources on another computer that they cannot directly (in physical terms) access [151]. This chapter explores the features of a network, the special demands of multimedia on networks, electronic mail, internet tools, and more.

9.1   Networks

Since the 1990s the popularity of large computers serving many users has given way to the situation in which many small machines connected via a network share resources. The kinds of sharing, the ways of communicating, and the applications of these *networks* are all vital to the modern organization.   For machines in a network to communicate many conventions must be established and followed.

9.1.1   Terms and Types

A computer network is a set of computers communicating by common conventions, called protocols, over communication media [151]. Each computer of any size in the network is called either a machine or a system, although the term system is sometimes used to denote the entire network. The machines in a network are called network nodes. Machines that users directly access are called hosts. *Hosts* have their own resources such as disks, user mailboxes, and user accounts. The building where a group of nodes is located is called a site. *Protocols* are used to manage the exchange of information in the network over the physical medium, such as wires or radio waves. Information is exchanged in discrete units called messages. Because of size limitations of either the physical medium or the protocol, messages are fragmented into packets. Packets may be routed into different networks and be reassembled into the original message when they reach their destination node. Computer networks may be combined and connected to form larger networks of networks. A host used to connect the networks may be referred to as a gateway.

The resources which networks might share include software packages and information storage facilities. This sharing may conform to the *client/server model* in which the machine containing the resource (the server) responds to requests from the other machines (the clients). In contrast, in a distributed model each machine contains some of the resource and the computers communicate on equal terms. In either case, coordination is critical.

One spectrum along which computer networks are described corresponds to their geographical dispersion. *Local area networks* (LANs) consist of collections of computers in a single building managed by one organization. In contrast, a *wide area network* (WAN) links machines that are widely separated, be it across a city or the world. The Internet is an example of a world-wide network. LANs are likely to be produced and serviced by one company. WANs are usually open in the sense that many different hardware and software systems from different companies can communicate effectively with a WAN.

9.1.2   Layers in General

The computers in a Wide Area Network to communicate they need to share a *common language*. Given the complexities of this communication, the common language is broken into parts or layers. The value of various layers in a communication system can be illustrated by analogy to a transportation system.

In this *transportation analogy* a company wants to send replacement parts to a customer in a distant city (see Figure 9.1). The company collects the parts and packages them according to the specifications of a shipping company. The resultant package is delivered to the shipping company and a shipping fee is paid. Responsibility for the parts has now passed to the shipper. Of course, the shipper does not view its responsibility as being specific to replacement parts. Instead, its task is to transport a package of a certain size and weight and under certain time and destination constraints. The shipping company will decide whether to put the package on a train, bus, plane or some other vehicle in accordance with various factors. If the package is to go onto a train, the shipping company may collect several packages that are to go via train to the same city and put them in a container that meets train transport specifications. The shipping company then passes responsibility for the container to the train company. The train company may put the container on a train that goes directly to the destination or route the container via some intermediate destination. In any case, the train company ultimately delivers the container to the shipping company at the destination city. The shipping company unpacks the container and delivers the packages therein to their appropriate addresses in the city [19].

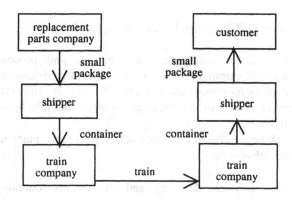

Figure 9.1: *Package via Train*: A small package goes from the replacement parts company to the shipper to the train company and then back via the shipper to its destination customer.

Just as the transportation of goods involves layers, so does the transmission of messages in a computer network. To manage the complexity of network protocols, *layering schemes* have been developed that allow a classification of protocols ranging from those close to the hardware to those close to the user. Interfaces are designed that allow protocols in adjacent layers to communicate directly. Applications are kept independent of the communication details so that detail can be changed to take advantage of the latest technological developments.

Communication software products translate the application requirements into a form that can be handled by the communication hardware and supervise the transmission process. Communication software is usefully viewed as concentric circles of software function surrounding the hardware (see Figure 9.2). From within each ring, the view is limited to what functions must be supplied to the outer containing one. These conceptual rings are called *levels of abstraction* or *layers of software.*

9.1.3   The OSI Layers

The need for standards to define the communication patterns in networks has lead to the adoption of the Open Systems Interconnection (OSI) standard. This describes the external interactions required of systems that need to be 'open' for communication with other systems. The *OSI reference model* is a functional description, in layers, of the services required for interconnection of systems. The model has layer boundaries with well-defined interfaces that allow for sensible implementations. The layers and boundaries indicate rules needed for conversation between systems.

The reference model for OSI has seven layers (see Figure 9.3):

1   The *Physical Layer* comprises the functions and procedures for the
         mechanical and electromagnetic interconnection of hardware components.
2   The *Data Link Layer* groups and interprets the bits. An important function of
         the data link layer is to detect transmission errors and take appropriate action
         to correct them.
3   The *Network Layer* chooses a transmission path from point to point in the
         network and delivers the data.

These first three layers, physical, data link, and network, are sometimes considered
together as a communications subnet because they were typical of the services
originally offered to the public by data communication network companies. The
higher level functions are increasingly related to applications:

4   The *Transport Layer* goes beyond the services of the network layer to ensure
         end-to-end communication. There may be multiple logical connections to be
         maintained between hosts, even over a single physical channel. The transport
         layer provides effective management of the logical paths and flow of data
         over those logical connections.
5   The *Session Layer* provides the dialogue for access and release of services,
         the integrity required to ensure completion of activities once begun, and the
         ability to recover from error situations
6   The *Presentation Layer* collects higher-level functions which would be
         commonly useful throughout the network system. Encryption and file transfer
         capabilities typically belong in this category.
7   The *Application Layer* handles a specific job in the information systems
         context such as data management, inventory control, and forecasting.

An example of the *practical utility* of the OSI reference model is provided by
describing for information communication as was described for transporting a
package but now using the seven layers of the OSI model. Assume that a user on the
west coast of the United States wants to transfer a file to a machine on the east coast.
The application layer on the west coast would handle the task of retrieving the file
from mass storage via the local operating system and passing it to the presentation
layer. The presentation layer may compress the file to reduce its length before passing
the file to the session layer. The session layer establishes a connection with the
machine on the east coast and releases the connection when the communication is
finished. The transport layer packages the file appropriately into units for the
particular network being used and attaches a final destination address to each unit.
The network layer handles the transmission via intermediate nodes in the network and
deals with the specific characteristics of the network in each link of the transmission.

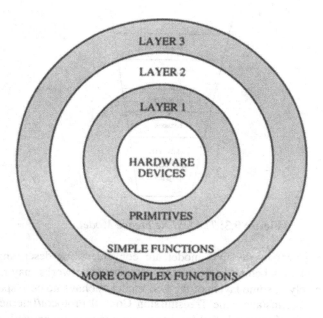

Figure 9.2: *Layers of Communication Software.* Starting from the inside, add one layer at a time in correspondence with extending the capabilities of the hardware by one group of functions at a time. Starting from the outside, strip away layer after layer of sophistication until reaching the core of primitive hardware functions.

The data link layer is responsible for accurate communication and may use error correction methods to this end. The physical layer converts the bit patterns into electrical or optical signals and transmits them over the communication line. After the data units are received at the east coast destination, each layer essentially reverses the process applied on the west coast so as to ultimately store the correct file on the machine on the east coast.

For each layer of the OSI model various protocols have been defined. For example,

- *physical layer* protocols include RS.232 and X.21,
- *data link layer* protocols include synchronous, asynchronous, and token ring, and
- *network layer* protocols include X.25 and packet radio.

Keeping track of these wide ranging protocols is difficult but allows for more effective and efficient communication than would be possible without standards for communication.

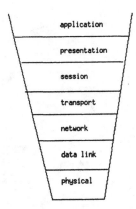

Figure 9.3: *The OSI Reference Model.*

While the seven layers of the OSI model are convenient for describing network architectures, the models behind some existing, important networks may have layers that correspond nicely to some layers of the OSI model but have no correspondence to other OSI layers. For instance, the Transmission Control Protocol/Internet Protocol (TCP/IP) suite is a set of protocols that has been very important in networking and has been used on nodes of different sizes ranging from supercomputers to personal computers. The primary goals of *TCP/IP* are to provide a fault-tolerant communications architecture and to support a variety of communication services over a wide range of networks. The TCP/IP suite does not deal with some of the layers in the OSI model. While the TCP/IP suite could be related to the OSI model, the relationship would make no use of several layers of the OSI model.

In the next two subsections two particular layers of the OSI model will be further elaborated. The *physical layer* includes wires and devices for communicating physical information. The *application layer* is at the other end of the model and holds the user or application programs that do the actual work for which the computers were purchased.

9.1.4   The Physical Layer

The physical layer is concerned with transmitting raw bits over the communication channel. Information can be transmitted on wires by varying some physical property such as voltage or current. Different media, such as a twisted pairs (two insulated copper wires twisted together) and coaxial cables, have different characteristics as transmitters of information. For more than a century, the primary international communication infrastructure has been the telephone system with its *twisted pairs* [182].

The traditional phone system when used to transmit digital data has a bandwidth in the tens of thousands of bits per second. *Integrated Services Digital Networks* (ISDN) is a digital telephone network that uses existing switches and wiring which have been upgraded in bandwidth. *Narrow-band ISDN* (N-ISDN) went into operation in 1988. With a transmission speed of about one megabit per second, N-ISDN service is limited to the transmission of voice, low- and medium-speed data, still pictures, and simple moving images.

Broadband ISDN (B-ISDN) is many times faster than N-ISDN. The *asynchronous transfer mode* (ATM) technique, key to B-ISDN switching, increases both speed and frequency bandwidth by a new transmission protocol. In N-ISDN, telephone, fax, video and TV signals are divided and passed through several different switching systems and then re-combined just before reaching the receiving terminals. ATM technology integrates these into a single net. The individual ATM transmitting terminal chops the information waves into cells of fixed lengths, assigns labels to them, and sends the 'wavelets' to the net. When these cells arrive at the receiving end, the various information signals, grouped by assigned label, are directed to appropriate terminals: telephones, computers, or TV conference terminals [109].

While the physical layer is concerned with how information is physically transmitted, it also concerns the *physical devices* which initiate and receive these signals. People using network computers often find themselves in situations where they have to work distant from the main network. The only way round this situation in the 1980s was to have a remote computer linked to the network via modem. But what if the user was planning to be constantly moving among a number of different sites? The expense of a remote terminal in each site would be unjustified for the amount of use it would receive, and so the laptop computer was born. These were small, briefcase-size, battery operated computers that could be taken anywhere, used, and then plugged into the network at a later date to update the group work. The *palmtop computers* of the early 1990s are smaller versions of these. Palmtops can communicate with their host computers by direct cable link or by infra-red beams (see Figure 9.4).

9.1.5   The Application Layer

Standards for formats on networks occur at multiple levels. At the level of the end-user (the *application layer)*, the concern is about the format of the information as the user sees it. For business purposes, one such standard naturally concerns the structuring of *business data*.

In the retail trade, particularly supermarkets, the balance of power in the industry was for decades with the giant manufacturers. In 1973 the 'Symbol Selection Committee' of a group of retailers agreed on a single standard code for their industry. Originally

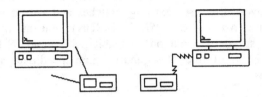

Figure 9.4: *Palmtop.* Shown roughly to scale are two personal computers and two palmtops. The palmtop on the left is connected by
infrared to the personal computer on the left, while the palmtop on
the right is connected via a cable to the personal computer on the
right.

introduced as a solution to the problems of long check-out lines and accounting errors,
the *bar code* afforded the means by which the supermarkets could begin to dictate to
manufacturers, rather than being dictated-to by them. A supermarket may stock
20,000 different items. The bar code and an optical scanner enable the retailer to keep
track of all these items, their sales, profitability, the timing of advertising, costs,
prices, discounts, location, special promotions, traffic flow, and so on. Thus the
supermarket knows more about the products it sells than the manufacturer.

More than retailers can use bar codes. As early as 1978, *American Hospital Supply*
began placing terminals inside hospitals and allowing them to connect via a network
to its computers. This made the process of ordering supplies simpler for hospitals.
Hospitals were thus able to cut back on their own inventories [185].

Electronic Data Interchange (EDI) is the electronic transfer of commercial and
administrative data. Use of EDI involves the exchange of information and messages
between trading partners or public administrations via electronic means of
communication. EDI may involve computers communicating directly with each other,
the exchange of magnetic media, or the use of telecommunications networks. In 1987
the International Standards Organization adopted the *EDIFACT* standard. EDIFACT
is actually a set of standards and guidelines which includes the *Syntax standard* which
provides the common grammatical rules used in EDIFACT messages and the Trade
Data Element Directory which specifies all allowed data elements and their meanings.
The ability to effectively link organizations' databases and electronic systems means
companies can form highly intimate partnerships. For example, the giant American
textile firm, Burlington Industries, sends its customers free software that allows them
to communicate directly with Burlington's mainframe and search through its stock and
place an order.

9.2   Multimedia on the Network

Computer networks have been important for organizations for some decades. The technology of the 1990's, however, makes *multimedia networks* more practical than they had been previously. With multimedia, new network considerations arise.

9.2.1   Multimedia Synchronization

A fundamental requirement of multimedia networks is *synchronization* — the coordinated ordering of events in time. The subsystems that deliver multimedia may introduce delay, jitter, and errors [124]. Managing resources to achieve synchronization is referred to as orchestration. Quality-of-service parameters are one basic tool of orchestration.

Because of the layered design of multimedia systems, the *granularity of synchronization* events is generally coarser at the application level, becoming more detailed at the lower levels of the system. For example, in synchronization of video the application layer may be concerned with the beginning and end of the video segment, the presentation system may be concerned with the relationship between one image and the next within the video, and the network may be concerned with packets of information which represent part of an image. Ways of representing information and synchronizing it at the different levels may naturally vary.

For a single media element which must be presented by time t, if the *delay* which might be expected in retrieving, generating, processing, transmitting, and presenting that element is D, then these steps must begin by time t - D. If 3 media elements from one object, such as 3 frames from a video segment, are to be presented one after the other with time deadlines of t1, t2, and t3, then the scheduling problem requires meeting the sequence of deadlines t1-D, t2-D, and t3-D. If the average delay which is experienced is less than D, then additional capacity exists to schedule other media elements. If media elements arrive prior to the presentation deadline of D, buffering is required to hold the elements in reserve until time t. In order to limit buffering requirements, the variation in delay, referred to as *jitter*, must also be bounded.

Media elements from two or more objects, such as a video segment and its associated audio, may need to be synchronized. Each element from the synchronized objects must arrive in time to meet the presentation deadline. Variation in delay between two synchronized media objects is called skew. *Skew* occurs when errors or delays in one media stream prevent the system from meeting the presentation schedule.

With *quality of service* parameters, service users specify to network services what the transmission requirements are. Quality of service parameters include transit delay, residual error rate, and throughput. The network service provider determines whether the quality of service parameters can be met.

9.2.2   Beyond OSI

In most existing communication architectures, the notion of quality of service is extremely narrow. In the Internet Protocol, the support of reliable data transfer was a primary goal and performance was only a marginal consideration. Furthermore, most current architectures are static in nature. In OSI protocols, the value of a *quality of service* parameter remains the same throughout the lifetime of a connection. Users can not dynamically adjust the connection. For example, users cannot choose to scale back the quality of an existing video connection from color to monochrome to allow the possibility of opening a new audio connection. If the provider is unable to maintain its commitment there is no mechanism to inform the user and allow her to request a suitably lower quality of service. The only option is for the provider to unilaterally close the connection [23]. For multimedia the communication architecture must be augmented beyond that provided by the traditional OSI architecture.

The basic layers of the OSI network model may be retained in the multimedia network, but another dimension is added to the model with three planes of multimedia control (see Figure 9.5) :

- the *protocol plane* distinguishes the control information from the actual multimedia content,
- the *maintenance plane* supports fine-grained resource tuning, and
- the *management plane* reserves resources, negotiates between layers of the OSI model, and implements coarse-grained maintenance.

The three planes work together to monitor and maintain a quality of service from the provider end to the destination end.

Another look at an architecture for multimedia networks sees new services [124], such as advanced call services (also known as teleservices). The advanced call services include media services [158]. Media services, in turn, involve media presentation and media control. Media presentation supports data format conversion among different representations for a given media type and multimedia data synchronization. Media control supports such activities as dynamic updates for shared data in a multiparty session. Several other services at the level of advanced call services are needed for a multimedia architecture. The network demands of multimedia are great.

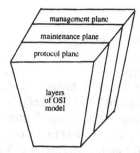

Figure 9.5: *Multimedia plus OSI.* The three planes are added to the OSI layers to properly support quality of service.

9.3 Electronic Mail

With *electronic mail* anyone with a computer account can create and send information to anyone who has a mailbox on any computer to which it is connected through a computer network. Depending upon software sophistication, the mailed information can be virtually anything digital from a multimedia document to a computer program. The recipient can read the information, edit it, save it, delete it, move it to another computer file, send it to other people, or reply to the sender, at his convenience [50].

9.3.1 Email Standards

Many different *standards for email* have been developed. One community has developed a standard called RFC 822 and its extension MIME. A different set of efforts are related to X.400.

The 'Standard for the format of Internet text messages' or *RFC 822* [36] defines an Internet message as consisting of two parts: a header and a body. The header consists of a series of field names and field bodies, after which a blank line marks the end of the header and the beginning of the body, which (according to RFC 822) consists of only plain text.

Several multimedia mail standards have been developed but one with particular interest is the *Multipurpose Internet Mail Extensions* or *MIME*. The syntax and semantics of all of the standard header fields defined by RFC 822 are retained in MIME. MIME defines a header field, called 'Content-type', which marks the entire message body as being a certain type of data. Importantly, MIME defines a Content-type, called 'multipart', which can be used to encapsulate several body parts within a single RFC 822 message body.

MIME enumerates several valid *content-types:*

- Text is the default content-type.
- The image content-type is for still images. Subtypes are image format names, two of which, 'image/gif' and 'image/jpeg', are defined by MIME. Mail readers that do not recognize an image format will at least know that it is an image and that showing the raw data to the recipient is not useful.
- The audio content-type is for audio information. Subtypes are audio format names, one of which is 'audio/basic', which is 8000 hertz audio data that is intended for telephone-quality audio.
- The video content-type for MIME is 'video/mpeg'.
- The multipart content-type is used to pack several parts, of possibly differing types and subtypes, into a single RFC 822 message body. Each body part is itself structured more or less as an RFC 822 message in miniature — in particular, possibly containing its own Content-type field to describe the type of the part.

Implementors can define new subtypes of established content-types.

X.400 is another standard for mail transport. X.400 defines a Mail Transfer System or MTS which provides the basic service of moving messages from one place to another. Messages may be digitized faxes, digitized sound tracks, or other computer files. MTS provides a number of services, including multi-destination delivery, grade of delivery service (priority), and non-delivery notification. MTS has no intrinsic limit on the size of a message, and mail can be stored at a node and later forwarded.

9.3.2   Email Filters

Paradoxically, the increased range of communication media and ever greater bandwidth that have been an enabling factor in the development of large, distributed organizations in the last century has also created a new communication problem for such organizations. Because sending information is so cheap, the amount of irrelevant information available makes it difficult to find the relevant information [93]. Information filtering systems address this information overload problem.

Information Lens, a research product [162][126], provides an intelligent assistant that can sort incoming messages into significant categories or *folders,* prioritize the messages based on importance and urgency, and automatically respond to certain kinds of messages. The system has four elements:

1   *Semi-Structured Message Templates* are the basis of the Information Lens
     system. Electronic messages already exhibit some structure in providing
     basic information such as To, From, cc, Date and Subject. Using templates
     containing appropriate fields makes it possible to automatically process a
     very wide range of information.

2   *Rule Sets:* Rules consist of a test imposed on the information in the fields
     (and possibly in the free-text part of a message) and an action.

3   *Display-Oriented Editors:* Information Lens provides graphical editors for
     composing messages, and for creating rules.

4   *The Anyone Server:* One can send a message to Anyone, in addition to the
     designated addressee or distribution list, indicating that the message may be
     automatically redistributed to anyone who is interested. Online services can
     also be fed into Anyone. The server then distributes its messages according to
     the processing rules that individuals have written for the Anyone Server.

Of particular advantage to work groups is the way in which by increasing the power of
their rules, they gain the ability to create applications that support a variety of
coordination and communication procedures, like task tracking.

9.3.3   Social Issues

An early case of organizational change brought about by the use of electronic mail
was provided by the *Mailbox System*, developed by Scientific Time Sharing
Corporation in 1973. It was used for exchanging mail on the mainframe machine
from sites in 20 cities. Various degrees of confidentiality were supported. In place of
the pyramidal hierarchy of the organization, groups or teams formed to handle tasks as
needed. One of the creators of Mailbox said of the system:

> "It has a flavor which is quite unlike any other form of
> communication, for example face-to-face exchange. For instance,
> you have whatever time is needed after receiving a message to get
> your own thoughts together and come back with a fairly incisive and
> coherent reply. You don't have the effect of thinking up snappy
> comebacks ten seconds too late. On the other hand, the messages go
> back and forth so rapidly, perhaps several times a day between any
> two particular participants, that it is completely unlike first-class
> mail, which is so slow that you really lose the interactive
> characteristic. It is unlike the telephone in a couple of important
> ways, too. I can communicate with someone at a time of my
> choosing, not wait for him to answer the phone or get filtered
> through his secretary. Nor is he interrupted by the message in what
> he is doing [148]. "

The Mailbox system affected organizational patterns by communication:

> "The way that this mode of communication affects the company is that it has a very strong democratizing effect. It would be almost impossible to enforce communication through the channels defined by an organizational chart. My boss may send a message to me with a copy to the people who report to me, and like as not one of them will have replied to it before I even see my 'mail'. This can make some people pretty uncomfortable. ...This kind of communication is not a substitute for face-to-face communication, as we've been discovering. We've got to get together occasionally to have round-table discussions. ...But the benefits are pretty substantial. Most time-sharing services that cover a wide geographic area have something similar. I think ours is one of the easier to use, and most flexible. We transmit 175 to 225 messages a day \(em that is the serial listing, because each of the messages might go to a large number of people [148]."

Email generally attenuates *social context cues*. In fact it eliminates the dynamic cues and minimizes the static ones. When information is sent via electronic mail, the only signs of organizational position and personal similarity for senders and receivers are names and addresses. There are few cues to evoke the knowledge of relevant social context information in the electronic mail situation. To counter these problems new email systems have additional features and users should be encouraged to use other media for communicating as well as email [125].

9.4   Electronic Libraries

Networks can make information of all sorts readily available. Historically, the archiving and provision of access for documents in the public domain has been done by *libraries*. New 'reading rooms' may be similar to automatic transaction money machines, in that people simply go to a computer, find what they want, and have it printed or read it online.

9.4.1   Public Libraries

Public libraries have served two goals, namely, to allow open *access* to published information and to *archive* written history for future scholars and posterity. The archiving goal is not sacrificed by loaning books since the limited public use does not destroy the books. However, with electronic distribution or publishing, making a copy is easy and inexpensive, and delivering a copy can be done without requiring a person to come into the library.

The unique aspects of *libraries* — service-oriented staff, lack of profit motive, prevalent locations, and the role in schools — can give them a more important role in the future than they had in the paper era. A new facility for access to literature, the 'Reading Room', protects and promotes publishers, while serving the public in the tradition of the branch library. A 'Reading Room' would offer patrons convenient access to published information, in printed form or for screen display, in many places in a town. One way to explain the idea is by analogy with the transition of the banking system from bank buildings to automatic teller machines (see Figure 9.6).

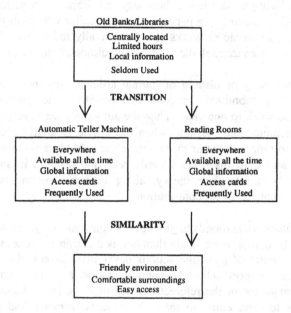

Figure 9.6: *Transition to Reading Rooms*: Technological changes have resulted in a transition from the public library service to the reading room, which offers users convenient access to information, not unlike the transition from the old banking system to the use of automatic teller machines which provide easier user access to numerous banking services.

A minimal design for a *Reading Room* would be a one-room store that had a few comfortable chairs, several computers for browsing and reading, and a printer and binder for making copies of documents. When a patron has selected a book or paper to take from the library, printing and binding can be done on demand. Current screen technology can be used effectively to find and browse documents, but a printer will still be preferred for reading long pieces. Since the Reading Room monitors all the books printed and viewed, it is easy to keep a record of this and reimburse the publishers either from library funds or by credit card payments from the Reading Room patrons. The current copyright laws are intended to ensure that authors, editors, and publishers get a fair stake from the use of their work, and Reading Rooms can help in this process. In fact, Reading Rooms help a publisher distribute and print works, so the publisher can lower costs of putting out a new volume. This cost savings might allow a flourishing of works that would have a more specialized audience [104].

9.4.2   Scholarly Refereeing

The ideas in scholarly journals make their way into libraries in a slow process that begins with an author submitting a paper to a journal editor who in turn distributes the paper to referees. Electronic networks can dramatically reduce the time required to get ideas from the authors through the referees and ultimately to the public.

In conventional scholarly publishing of journal articles, new ideas and findings are written up and then submitted for *peer review* [80]. The refereeing may take anywhere from one week to one year. Then the author revises in response to the peer evaluation and recommendations, and when the article is finally accepted, it again takes from three to nine months or more before the published version appears. Next the author must wait until his peers actually read and respond in some way to his work, incorporating it into their theory, doing further experiments, or otherwise exploring the ramifications of his contribution.

By the time the literature responds to an author's contribution, years will have passed and by that time the author, more likely than not, is thinking about something else. So a potentially vital spiral of peer interactions never materializes. However, the new technologies could support scholarly communication at a fast tempo while still retaining the permanence of the refereed written medium [82]. Electronic networks allow individuals to send email to many individuals instantly and simultaneously. This rapid global interactiveness can be used to speed the *refereeing* of scholarly documents.

Review of a scholarly communication would occur through a hierarchy of email groups, the height of each depending on degree of expertise. An accredited group of peers at one level would referee the work of those at a lower level. An individual with an established record of work experience could eventually be voted up a level [81].

Scholarly inquiry in this new medium might proceed quickly, interactively, and globally. An electronic bulletin board, called *Psycholoquy* became in 1989 a refereed electronic journal. One of *Psycholoquy's* principal scholarly objectives is to implement peer review on the electronic networks in psychology and its related fields. All contributions are refereed by a member of *Psycholoquy's* Editorial Board. The refereeing of each contribution is done very quickly, sometimes within a few hours of receipt.

9.5   The Internet and its Access Tools

New and vast libraries of material are available via network. One of the most heavily used network systems uses the Internet Protocol and is called the *Internet*. Many non-Internet networks have provided connections to the Internet so that it has become indirectly a connector of the world's networks. Three particular tool sets for accessing this material on the Internet have become popular. Gopher supports a kind of hierarchical file browsing across Internet hosts. WAIS does free text searching across the Internet, and the World Wide Web supports hypermedia browsing [75].

9.5.1   Internet

The term Internet originates from the protocol on which the Internet depends, namely the *Internet Protocol* (IP). The basic mechanism of the network is that one computer sends a message to another computer. To send a message on the network, a computer puts its data in an envelope, the IP packet, and addresses the packet to the target computer.

In the United States in 1969 the Advanced Research Projects Agency (ARPA) demonstrated the viability of a IP computer network called *ARPAnet* . The original motivation for development was resource sharing, as ARPA noticed many contractors were tending to request the same resources. The network was designed to be tolerant of failure of nodes within the network. Each computer can talk to each other computer in the network as a peer and must assume some responsibility for the integrity of the messages it sends and receives.

Researchers almost immediately began using the ARPAnet for collaboration through electronic mail and other services. The high utility of the network led people to want *increased connectivity*. By the early 1980s, local area networks of Unix workstations began to be popular. These systems typically included IP networking capability. Many organizations in which these networks were placed wanted to connect the ARPANet to their local network so that each user of the local area network would also through that network have access to the ARPANet.

Other networks that were harmonious with the ARPANet also began to appear. In the late 1980s the American National Science Foundation (NSF) developed a network to allow educational and research institutions to access the nations five supercomputer centers. This *NSFNet* used the ARPANet's IP technology. Special, 56,000 bit per second telephone lines were used to connect the supercomputer centers with one another and with regional centers. Within a region, an institution could use the regular phone lines to connect to the regional center and through that center access the supercomputer center. The NSFNet traffic increased to the point were upgrades on the network were needed and in 1987 faster telephone lines and computers were installed to control the main links to the supercomputer centers (these main links are called the backbone of the NSFNet). The most important point of the NSFNet experience is that it allowed wide-scale access to the network. The NSF promoted universal educational access by funding campus connections only if the campus had a plan to spread the access so that everyone on the campus could become an Internet user.

In the late 1980s one could say that the Internet was all the networks using the IP protocol that cooperate to form a seamless network for their collective users [112]. However, other networks, such as *Bitnet* and *DECNet,* have developed translators that take Internet messages and send them to Bitnet or DECNet addresses and conversely. These translators sit on computers called gateways and the Internet in a sense extends over these gateways across a wider set of computers than those literally using the IP protocols.

The Internet has a strong 'grass roots' character. The ultimate authority for the direction of the Internet rests with the *Internet Society.* The Internet Society is a voluntary membership organization whose purpose is to promote global information exchange through Internet technology. The Society appoints a group of volunteers to approve new Internet standards, to develop rules about the assignment of addresses, and to take other management-like positions. This group is called the Internet Architecture Board and is again composed of volunteers.

The Internet is not owned by any one company. Instead *everyone owns* and pays for their own part. NSF pays for the NSFNet. A college or corporation pays for its connection to some regional network, which in turn pays a national provider for access. This arrangement is somewhat like the international telephone network.

Internet growth has been phenomenal. In January 1993 about 1,300,000 different sites were hosts on the Internet and in January 1994 that number had risen to 2,220,000, an impressive 70% increase [62]. By May 1994 the Internet included over 31,000 networks with one network being added every 10 minutes; the number of computers connected through the Internet exceeded two million; and over 20 million people had access to Internet resources [114]. While the Internet was originally developed for research-related purposes, by May 1994 commercial users had exceeded 50% of the connected base and commercial usage was growing most rapidly.

9.5.2   Gopher

The *Gopher system* began at the University of Minnesota as a distributed campus information system. The school administration could have a computer for administrative information, while the athletic department could maintain a sports schedule on its server. Each academic department could have a computer on the network which described its class offerings, the members of the teaching faculty, and so on. Gopher developers then provided a transparent interface to this network of campus information. Information is organized as menus with each server providing another submenu. From Gopher the user can launch various activities, such as file transfer, and phone directory search systems, but basically the user browses the menus and does not need to realize that different submenus are on different machines. Given that Gopher worked for a Internet network at the University of Minnesota, it was simply connected to the world-wide Internet.

Gopher is based on a client/server architecture. When a user starts a Gopher client, it contacts its home server and retrieves a main menu. The client then displays this *menu* (see Figure 9.7). The user may proceed downward through menus activating other menus. At some point the menus will not continue and the user has the option to select either files to read (see Figure 9.8) or searches to initiate.

Sites that want to meaningfully provide Gopher access to their information store must create the submenus which are added to the massive network of menus which exist in Gopher-space. Unfortunately, the menus at different locations may not follow a *standard pattern* and users may need to learn by trail and error what is meant by a menu at one site versus a similar looking menu at a different place. The challenge to organizing the information in Gopher space is similar to that of organizing information in libraries, but much remains to be done to harmonize the entries on Gopher across the world.

Informal guidelines are developing to guide creators of information. The most time consuming aspects of preparing a Gopher site concern:

- the organization of the information,
- the quality of the information, and
- supporting documentation.

At a more detailed level there are menu presentation suggestions (see Figure 9.9).

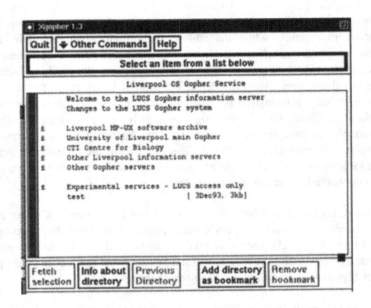

Figure 9.7: *Main Gopher Menu*: This window was captured from a screen at the University of Liverpool and shows the main menu of the University of Liverpool Gopher server.

9.5.3   WAIS

The *Wide Area Information Service* (WAIS) was started by the three companies Apple Computers, Thinking Machines, and Dow Jones Information Service. WAIS is a client/server system for finding information on the Internet. To make a document available through a WAIS server, someone must create an index for that document on the server. Every word in the document is usually indexed.

The WAIS interface presents a question field and a source field. In the source field, servers are specified. Each server has its own *index file*. In a sense each server is a library with its own catalogue. One server has been provided with a meta-index whose index terms point to other servers rather than to specific files. A common way to search WAIS is to begin by specifying a set of words in the question field of WAIS and to choose the meta-index server for the source (see Figure 9.10). In this way the search may be next narrowed to a part of the WAIS information space.

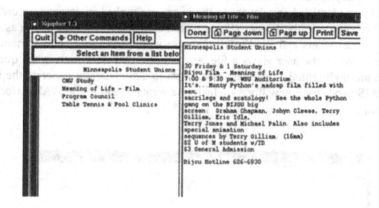

Figure 9.8: *File seen through Gopher.* The user has gone from the home menu to other Gopher servers in the world, then to the University of Minnesota server, and after several, further steps to information about the 'Meaning of Life - Film' which is being played at the Minneapolis Student Unions on Friday and Saturday.

The main menu should be limited to one page (18 options).

The first option should be "Welcome -- Press Enter key and READ THIS FIRST!" and include: why you have the gopher, what types of information it has, who the target audience is, who runs the gopher, how that person(s) can be contacted.

Don't put information in an area that does not fit the topic. Stick to the topic! This is a common mistake on gophers.

Identify all items that originate from your site.

Don't try and build a subject tree of all categories of information. There are at least 26 good subject trees out there you can point to. Concentrate on the information your gopher was established to deliver.

DON'T USE ABBREVIATIONS! Especially your organization's name!!!

Alphabetizing is not the desired method of organizing menu options

Figure 9.9: *Menu Tips*: These tips for organizing menus on Gopher were extracted from a larger list distributed on the Internet news [160].

Subsequently the user would generate a new *query* and would add source(s) found from the first search. In this second round, the user would expect to get names of actual files rather than just pointers to servers. The user might then view a file found on this second search (see Figure 9.11).

WAIS offers sophisticated *methods for searching* based on words. The sources or files which are identified as relevant to the query are ranked in descending order of a computed relevance to the query. The user can also select a source or file as similar to what the user wants and WAIS will then use words from that 'similar item' in its next query. When the user views a file, any word(s) that were both in the query and in the file are highlighted. Software also exists to automatically generate the indices which WAIS needs for a new library which one wants to add to the WAIS information space [112].

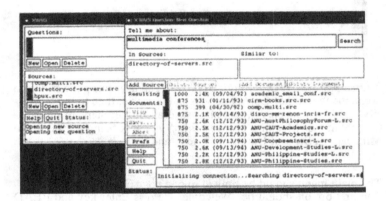

Figure 9.10: *First step in WAIS*: The user has first selected 'New' under the Question option in the left-hand window. The resulting 'New Question' window has then been used to execute a search for sources that are relevant to the query 'multimedia conferences'. The sources relevant to this query are returned in the lower-right-hand box with 'academic-email_conf.src' being ranked highest.

9.5.4   World Wide Web

The *World Wide Web* (WWW) was developed to be a pool of human knowledge which people across time and space could share. The WWW began at the European Particle Physics Laboratory (called CERN) in Geneva, Switzerland. There scientists collaborate with many other scientists around the world on the subject of high energy physics. A small collaborative hypertext system was developed at CERN to facilitate electronic collaboration. This initial Web was designed so that if used independently for two projects across which connections were later discovered, then these connections could easily be added to the Web information space without having to rewrite the information [11]. This property of the Web has facilitated its connection to other sources of information on the Internet and ultimately to a world-wide information space.

Three key features of the WWW are:

- the address system,
- a network protocol, and
- a hypertext markup language.

These three features are extensions of the *Internet* and fully compatible with it. They allow properly structured Internet information to have a new kind of accessibility.

Figure 9.11: *Second step in WAIS*: In the upper window the user has chosen the source 'academic_email_conf.src' and repeated the search on the query 'multimedia conferences'. One of the retrieved files is 'Readme: 8th Revision Directory of Scholarly Electronic Conferences' and the user has chosen to view this document. In the lower window the content of that document is shown.

The address system is based on *Universal Resource Identifiers* (URIs). URIs are strings which address objects on the WWW. URIs are universal in that they encode members of the universal set of network addresses. The URI syntax reserves the '/' as a way of representing hierarchical space. Relative names exploit the hierarchical structure and allow links to be made independent of the higher parts of the URI, such as the server name. The prefix of the URI is often the string 'HTTP' which refers to the hypertext transfer protocol, but the prefix could also be 'Gopher' or 'WAIS' to indicate a connection to that part of the Internet information space.

The *HyperText Transfer Protocol* (HTTP) is a protocol for transferring information efficiently and for retrieving documents in an unbounded and extensible set of formats. The client sends a weighted list of the formats it can handle, and the server replies with the data in any of those formats. This allows proprietary formats to be used between consenting programs in private. HTTP is an Internet protocol that uses basic commands like Get, Put, and Post as does the File Transfer Protocol of the Internet.

The *Hypertext Markup Language* (HTML) was designed to be sufficiently simple to be easily produced by both people and programs, but also to adhere to the SGML standard. A valid HTML document, if attached to SGML declarations including the HTML Document Type Definition may be parsed by an SGML parser. HTML includes simple structure elements, such as several levels of headings and bulleted lists. Files do not need to be stored in HTML format to participate in the WWW information space. Servers may store files in other formats and then generate a basic HTML on the fly with each request.

The first WWW access programs were written at CERN. Subsequently, the National Center for Supercomputer Applications at the University of Illinois made available a viewer called *Mosaic* which became very popular. Many viewers or browsers are now freely available.

A user typically begins a trip in the WWW from a *home page* of her own institution (see Figure 9.12). This home page should also provide routes to the rest of the WWW. One of the big attractions of the WWW over Gopher or WAIS is the ease with which graphics and, more generally, *multimedia* are available. In addition to the hypertext links which readily take one from one section of text to another, a WWW document readily links to sounds, videos, or animations (see Figure 9.13).

The WWW has attracted more and more interest in the world. Data on usage on one network provides a telling story (see Figure 9.14). In January 1993 the information transmission for HTTP was less than that of WAIS or Gopher. By March 1994 the information transferred with HTTP exceeded that by WAIS and equaled that on Gopher [11]. The trend was clearly in the direction of *HTTP usage* exceeding either Gopher or WAIS usage.

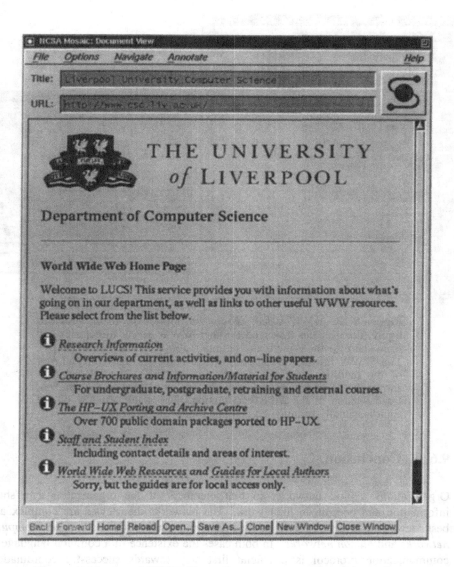

Figure 9.12: *Local WWW Home Page*: An example of accessing the WWW from the University of Liverpool with the Mosaic viewer.

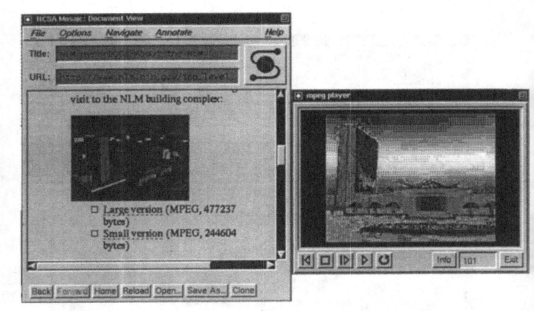

Figure 9.13: *WWW Video:* From the home page in the previous figure, the user has traversed to other WWW server directories and from there to the American National Library of Medicine (NLM). The WWW information about the NLM includes an animated tour of the facilities which is encoded in MPEG. The left window shows the Mosaic interface with the option to choose the small or large version of the MPEG animation. The small window on the right is actually running the animated view of the NLM.

9.6   Conclusion

Organizations exploit networks so that members of the organization can share information and coordinate their work. The networks themselves are complex and best viewed in layers. In fact, many interesting analogies exist between *computer networks* and *human networks*. In both cases the existence of a common language or communication protocol is a crucial first step towards successful coordination. Between two computers a very low level of common language might be the voltage level which defines a bit of information. Between two people(s) a common alphabet is an early prerequisite to successful communication.

The model for a computer network includes at the high level the *application* which the end user sees. This application must communicate with the level beneath it and also with other applications. One important application for businesses is exchange of orders for supplies. Protocols for such exchange go under the general heading of

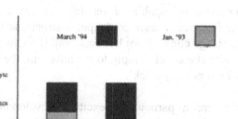

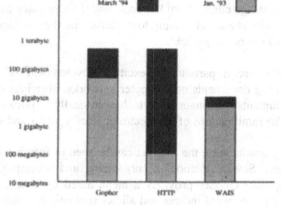

Figure 9.14: *HTTP Usage.* The amount of information transmitted is indicated on the vertical axis with each step upward representing a tenfold increase in traffic. Traffic is shown for each of the three services, Gopher, HTTP, and WAIS. The top of the lightly shaded boxes indicates the January 1993 traffic — less than 100 megabytes was HTTP information; about 5 gigabytes was WAIS information; and about 50 gigabytes was Gopher information. By March 1994 HTTP traffic and Gopher traffic were equal at about 500 gigabytes and WAIS traffic was about 10 gigabytes [11].

Electronic Data Interchange (EDI). EDI, along with such labeling methods as bar codes, has revolutionized the practices of retail stores.

For multimedia networks, *synchronization* is very important. Failure to properly synchronize introduces delays, jitters, or errors. To control the quality of the service, the architecture of the computer network must be extended with specific multimedia synchronization functionalities.

Electronic mail is one particularly popular application of computer networks. Originally, email was simply text but the acceptance of new protocols, such as the Multipurpose Internet Mail Extensions, and the wide availability of multimedia, networked computers have helped make *multimedia mail* practical. A MIME email message has various headers to introduce its different media components, such as a video or a text block.

The vast usage of email has led to *information overload* for many email recipients. The computer, however, is capable of reading the email and *filtering* it or even replying to it. For instance, a user could put instructions in her email program to detect whether a message comes from her boss, and if so, to place that message at the top of the high priority stack and to reply to the boss with the message with 'your mail is at the top of my high priority stack'.

Electronic libraries are a particularly exciting development of hypermedia and networks. By storing documents on computer networks, librarians change the nature of libraries. Documents no longer have to be physically duplicated in order to be widely shared. The ramifications of the electronic library go far and wide.

Information freely available on the Internet can be seen as forming a vast network of electronic libraries. Several methods of organizing and accessing this information have become popular. Gopher provides a menu-based approach. The Wide Area Information Service uses word indices and allows sophisticated searches for words in documents across libraries. The World Wide Web is based on a hypertext structure of information, supports browsing across hypertext links, and makes graphics and other media readily available. This new library system is dependent on computer networks.

10
Organizational Case Studies

The use of *information technology in organizations* has been fundamental to the success of some organizations for decades. The ever increasing availability of powerful information technology makes the importance of exploiting this technology ever more important. This chapter looks first at some important examples of how information technology is developed in organizations. Then the development of educational interactive media in universities is studied. Experiences with a networked hypermedia information system for a research organization are then presented, and finally organizational experiences with telemedicine are described.

10.1 Developing Organizational Applications

The following four cases illustrate methods of *developing organizational information systems* of which networks are a part. The first two cases concern the SABRE airline reservation system and the Lockheed decision support system. The second two case studies both involve the popular Lotus Corporation product called Notes. Careful attention to users and usability mark the successful organizational product.

10.1.1 The SABRE Online Database

The *American Airlines* SABRE system was built in 1963 and remains a prime example of good design and implementation [119]. It involved the maintenance of a massive international database of reservations and other airline information with access under real-time constraints. SABRE's main initial purpose was to support customer reservations. In addition, information was provided about flight crews, the maintenance operations, and financial information.

When system requirements were analyzed, American Airlines was very careful to involve the *user*. The company had users detail the functional specifications of a reservation system. These users were told not to be biased by programming considerations nor by how the information could be stored. System inputs, outputs, and data flow were prepared also with the help of users.

Before programming was begun, the company issued a programming standards manual for the *SABRE* program. Each program was flow charted in advance with standard programming rules. Among the rules were:

- the programs were to be coded in segments of 250 or less words,
- each segment was to be self contained, and
- tests were to be utilized for each program segment before the program as a whole was tested.

Also the team approach was emphasized. Each problem type was assigned to a project manager who in turn assigned specific coding requirements to individuals of the team. The final program included about one million instructions. The SABRE system was enormously successful and new versions of it continue to be released.

10.1.2   Decision Support at Lockheed

The development of the SABRE airline reservation system illustrates how a large, networked information system is successfully built by carefully involving the users from the beginning. Another example of a corporate information system that was developed with user involvement has a rather different flavor as the key users were senior executives. The *Management Information and Decision Support* (MIDS) [92] system provides information for executives so that they can make timely decisions with the correct and latest information.

Lockheed Georgia is a subsidiary of the Lockheed Corporation and manufactures aircraft. The President of the corporation requested an information service that was tailored to the needs of executive decision makers and in 1978 development of MIDS began. No feasibility study was performed. The justification was informal—the *President* wanted it.

A team of 4 professionals was assigned to the project and reported directly to the vice-president for finance. This group began by studying the information requirements of the President and his senior staff. *Standardization* and *simplicity* were deemed critical. For instance, color was used in a standard way:

- Under budget or ahead of schedule is in green.
- On budget or on schedule is in yellow.
- Over budget or behind schedule is in red.

The information available on a display was designed to be clear and to emphasize only a few points. The person responsible for the information content of a display was listed with each display. Executives were taught to use MIDS in a 15-minute tutorial. No written instructions were provided, and the system was easy enough to use that no written instructions were needed.

The initial version of MIDS took 6 months to develop and gave the President 31 displays. Eight years later the system had evolved to include 700 displays and was in use by 70 top personnel at Lockheed-Georgia. The stimulus of the President combined with rapid prototyping and an emphasis on *usability* led to a successful product.

10.1.3 Lotus Notes Success

Lotus Notes connects people and information. Many companies have adopted Notes as a major part of their corporate information technology approach [14]. This section will first describe some of the basic features of Notes and then the evolution of its successful use by Lotus's own Information Resources Group. In the subsequent section a less successful use of Lotus Notes is described.

Lotus Notes is software that allows people to access, track, and organize information. It was first released in 1989 and has become one of the world's most commercially successful software products [117]. Lotus Notes has a number of database features [122]:

- text handling,
- information integration,
- standard database interface,
- simultaneous user access to databases,
- multisite access to identical data, and
- integrated electronic mail.

Lotus Notes documents can contain large amounts of text. Notes also handles compound documents, integrating graphics, text, images, sound, video, and other multimedia formats. Because electronic mail is integrated with the database features, *database documents* can be mailed between Lotus Notes users.

There are four main application types for which Lotus Notes is particularly suited:

- *tracking applications* allow users to track activities, such as project progress, and typically have many users and are continually updated.
- *broadcast applications* are made available to a large audience where information is time-critical but remains static thereafter. Newsletters and meeting agendas are example of items which might be appropriately broadcast.

- *reference applications* provide document libraries.
- *discussion applications* function like electronic bulletin boards where users address new topics and respond to others.

A Lotus Notes database has four components: fields, forms, documents, and views. *Fields* are defined in a form and can be arranged on the form as desired, such as user prompts, headings, and such. A *form* can have an unlimited number of fields. A database *document* is a result of information entered into a form. Documents are accessible for reading, printing, and editing by means of the *view*. Views can be designed to select documents matching a particular criterion, such as author or keyword.

The *Information Resources Group* (IRG) at Lotus Corporation has been providing library-like services and information to other staff at Lotus Corporation since 1983. The Corporation itself was formed in 1982 and by 1983 had about 100 staff. In 1984 the IRG began subscribing to electronic news services and using electronic mail to help distribute information.

In 1986 Lotus's director of marketing suggested that library information be distributed on the new product Lotus Notes. The IRG tried Notes but not enough employees at Lotus were using Notes to make this a practical delivery vehicle. IRG continued to provide an increasingly wider range of services to Lotus staff that involved unfortunately an increasingly diverse range of *incompatible interfaces* [118].

In 1990 Lotus Corporation decided to standardize its email and database delivery *corporate-wide on Lotus Notes.* The number of staff in the company had by 1990 grown to 4,000. IRG began to evaluate all its services in light of their suitability for Notes delivery.

The IRG has been able to integrate its services with Notes and to provide to users a *consistent interface* and wide availability. For instance, IRG receives daily news stories from more than a hundred newswire sources. Special software monitors the news sources to find topics of relevance to Lotus Corporation. The stories are then reformatted into documents in a Lotus Notes database and made available daily to Lotus Corporation staff. A manager may specify his profile of interests to the system. On a daily basis this profile may be matched against the latest news, and stories that match the profile will be routed to the manager.

The IRG originally maintained a library of thousands of physical holdings such as books and videos. The catalogue for this library was moved into Lotus Notes and items are now lent with *no recall date.* When a searcher wants an item that someone else has already borrowed, then the searcher contacts the borrower and requests the copy.

IRG's electronic library includes various maps and *help systems.* Further, the user can request assistance from the IRG staff by completing a form online. When the form is saved, Lotus Notes automatically routes it to the library staff with the help of the Notes integrated electronic mail facility. The electronic library at Lotus has proven highly successful and other companies are adopting similar electronic libraries.

10.1.4 A Less Successful Case with Lotus Notes

In the late eighties a few senior staff at a large, international management consulting firm (hereafter to be called Alpha Company) realized that the company was underutilizing information technology. A new position of *Chief Information Officer* (CIO) was created with responsibility to create firm-wide standards for personal computing environments. It was while reviewing communication software that the CIO was introduced to *Lotus Notes.* He decided that this was revolutionary technology and within a matter of days bought a site license to install Notes throughout the firm [143].

The CIO began a vigorous international campaign within the company to promote the use of Notes. The physical deployment of the technology proceeded rapidly throughout the firm. The system was widely used for electronic mail, but was not widely used for its other intended functions. Interviews with staff in one office before installation of the software revealed that they had little idea of what the new software was intended to do and felt that it was being forced upon them. The CIO felt that *rapid deployment* and *critical mass* was the key to success and that training or pilot studies would be too costly.

Within Alpha there is an expectation that all or most employee hours are *billable,* that is charged to clients. Employees carefully avoid non-billable hours. Unfortunately, for the deployment of Notes, its use was viewed as non-billable. The most senior people at Alpha are paid based on company profit rather than on billable hours. While they were persuaded to use Notes, they did not appreciate that the other consultants were afraid to use Notes because the time required to learn it was not billable.

The technological push to install Notes had not addressed the issues of *ownership* and *confidentiality* of information put into Notes. Consultants were hesitant to put information into the system without a clear understanding of who would control the information. Alpha shares with many other consulting firms a competitive culture at levels below the principals. The hierarchical 'up or out' career paths promotes intense competition among consultants. This lack of a precedent for sharing information and cooperating with colleagues was another disincentive to use Notes. Thus at all but the principal level (where this competition does not exist) the use of

Notes in Alpha tends to be limited to an individual productivity tool rather than a networking tool. If the culture, policy, and rewards of an organization do not encourage sharing of information, then technology such as Notes may have difficulty being widely used.

10.2   University Teaching

At many universities the vision is that students can sit at any terminal or their personal computer at home, and have access to stimulating learning packages which they can study at their own pace and at their own convenience [189][186]. This section examines the development of such courseware at universities through several case studies. As *courseware development* is a new enterprise, there are many cottage forms of it - namely small numbers of people, sometimes just one or two, who decide that they would like to experiment with the technology and demonstrate that it can be effectively used within a particular context. Some universities have, however, witnessed large multi-year, multi-person courseware projects, and the lessons from two such projects will be described here.

10.2.1   Athena Project

The Massachusetts Institute of Technology Athena Project was set up in the 1980s (ending in 1991) to examine diverse uses of computing in a university. It included educational, technical, and organizational aspects and was intended to explore the following questions [91]:

- What does it take to design, implement, and operate a fully-distributed computing environment for a university?
- How do students and staff use such an environment?
- Who should maintain and manage the environment?

The *Athena project* had over 600 publicly-accessible workstations which students and faculty could access 24 hours a day, 365 days a year.

The Athena Project had successes and failures. Some of the latter were due to the experimental nature of the project itself. It was intended to produce a system which would allow for *standardization* of procedures and greater *portability*. Athena developers were pioneers in the area of distributed network computing and as such discovered the pitfalls and the benefits.

During the first stages of Athena, it was claimed that too much time and effort were needed to build courseware because no authoring system or development tools existed. It was important that courseware production should be cost-effective. Consequently in the mid-1980s the Athena project built its own *courseware authoring environment* called AthenaMuse.

Initially, the Athena environment consisted of expensive hardware platforms and a single operating system. Later a more heterogeneous mix of hardware platforms and systems was possible through the increased power of personal computers. Consequently, Athena moved from the idea of hardware and operating system coherence to that of data and *application coherence*. This refers to the interchange of data among computers and utilizes services such as electronic mail and on-line course catalogues. So people can use commercial software in the hardware and operating system of their choice and easily access common services.

Athena began with concerns for usability but then spent the major part of its early years dealing with *technical challenges*. In the early years of the Athena Project the systems and services changed rapidly. This led to the perception among some users that the project was unstable and unreliable. Nevertheless the Athena Project produced many excellent results, as manifested in part by the success of its TUDOR courseware projects.

The *TUDOR project* was concerned with Fluid Mechanics. Teaching staff were interested in using the computer to provide graphics and animations to demonstrate solutions of complicated equations and motion of an invisible medium. An evaluation of the project by members of staff showed clearly that the simulations were useful. However, there was some concern that computers might threaten the traditional relationship of student and tutor or hurt the theoretical side of the subject.

The conditions surrounding the actual construction of TUDOR had an affect on traditional educational structures. Students were encouraged to produce material and modules for the project, and this was seen by most as a successful method of course production. Not only did it reduce pressures on busy teaching staff, but it also ensured that the focus was directed on areas which were considered important or problematic by the students themselves. Using workstations was found to have an effect on the students and staff. Substantial use of electronic mail, electronic discussion groups, computer-based course work, asynchronous access to teaching staff, and on-line library information all helped to encourage *communication* and *collaboration* among students and staff.

10.2.2 Purdue's Escape

The *Engineering Specific Career-planning and Problem-solving Environment* (ESCAPE) was created at Purdue University to inform students of the role of an engineer and to offer them advice on career planning. The project's premise was that the computer could provide a more dynamic and stimulating insight into engineering than more conventional forms of presentation [91].

One of the goals of the ESCAPE project was to make education fun. To achieve this, *multimedia* techniques, including digitized sound, color graphics, and video, were employed. However, this was not an overall success as the project suffered technical difficulties which resulted in the production of less than was anticipated in this area.

Initially HyperCard was thought to have the capability to represent both the engineering structure and content through databases of linked text or graphics and simulations. These functions were useful, but they were found to be too simple and therefore eventually limited the development of the project. It was decided to switch from *Macintosh computers* to the Engineering Schools newly acquired *Sun workstations*. The high speed processing capabilities, high resolution graphics, and large memory were advantages of moving to workstations, but the transfer to workstations required a restructuring of the entire system.

An emphasis on the role of *networks* came fairly late in the ESCAPE project. This resulted in the project's educational goals not really being revised to take into account any benefits afforded by student-student interaction across networks. Networks were used in a more traditional sense - to provide access to a central dataset and allow for easy access and maintenance.

10.2.3   Organizational Issues

In the Athena and ESCAPE projects [91] courseware production was based on a *team approach*. The reasons for the existence of a team and of its constituents varied from project to project. For instance, some can be seen as software design teams and others as courseware design teams. There are important differences between the two. Larger teams were required for developing software than for courseware.

While some of the courseware developers had taken courses related to design and development, most kept plans and processes in their heads. There were few formal planning activities and the main form of communication was verbal. This is possibly due to the informal nature of academia. Faculty have tended to see courseware projects in the same way as they would a publication, i.e. once it is finished and delivered that is the end of the matter. This is highly detrimental to the longevity of the courseware. Athena recognized this and attempted to solve the problem by having as one of its goals to help the faculty produce *maintainable courseware* and watch over it once it was created.

The two most important resources for the initial creation of courseware are human and technical, but its continuation and expansion are mainly dependent on organizational resources. Three organizational models support courseware development and its processes (see Figure 10.1):

- the creator organizational structure,
- the integrator organizational structure, and
- the orchestrator organizational structure.

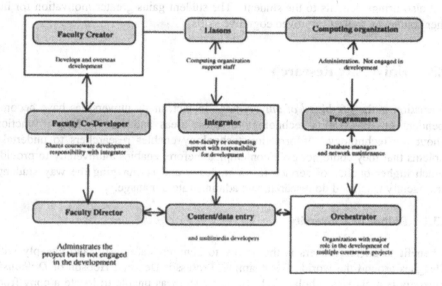

Figure 10.1: *Courseware Organization.* The creator, integrator, and orchestrator roles are depicted here.

The *creator organizational structure* is the traditional academic structure for course design and implementation. An individual faculty member takes on the responsibility for both administration and creation. A person who performed this role in the various projects was called an author or a creator. Where faculty created courseware there was an emphasis on the need for technical resources which would allow a great deal of adaptability and availability. This type of structure does have limitations, as it is dependent on the enthusiasm and talents of an individual who doubtless has other commitments and interests.

The *integrator organizational structure* is characterized by the role of an individual integrator who is engaged in a partnership with the faculty. The *orchestrator organizational structure* is characterized by the role of a third organization to support the development of courseware. A mutually beneficial relationship is created by using the strengths of the departmentally-based projects to provide the content and part of the human resources, while the orchestrator provides support in the form of technical resources and advice.

There is perhaps another organizational model that can be considered which leads from the effect that student contributions can have on the courseware development process. The issues of limited time and skills which are prominent problems in faculty-based development are often missing from student-based development strategies. Not only does *student-based development* have advantages for the project but it also brings benefits to the student. The student gains greater motivation for his or her course, as well as improved cognitive skills.

10.3   University Research

Information is the *life-blood of universities*. In fact, many universities have become dependent on information technology in most areas and can no longer function without the technology. Information technology enables researchers to undertake problems that they could not even contemplate before, enables a university to provide a much higher quality of service to its students, and is changing the way students learn, faculty teach and do research, and administrators manage.

10.3.1 Dalhousie University

Of benefit to all researchers is the ability to communicate easily and cheaply with colleagues around the world. For example, Professor Deborah Hobson of *Dalhousie University* is a classics scholar [31]. Recently she was unable to locate a copy from local university libraries of a rare book from which she needed vital information. She sent electronic mail to fellow colleagues around the world asking for help and twenty minutes later the two pages of the book she needed were faxed to her by a fellow researcher in Amsterdam. Researchers and others are realizing similar benefits on a regular basis and together they constitute a significant payoff.

At Dalhousie University electronic communication is being used increasingly to better prepare staff for *committee meetings* through asynchronous exchanges of views using electronic mail prior to meetings, to setup meeting times, and to distribute information. The latter saves paper, reduces the load on the campus paper mail, and is quicker than traditional methods. Some committees now do most of their work in this manner. In fact the technology can significantly reduce the number of necessary meetings and could even eliminate the need for them altogether in some cases.

The payoff of information technology is very real and extensive but, in most cases, difficult to measure. It is clear that universities must make effective use of information technology to remain competitive and maybe to survive. But with decreasing budgets, increasing emphasis will have to be put on cost-effective use. This means, that despite the difficulties, better ways will have to be found to measure the payoff. This might mean more fees for specific information technology related services and allowing *market forces* to determine the value of the services.

10.3.2 A Research Organization

Large research projects within a university depend on external sources for funds [98]. The Many Using and Creating Hypertext *(MUCH)* project was richly funded by external sources [111] and grew from a group to an organization in a rather short time, by passing through several stages. An electronic planning document reflecting the visions, objectives, and activities was introduced to support this growth [63].

In the first stage of the MUCH project, the MUCH staff was just five people. Control was completely in the hands of the one professor. At this stage, little was formalized, there were no job descriptions and no formal communication channels because the work could be done through direct *face-to-face* contact.

The rapid growth of the project generated the need to induct and supervise new staff. The traditional communication modes (face-to-face meetings and email interaction) between the research professor and the research workers that had been used previously were no longer sufficient to cope with the number of people and range of activities. As the project grew to thirty staff a *hierarchical organization* was instituted in which power was largely centralized, although some control was delegated down the organizational layers.

Consistent with the ethos of a *learning organization,* it was decided at this stage that a survey should be conducted to collect data on current operations. A questionnaire was circulated among the members of the organization. The results showed that members were suffering from role and task ambiguity. Their comments were not atypical in organizations undergoing change [178]. Ambiguity forms a major source of stress. The goal to be achieved, the methods used, and the criterion by which members of an organization recognize success, any or all of these can become more ambiguous during times of change.

The initial response to the findings of the field study was the restructuring of the research organization to take the form of a loose *matrix*. The organization was divided into groups, but group members frequently worked on different projects at the same time, reporting to one or more project managers as well as a group manager.

Embodied within this new structure were formalized changes in the approach to management which attempted to address the problem of role and task ambiguity.

A *plan document* was drafted and entered into the MUCH system. The plan document reflected visions, objectives, and activities [26]. The document was also designed to permit individual users to maintain schedules, 'to do' notes, and progress reports (see Figure 10.2). The introduction of the plan into the MUCH system was aimed at increasing the level of information sharing among members. Each member would have access to the plan document, could get a clearer picture of the tasks she is required to perform, could identify with whom to consult or cooperate, and could update the plan each time a task is completed, so reducing role and task ambiguity. In addition, the managers could keep track of each of their subordinate's progress by checking the updates of the document.

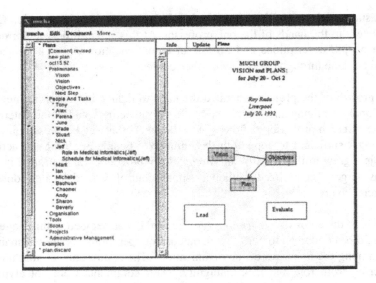

Figure 10.2: *MUCH Plan Document.* The title of the document is 'Plans' (the top node in the tree). The outline of the document has been expanded or unfolded to show some of the nodes in the document. The level of expansion is indicated by the level of indentation. The 'People and Tasks' node has been expanded further (Jeff). The top node, Plans, is highlighted in bold to indicate that this node has been selected for viewing, and its contents appear in the right hand part of the screen, a separate scrolling window.

In order to be able to better assess the viability of the Plan Document, a statistical review of actual Plan usage was undertaken. Measurements were derived from data maintained by the MUCH system. Long-term matters such as visions, plans, and objectives were relatively infrequently accessed for reading and writing by comparison with shorter-term matters. The tendency was to access nodes relating to visions and plans in order to become aware of and familiar with the longer term as a form of high level reference, with an average of one access per member. 'People and Tasks' nodes, however, being more concerned with the immediate future and being more personal, tended to be accessed and updated more frequently. Even here, though, the access rate was less than one per day and updating was infrequent. The overall impression was that the Plan Document was *not being used* by the members of the organization as a whole, being rarely consulted and updated. The usage did, however, tend to increase when going from the long term to the short term and from the group to the individual. This tendency influenced the design of a new plan document.

It was evident from the field study that group members required clear organizational structure with clear roles. The Plan Document was refined in the presentation of planning and the timetabling of objectives. The translation of long-term visions into *short-term objectives* and weekly schedules was introduced. Since, however, the longer-term visions and objectives (down to four months) should require only infrequent consultation and amendment, as indicated by the statistical measures, it was decided that they should be in a separate document from the weekly schedules (see Figure 10.3).
The role of *group managers* includes assisting in the establishment of weekly plans that are stored in the MUCH system (see Figure 10.4). Group managers report on their group's progress at weekly, face-to-face executive meetings. They are also involved in ensuring that current activities are in accordance with the visions and objectives and that these are being pursued.

The MUCH experience highlights some of the potential problems that may be encountered by research groups as they become organizations and attempt to employ computer support to facilitate systemization. The challenge for the future is to look beyond the systemization phase and the MUCH organization is taking steps to facilitate movement into the *integration phase* [178]. These steps include:

- Managing the interaction between people and technical systems, and
- Encouraging people to manage themselves in small groups and take responsibility for their own development and motivation.

The cycle of evaluation followed by change has led to both organizational development and the revision of the MUCH Plan Document.

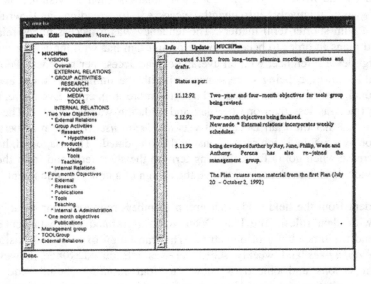

Figure 10.3: *Second Plan Document* This screen illustrates the structure and outline of the new Plan Document. The structures of visions, two year objectives, and four month objectives are near-identical.

10.4   Telemedicine

Health care is being transformed by advances in computers and telecommunications, as previous examples in this book have shown. This section provides examples of the way in which the technologies of fiber optics and satellite, combined with computing power, are making advances in medicine more widely available. Once again, networks help to overcome the problems of isolation of individuals, groups, organizations, and even whole countries and continents.

10.4.1   History of Telemedicine

Mirroring the development of commercial computing generally, hospitals have over the years acquired a multitude of different types of separate computer systems. Only recently have these systems begun to be networked into hospital-wide local area networks. In parallel with this has been the development of standard patient records. Electronic management and transport of *patient information* offers great savings in terms of money and time. The first large, interactive audio teleconference system in

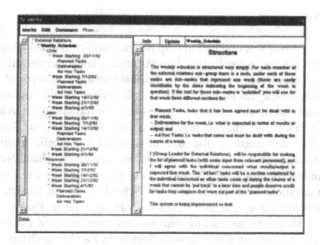

Figure 10.4: *External Relations Group.* This screen shows information on the External Relations Group. At any point it is possible for any group member to inspect the nodes and see what the group and its individual members are doing for the current week and previous weeks.

health was developed in Wisconsin around 1966. In 1968 at Massachusetts General Hospital an interactive telemedicine hookup was used as a way of staffing the hospital's airport clinic and relieving the doctor on call of a daily three-hour drive. Now Massachusetts General Hospital has a fiber optic network for quick transfer of images and records among sites in three cities.

Memorial University of Newfoundland was an early participant in the Canadian Space Program. The University's Telemedicine Center used the Hermes satellite in a one-way television/two-way interactive audio configuration. Four remote hospitals were linked to a central site. In the 1980's, *Memorial's Teleconference System* linked 170 teleconference sites in 80 communities throughout the province of Newfoundland. Hospitals transmitted electroencephalogram tracings to a central site where they were interpreted by experts. This service proved acceptable over a decade of use.

Early *telemedicine* efforts had to make do with bulky and expensive equipment. Recent advances have cut costs and led to less bulky equipment. The speed, precision and versatility of digitized transmission has sharpened the picture and sound. Other advances include the ability to hook stethoscopes, endoscopes, otoscopes, microscopes, electroencephalograms, and other diagnostic devices directly into the system to send images and sounds instantaneously.

10.4.2   HealthNet

In Spring 1992 HealthNet was initiated to help health workers in developing countries generally and rural Africa in particular. *HealthNet* is a telecommunications system providing health professionals with access to medical literature, to medical databases, to each other, and to colleagues in other countries. It utilizes satellite technology with appropriate ground stations, personal computers, information providers, and information receivers. The parent organization of HealthNet is SatelLife, an international charity dedicated to the use of space for peaceful purposes, and especially for the furtherance of health in developing countries. HealthNet provides doctors in developing countries with on-call access to organizations and institutions. Participating organizations include the Harvard School of Public Health, Liverpool School of Tropical Medicine, and the Oswaldo Cruz Institute in Brazil. In Africa, medical doctors in Mozambique treating patients with rare forms of sickness use the system to share clinical reports and data with doctors in Zambia to determine if they have seen similar cases.

HealthNet makes use of technology which allows small, low orbit satellites to be used as orbital post-boxes at a cost of about $1 million. This contrasts with the $100 million price tag of a satellite broadcasting station. A satellite, called HealthSat, was commissioned by SatelLife for use exclusively for communications on health with and between *developing countries.*

HealthSat is a *store and forward satellite.* This technology relies on radio waves to transmit messages to and from the satellite (see Figure 10.5) so there are no transmission costs. HealthSat does not depend on international telecommunications links and is therefore not affected by congested circuits, unaffordable service charges, or frequently disrupted service. The ground station required to send and receive messages comprises a personal computer, a two-way radio, and an antenna.
HealthSat has a 500 mile, low-earth orbit, continually passing over the North and South Poles. As the satellite travels in a north/south plane, the earth rotates east to west; each *orbit* takes approximately 100 minutes. Every place in the world is within each of the satellite's signal at least twice a day. A HealthNet user sends a message composed at the ground station's computer via a radio to a computer in the satellite. The satellite's computer stores the message. When the satellite passes over the ground station for which the message is destined, it forwards the message to that station.

10.4.3   Rural Practitioners

A computer telecommunications network links primary health care practitioners in isolated areas of Australia [187]. It consists of a collection of personal computers linked via telephone. It has been designed by a group of ten *country doctors* in conjunction with a medical informatics team. The objective is to improve

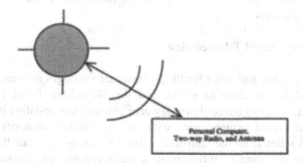

Figure 10.5: *Satellite*: Radio waves transmit messages to and from the satellite, removing dependence on ground-based telecommunication links.

communication between general practitioners working in rural areas and those working in urban medical centers.

In *Australia,* small towns and farming communities are scattered across the middle of the country in isolated areas often separated by hundreds of miles of desert. In these settlements, there may be only one doctor working alone. The nearest hospitals are many hours away.

The facsimile machine has improved the lot of the country doctor. Many doctors use the *fax* to receive pathology results and send electrocardiographs to colleagues for a second opinion, however the slowness of transmission and the poor quality reproduction can be frustrating. The cost of transmitting large amounts of data over a large distance is expensive and the end product is flimsy, difficult to file, and soon disintegrates. Nevertheless, a telephone and fax machine do give a doctor a link to millions of fellow telephone users around the world, as well as the capacity to send and receive visual images of poor quality. Neither of these systems is totally adequate for the day to day needs of general practitioners.

The pilot test of the new system involved one hundred physicians, each with a personal computer plus a modem. The first step was to establish *electronic mail* contact. A bulletin board facility was added and was used for sharing clinical information and seeking consensus standards of management and ideas on office procedures. The continuing medical education needs of the doctors were addressed with the inclusion of computer-based teaching programmes on the network.

Referral to specialists on the system was important. In one dramatic case, a solo doctor in a very isolated region received a quick response and advice from a pediatrician on the management of a sick child. The users started to generate their own patient information handouts on common conditions and these were used and refined by members of the group. File transfer, primarily of word processing documents, was widely utilized. Several doctors made use of the ability to access medical journal databases.

10.4.4   Winnsboro Rural Telemedicine

In response to physician and other health professional shortages in rural health areas, the University of South Carolina established the Winnsboro Rural Primary Care Education Project. In 1993 a model primary care practice was installed in Winnsboro, an *impoverished rural community* with a substantial minority population approximately 35 miles from the University. The University contends that training in the model practice will strongly influence its medical and nurse practitioner graduates to take up careers in rural community practice, an objective which is very much in accord with its overall institutional mission.

The advancement and reduction in cost of *network technologies,* using interactive audio and video, high resolution monitors, and fiber optics, are resulting in cost effective advantages to interactive communication technologies. At the foundation of the Winnsboro Telemedicine Project is a dedicated network that connects the various sites. The network is a high-speed digital circuit that is capable of transferring data at speeds of 1.5 megabytes per second.

The telemedicine system allows effective and efficient use of the medical resources available at the medical center to support the primary care physicians. A camera having the capabilities to connect various medical instruments, i.e., otoscope, ophthalmoscope, sigmoidoscope, and endoscope, is available to provide viewing of procedures performed by the remote site and facilitates consultations with the medical center. Physicians at both sites can view each other, discuss cases, conduct patient interviews, and interact effectively to improve the quality of patient care. The high-resolution *patient camera* has remote control capabilities and can be operated by either site. Real-time echocardiograms have been transmitted from the Winnsboro site to cardiologists located at the host site at the University of South Carolina successfully.

The most important key to the success of this and any like project is a capacity to identify and invite *stakeholders* — community members, healthcare professionals, educators, and information technology departments — to join in its development as soon as possible. When done properly, health care professionals will provide the project with advice and market the project to other potential users. Many projects do not bring in these professionals early enough and end up with a telemedicine solution without a user base sufficient to maintain success [60].

10.4.5   Radiological Multimedia Communication

The ultimate goal of a *multimedia archiving and communication system* in medical care is to provide various kinds of medical data in such a way that they can be quickly retrieved and reviewed by authorized personnel. Typical examples of such data are radiological images that might be enhanced and processed, movies made from serial images, dictated diagnostic reports electronically linked to examination results, and real-time conferencing set up for better diagnostics. Especially because technology is still so expensive, those applications should be identified that benefit most from what can be realized for practical use today.

Currently, information exchange between *radiology* and other clinical departments is based both on regular group meetings as well as on unstructured individual contacts. Concerning the latter, a referring clinician often needs to arrange a meeting with a particular radiologist to discuss the problem because this hardly can be done over the phone, as images and other data are involved. Hence there is an incentive to (partially) replace such contacts by a computer-assisted system.

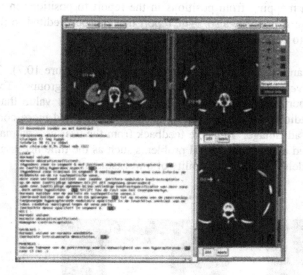

Figure 10.6: *User interface for report creation.* Examples of active labels are shown in the text window as black-on-white [x] character strings, where x is a numeral. An annotation is composed of an arrow and the [x] label. The appearance of such annotations can be changed by the user (as shown in the upper right corner). The radiologist can add text and labels.

Current medical imaging examinations usually result in large sequences of images of which the radiologist must be able to get an overview. Traditionally, such a sequence is stored on film and evaluated on a light-box. If this activity must be replaced by a *radiological workstation*, it is essential that a sufficient number of images can be displayed with a high quality. When using a workstation, features such as the ability to change contrast in real-time or to display video sequences compensate for the lower quality of images displayed on a monitor.

The *RAdiological REporting using MultiMedia ANnotations* (RAREMMAN) system is a prototype report creation and presentation system developed on Unix workstations. RAREMMAN offers the reporting radiologist an image window to view the diagnostic images needed and a text window to enter the text of his report. The image window is implemented by an image manipulation program. The text window is implemented by a program that has been extended to allow the entrance of active labels (see Figure 10.6). When such a label is entered in the text, RAREMMAN gives the radiologist the opportunity to choose an image and by a simple mouse click, to put an annotation at a spatial position in the image. Active labels realize a mapping from positions in the report to positions in an image. The inverse mapping is possible also. The report that has been edited in this way can be saved and sent to the corresponding clinician.

The clinician can also annotate the report by voice (see Figure 10.7). The possibility to employ *active annotations* is well appreciated by user groups. To clinicians the multimedia reports are considered of a higher educational value than the classical reports. For radiologists the possibility to make shorter and more concise reports is regarded as an advantage. Negative feedback from the user groups mainly concerned hardware-related and organizational problems such as the time necessary to load up a report and the delays before availability of a workstation [32].

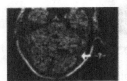  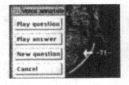

Figure 10.7: *Handling voice annotations.* Images from the RAREMMAN screen which illustrate the handling of voice annotations. As shown on the left of the figure, a '-?-' can be put at a certain position in the image and the clinician can speak in a question. The radiologist now receives the document with the voice annotations displayed. He can activate these annotations as shown in the middle of the figure. By clicking on the arrow, a menu pops up to listen to the question or to answer it. When the question is answered the annotation changes to ?!.

10.5   Conclusion

Developing organizational, networked applications requires close *cooperation between users and developers.* The famous American Airlines reservation system was developed by including both airline reservation staff and software engineers on the same team and by regularly testing prototypes. While the airline system did not include sound or video, the lessons it provides for system development apply to systems of today. The introduction of Lotus Notes within two different organizations, one successfully and one unsuccessfully, has also highlighted the importance of a close fit between the work habits of individuals in the organization and their information technology.

Universities and their staff, while excited about the possibilities of networked hypermedia courseware, are uncertain as to how to proceed. Experiences of such technologically-sophisticated institutions as Massachusetts Institute of Technology and Purdue University have shown the importance of organization-wide commitment to *courseware development.* The technological infrastructure for courseware continually changes, and the courseware will need updating simply to keep pace with the new technology. An academic working alone may not readily have the resources to commit to the exhausting development and repeated maintenance.

Various network and hypermedia services support *healthcare functions.* X-rays may be transmitted to a doctor's home so that emergency treatments can be sanctioned without the doctor having first to travel to the hospital. Hospital personnel may create and share hypermedia patient reports, viewable simultaneously by various specialists.

The advent of new technologies brings *new opportunities* for system development, but these developments are unlikely to succeed unless they benefit from the experiences with earlier systems. The past failures and successes illustrate how high technology relates to organizations. Successful systems fit into the organizational work flow.

11
Conclusion

Hypermedia is usually considered as a new approach to the computer-based organization of information. But it is equally a new approach to the computer-based organization of communication. This reflects the increasing difficulty of differentiating between information and communication. Traditionally, information was what one found in books, television, or radio programs. A key characteristic of the media of information was that they were non-interactive media, in contrast to the new *interactive media*, where the presentation of information becomes much more explicitly a process of communication. The integration of information and communication is the result of digital technology. Indeed, until recently market analysts could distinguish between information processing companies and communication companies. But as new products and services have integrated the two technologies, they have merged into one communication-information industry, and analysts can no longer distinguish clearly between them [90].

11.1 New Technologies

The proliferation of computer and networking technology leads to the investigation of *new ways of working*. The concept of individual use of computers has been expanded to group and organizational use. Individual, group, and organizational activities are related, and innovative technologies can support these activities.

The changes introduced by the sequential advent of *speech, writing,* and *print* had qualitative effects on how people think. Speech made it possible to make propositions, and hand-writing made it possible to preserve them speaker-independently. Two features conspire to make writing unnatural [67]. One is the constraint it puts on the speed with which it allows thoughts to be expressed and the other is the constraint it puts on the interaction of speaking thinkers. Oral speech not only matches the natural speed of thought more closely, it also conforms to the natural tempo of interpersonal discourse. In comparison, written dialogue on paper has served a different kind of relationship. With the invention of movable type and the printing press, the laborious hand-copying of texts became obsolete, and both the tempo and the scope of the written word increased enormously. Texts could be distributed so much more quickly and widely (see Figure 11.1) that again the style of communication underwent qualitative changes.

Figure 11.1: *Books on the Wall.* Many volumes of text are readily available through libraries.

Another qualitative change has begun with the spread of computers and networks. In a seminal article from 1963 that continues to inspire research, Engelbart [47] envisaged a hypermedia and groupware system that would "increase the capability ... to approach a complex problem situation, ... and to derive solutions to problems." With the advent of electronic communication over computer networks, people can communicate in writing and other media across distances arbitrarily quickly. New kinds of *relationships among people* are created.

With some hypermedia products, *authors* and *readers* are separated. Once the hypermedia is installed in the delivery format, the reader can only follow the links that have previously been created, not add his own. A larger role for hypermedia entails eliminating the distinction between authors and readers. In most engineering projects, information is created, analyzed, revised, reviewed, and approved through a complex series of human interactions, both formal and informal. Hypermedia could support collaboration by showing relationships among all elements of the project at all phases of its life, by providing access to all the data elements regardless of where they may be, and by helping users augment the content. Participants in asynchronous, distributed virtual meetings could share views of the same hypermedia object, while being able to create and use private links. Hypermedia has always been seen by its visionaries as more than merely a delivery mechanism, but as an authoring environment as well, wherein new material can be easily linked into the existing corpus.

People form teams to solve problems and perform tasks that a single person would not be able to perform. Although teamwork may be necessary, coordination costs may counteract its value. In the past, groups have employed a variety of techniques to reduce coordination costs. The latest techniques exploit groupware. The introduction and use of groupware creates a co-evolution between the tools and the people using them. Groupware may participate in a human-computer-human interaction and improve the capacity of the human-human interaction. The move from software to groupware will allow the creation of people-centered systems that can clarify and simplify the *coordination* of human action.

11.2   Measure of Success

In modern times, the television has become simultaneously the most common way of transmitting a social message and an image of yet unrealized potential - namely, the potential to marry with the computer and provide interactive media. Hypermedia, groupware, and networks empower people to make contributions. Those who do not *exploit* this technology are at a competitive disadvantage against those who do exploit it. With this technology people can find information, copy it, modify it, and retarget it more quickly than without the technology.

Based on an evolution metaphor, a *measure of success* can be made precise. Success occurs along two dimensions: the amount of information and the amount of time. Short-lived success occurs when information is widely disseminated but quickly disappears (see Figure 11.2). For example, the disk jockey who persuades a stadium full of people to dance may have a short-lived but large impact. A small, long-lived success occurs when information is seldom noticed but survives a long time. An illustration of this case might be the philosopher whose published work is referenced by one other person after many years but not noticed by other people. Successful messages are copied by others when they create their own messages [55]. For this reason, academicians may be evaluated by how frequently they are cited, or advertisers by how frequently customers use their product names.

In ancient Egyptian times the writing was literally on the wall (see Figure 11.3). Libraries with books on the wall where a hallmark of information storage and communication through most of the last few centuries. In a modern store, one is likely to see videocassettes on the wall (see Figure 11.4). Arguably, more people are influenced by videos these days than by books. The writing on the wall is increasingly done with hypermedia, groupware, and networks, and successful communicators may exploit these new tools.

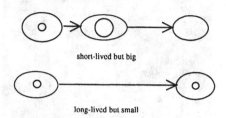

Figure 11.2: *Growth in Sets*: The large ellipse is the World relative to which the analysis is being made. The circle is the local community whose success is being measured across time. In the top sequence the circle has grown quickly and then disappeared. In the bottom figure the circle has not changed in size over a long period of time.

Figure 11.3: *Writing on the Wall*. Egyptian hieroglyphics are chiseled into the stone on the wall.

11.3   Organizational Learning

The failure of some computer systems may be due to their failure to take account of the increasingly co-operative nature of work in organizations. Some years ago a survey of office automation revealed [150] three factors as contributing to this perception of *failure* [70]:

Figure 11.4: *Videocassettes on the Wall.* Videocassettes on display on a store wall.

- the disparity between those who will benefit from an application and those who must do additional work to support it,
- a tendency of managerial decision-makers to favor applications that benefit themselves at the expense of others, and
- the difficulty of realistically evaluating the collective benefits and costs of these applications.

In general, the failure rates for systems increases as the activities they are designed to support gain in *complexity*. The most successful applications are those to do with text-processing. Less successful are those designed to support case-handling. Case-handling or casework is the major activity of organizations engaged in complex service provision, where a team of expert staff will co-operate in dealing with a single case. Examples of this kind of work might be all the police working on a major crime, or a medical team dealing with a particular patient. The primary reason for system failure is the difficulty of matching generic software products to the complex ways people need to share and exchange information [42].

The post-industrial environment is marked by more levels of knowledge, complexity, and turbulence [93]. Increased knowledge means increased specialization of people, products, and services. In such an environment, there will be needs for more continuous and wide-ranging *information acquisition and distribution*. For organizations evolving from old hierarchical, bureaucratic structures towards more fluid, matrix-type structures in order to survive in the rapidly changing environment of today, greater democracy is something that might be usefully encouraged. Systems implemented in organizations of this kind will emphasize lateral information flow, as well as top-down flow.

Early information systems products focused on large, dedicated production operations, where costly integration could yield acceptably large payoffs, like materials requirements planning systems. New information systems design methods enable the combination of technological and organizational design. *Socio-technical design* includes analytic methods to scrutinize work, redesign organizational arrangements, and propose technology enhancements [145].

The potential of the new technologies is not always the same as the reality. This book has documented new technological developments which have failed to help the *customer*. Some hypermedia products lose the customer in a too complicated information space, the first television-phone ruined a communicator's visual image of the speaker, and some organizational information systems slow an organizations ability to respond to a new situation. Technologists and their customers must work closely together.

The way information is organized tends to reflect the way people are organized [185]. Thus a hierarchical organization will probably favor a hierarchy of information, as in traditional documents, whereas a matrix organization might be expected to favor a network of information, as in hypermedia documents. Where information needs to flow widely, hypermedia, groupware, and network tools can facilitate this *flow of information*.

12
Exercises

Exercises are important for learning. An individual exercise might be of the sort:

Working alone, write an essay on some hypermedia-like system. Analyze what you did from the theoretical perspective as captured in the book. Describe what kinds of tools you used and why.

A good way to learn the material about groups and organizations involves working with groups and organizations. In the classes in which this book has been used at the University of Liverpool, the students all worked on the MUCH system and their exercises were submitted via the MUCH system.

For the group exercise at Liverpool, students are divided into small groups of 3 students each. Each group collaboratively writes a short essay of about 1 page. Students are evaluated by the extent to which they:

- work effectively as a group and make a group product, and
- produce individual reports of the group experience.

The individual report should describe what happened in the group and how each student did what.

12.1   Essay Topics

Sample essay topics have been divided into Individual, Group, and Organizational categories.

Individual essay topics:

- What are the relationships among task, information space, and method of information access?

- Describe the 3 layers of the Dexter hypertext model.

- Describe some applications of hypertext to either education or software engineering.

- How might the timing of multimedia be represented?

- Describe various issues germane to compression of video.

- What are CD-ROMs and why might they be important in the dissemination of multimedia?

- How does the Amsterdam Hypermedia Model extend the Dexter model?

- What is the difference between converters and containers as used in hypermedia?

Group essay topics:

- Describe coordination theory and relate it to roles in a group.

- Why are software engineers particularly likely to use groupware tools?

- Describe an extension of the Dexter model to support collaborative work.

- What are some of the dimensions along which groupware might be usefully classified? Give examples of kinds of technology that belong along these dimensions.

- How is the MUCH system used to support peer-peer assessment and what other tools might beneficially be employed for such purposes?

- Under what conditions will new technology to link groups succeed? Why was the PicturePhone not successful?

- What is a shared workspace system?

Organizational essay topics:

- Describe the environmental conditions of organizations.

- Compare and contrast the Hierarchy and Matrix structures of organizations.

- What is the relationship between the number of communication links and the number of people in an organization?

- How can an organization become more innovative?

- How might the OSI reference model for networks be extended to better deal with multimedia synchronization problems?

- What is the World Wide Web?   How does it relate to the Internet and what kinds of software tools have been developed to help people access the World Wide Web?

- There are several social issues concerned with the use of electronic mail. Discuss these.

- 'The process of scholarly communication is currently undergoing a revolution comparable to the one occasioned by the invention of printing'. Discuss this statement.

- Lotus Notes has been successful in many organizational environments but not all. What constitutes a good match between the Notes facilities and the organizational characteristics?

- What impact can new telecommunications technology have on health care?

12.2   Organizational Exercise

Organizational exercises for the class have been handled over the years in a variety of ways. In a typical example, the teacher randomly assigns people to companies of three groups where each group itself consists of several students. Students are evaluated on the extent to which they work effectively as a company, as well as the extent to which the company makes a product. The company is expected to develop a hypermedia product design which other students in the university would find useful.

The groups within the company are marketing, management, and design:

- The marketing group determines a market need and then interacts with customers to refine a preliminary requirements document which is used by the design group. The marketing group is also responsible for taking the resulting design to the customer and getting customer feedback on its value.

- The design group chooses a design methodology and works closely with marketing in developing the design.
- The management group includes a leader, an internal manager, and a finisher whose roles are as follows:
  - The leader directs the company and liaises with the teacher to resolve any problems which may arise.
  - The Internal Manager acts as an assistant to the leader and coordinates the communication between the marketing and design groups.
  - The Finisher collects all completed work from each group and formats it in a comprehensive fashion.

The marketing (design) group is also expected to choose someone to assume the role of marketing (design) leader.

The company is responsible for producing a management report, a marketing report, and a system design made respectively by the management, marketing, and design groups.

- The management report contains:
  - the executive summary of the project,
  - the organizational structure of the company,
  - the roles of the company members, and
  - the phases of the project with deliverables and deadlines.
- The marketing report assesses the needs of the customer and the match of the design to those needs.
- The system design presents a storyboard for a hypermedia product.

In all of this work the students are expected to be considering and exploring the use of technology to support the work of the organization. What channels of communication are most useful for what purposes? For instance, does email help arrange meetings, is a cooperative database good for writing, and so on? This kind of thinking is reflected in a report which each student is required to write about his/her experiences in this exercise.

The assessments are produced as follows:

- Each leader within a group assesses the individuals within the group and the individuals within the group assess the leader of the group.
- Each student in the group inherits the grade which the group product earns.

   Each individual report is assessed.

At the end each student receives a grade that is in the sum of the grade from the above three items.

13
Selected Abbreviations

AME - (Activity Model Environment) a method and a tool for representing organizations to facilitate coordination.

ASCII - (American Standard Code for Information Interchange) a standard code introduced to promote compatibility in terms of representation of characters and symbols.

ATM - (Asynchronous Transfer Mode) protocol for transmitting messages on networks, key to B-ISDN switching, which chops the information into cells of fixed lengths, assigns labels to them, and sends the cells to the network. When these cells arrive at the receiving end, the various information signals, grouped by assigned label, are directed to appropriate terminals.

AVK - (Audio-Video Kernel) a software environment for processing audio-video material.

B-ISDN - (Broadband Integrated Services Digital Network) a high-bandwidth communication network whose protocols and devices allow transmission at many times the rate of N-ISDN and can accommodate HDTV.

CASE - (Computer Aided Software Engineering) software tools which support the development of other software

CD - (Compact Disc) the standard, 4.75 inch diameter, plastic disc on which data is stored by creating pits in the reflective surface of the disc which can be subsequently detected by a laser beam.

CD-DA - (Compact Disc-Digital Audio) is a CD for the music industry which records data in the Red Book Standard format.

CD-ROM - (Compact Disc Read Only Memory) is a CD for use as a data storage device for a computer with over 600 megabytes of data stored, typically in the Yellow Book Standard format.

CMC - (Computer-Mediated Communication) computer networked services for human-human communication, such as computer conferencing, bulletin boards, and electronic mail.

CSCW - (Computer Supported Cooperative Work) cooperative work which is supported by information technology. The term 'CSCW' also refers to the discipline which studies this subject.

DDE - (Dynamic Data Exchange) a program or feature that is able to import and export data in real-time.

EDI - (Electronic Data Interchange) the electronic transfer of commercial and administrative data.

Email - (Electronic Mail) transmission and reception of messages via electronic means.

GDSS - (Group Decision Support System) an interactive computer-based system that facilitates the solution of unstructured problems by a set of decision makers working together as a group.

HAM - (Hypertext Abstract Machine) a hypertext infrastructure based on nodes and links which is the underlying storage mechanism of several hypertext systems.

HDTV - (High-Definition Television) television which requires equal use of the compression and the decompression process and provides a significant improvement in picture clarity and quality mainly by increasing the number of scanning lines from 525 (the American production standard for over 40 years) to about 1000 lines.

HTML - (Hypertext Markup Language) the markup language which supports hypertext features and is used on the World Wide Web.

HTTP - (Hypertext Transport Protocol) an Internet protocol which supports message transport for the World Wide Web.

IBIS - (Issue-Based Information System) a hypertext system which supports people in discussing issues.

N-ISDN - (Narrowband Integrated Services Digital Network) a digital telephone network that use existing switches and wiring, transmits at 1.5 megabits per second, and can handle simple moving images.

ISO - (International Organization for Standards) an international body whose members are countries and which manages the consensus process for making standards and then copyrights and publishes the standards.

JPEG - (Joint Photographic Experts Group) a group that has made an ISO standard for formatting still images.

Memex - (Memory Extender) a device proposed about 50 years ago in which an individual stores items of information in a miniaturized form which allows these items of information to be consulted and processed with speed and flexibility.

MIDI - (Musical Instrument Digital Interface) a digital protocol for the transmission of musical sounds which encodes the sequence of actions taken by an instrument.

MIME - (Multipurpose Internet Mail Extensions) the format of an electronic mail message so that multiple media types can be practically conveyed in the mail.

MPC - (MultiMedia Personal Computer) a personal computer with sizable storage, a color screen, audio devices, and so on. The Multimedia PC Marketing Council has defined the minimal features for such a multimedia PC.

MPEG - (Motion Picture Experts Group) a group which has made standards for representing motion video. An MPEG video is one which has been digitized and compressed into MPEG format.

OSI Model - (Open Systems Interconnection Model) a model which describes the external interactions required of systems that need to be open for communication with other systems. The OSI Model is an ISO standard.

SGML - (Standard Generalized Markup Language) a formalization for describing the way in which documents are logically organized.

TCP/IP - (Transmission Control Protocol/Internet Protocol) a set of protocols for computer networking and on which the Internet was originally based.

WAIS - (Wide Area Information Service) an information organization and retrieval tool that works across the servers of the Internet and points to files based on word indices.

WWW - (World Wide Web) an information service that allows properly structured information to appear as part of a seamless, world-wide hypertext across the Internet.

References

1. Ahuja, S. R., Ensor, J. R., and Horn, D. N., "The Rapport Multimedia Conferencing System," *The Proceedings of the Conference on Office Information Systems*, pp. 1-8, ACM Press, New York, 1988.

2. Allinson, Lesley and Hammond, Nick, "A Learning Support Environment: The Hitch Hikers Guide," *Hypertext: Theory into Practice*, pp. 45-61, Ablex, Norwood, New Jersey, 1989.

3. Alty, James L., "Multimedia - what is it and how do we exploit it?," *Proceedings of the HCI '91 Conference: People and Computers VI*, pp. 31-44, Wiley, 1991.

4. Annis, P., *Use of telephones and computers in the classroom at Boston University*, 1992. (this work was distributed electronically to various newsgroups in 1992, copy can be obtained from the author at email address annis@crca.bu.edu)

5. Arman, F., Depommier, R., Hsu, A., and Chiu, M. Y., "Content-based Browsing of Video Sequences," *Proceedings ACM Multimedia '94*, ACM Press, New York, 1994.

6. Bannon, L. J. and Schmidt, K., "CSCW: Four characters in search of a context," *Proceedings of the 1st European Conference on Computer Supported Cooperative Work*, pp. 358-372, Computer Sciences Company, Slough, England, 1989.

7. Barnard, P., Ellis, J., and MacLean, A., "Relating ideal and non-ideal verbalised knowledge to performance," *People and Computers V*, pp. 461-473, Cambridge University Press, Cambridge, England, 1989.

8. Barnsley, M., "SMARTbook," *BSC Computer Bulletin*, Frax Ltd., Aberdeen, England, February, 1994.

9. Belbin, R. M., *Management Teams: why they succeed or fail*, Heinemann, London, 1981.

10. Bennis, Warren G., "A Funny Thing Happened on the Way to the Future," in *Readings in Managerial Psychology*, ed. Leavitt and Pondy, pp. 760-787, University of Chicago Press, Chicago, 1964.

11. Berners-Lee, Tim, Cailliau, Robert, Luotonen, Ari, Nielsen, Henrik Frystyk, and Secret, Arthur, "The World Wide Web," *Communications of the ACM*, vol. 37, no. 8, pp. 76-82, August 1994.

12. Bertino, E., Rabitti, F., Thanos, C., Converti, A., Savino, P., Eirund, H., and Kreplin, K., "MULTOS - a filing server for multimedia documents," *EURINFO '88*, pp. 435-442, North-Holland, Amsterdam, 1988.

13. Bigelow, James, "Hypertext and CASE," *IEEE Computer*, pp. 23-27, March 1988.

14. Black, G., *What's New in Computing*, pp. 21-2, May 1994.

15. Bolt, R., "Put-That-There: Voice and Gesture at the Graphics Interface," *ACM Computer Graphics, 14, 3*, pp. 262-270, July 1980.

16. Borenstein, N. S. and Thyberg, C. A., "Power, ease of use, and cooperative work in a practical multimedia message system," *International Journal of Man Machine Studies*, vol. 34, no. 2, pp. 229-259, 1991.

17. Botto, A., "Compact Disc Interactive," *Electronics*, vol. 65, no. 8, p. 27, 1992.

18. Bowers, J. and Churcher, J., "Local and global structuring of computer medicated communication: Developing linguistic perspectives on CSCW in Cosmos," *Proceedings of the Conference on Computer-Supported Cooperative Work*, pp. 125-139, ACM Press, New York, 1988.

19. Brookshear, J. Glenn, *Computer Science: an Overview,* Benjamin/Cummings Publishing Company, Redwood City, California, 1994.

20. Brothers, L., Sembugamoorthy, V., and Muller, M., "ICICLE: groupware for code inspection," *Proceedings of the Conference on Computer Supported Cooperative Work*, pp. 169-181, ACM Press, New York, 1990.

21. Brown, M. A. and Slater, M., "A review of interaction technologies as applied to virtual reality," *Computer Graphics*, pp. 309-327, Blenheim Online, Pinner, England, 1991.

22. Brown, P. J. and Russell, M. T., "Converting Help Systems to Hypertext," *Software Practive and Experience*, vol. 18, no. 2, pp. 163-165, 1988.

23. Campbell, Andrew, Coulson, Geoff, and Hutchison, David, "A Quality of Service Architecture," *Computer Communication Review*, vol. 24, no. 2, pp. 6-27, April 1994.

24. Campbell, Brad and Goodman, Joseph M., "HAM: A General-Purpose Hypertext Abstract Machine," *Communications of the Association of Computing Machinery*, vol. 31, no. 7, pp. 856-861, 1988.

25. Card, S. K., Moran, T. P., and Newell, A., *The Psychology of Human-Computer Interaction,* Lawrence Erlbaum, Hillsdale, New Jersey, 1983.

26. Caroll, S. J. and Tosi, H. J., *Management by objectives,* Mac Millan, New York, 1973.

27. Chapanis, A., "Interactive human communication," *Scientific American*, vol. 232, no. 3, pp. 36-42, 1975.

28. Charnock, Elizabeth, Rada, Roy, Stichler, Steve, and Weygant, Peter, "A Rule-Based Task-Oriented Method of Creating Usable Hypertext for Commercial Audiences," *Interacting with Computers*, vol. 6, no. 3, pp. 275-287, September 1994.

29. Chen, Chaomei, Rada, Roy, and Zeb, Akmal, "An Extended Fisheye View Browser for Collaborative Writing," *International Journal of Human-Computer*

Studies, 40, pp. 859-878, 1994.

30. Ciborra, C. and Olson, M. H., "Encountering electronic work groups: A trans-action costs perspective," *Proceedings of the Conference on Computer-Supported Cooperative Work*, pp. 94-101, ACM Press, New York, 1988.

31. Clark, Howard C., Jones, H. S. Peter, and Maharaj, Ken R., "What Presidents Need to Know about the Payoff on the Information Technology Investment: The View from Dalhousie University," *retrieve electronically by sending e-mail to HEIRA@CAUSE.colorado.edu*, Background paper for HEIRAlliance Executive Strategies Report #4, September 1994.

32. Cleynenbrengel, J. Van, Bellon, E., Marchal, G., and Suetens, P., "Design and Evaluation of a Demonstrator for Radiological Multimedia Communication," in *Medical Multimedia*, ed. Roy Rada and Claude Ghaoui, pp. 24-41, Intellect Books, Oxford, England, 1995.

33. Conklin, Jeff, "Hypertext : An Introduction and Survey," *Computer*, vol. 20, no. 9, pp. 17-41, September 1987.

34. Conklin, Jeff and Begeman, Michael, "gIBIS: A Hypertext Tool for Exploratory Policy Discussion," *ACM Transactions on Office Information Systems*, vol. 6, no. 4, pp. 303-331, 1988.

35. Corvetta, Angelo, Pomponio, Giovanni, Salvi, Aldo, and Luchetti, Michele M., "Teaching medicine using hypertexts: three years of experience at the Ancona Medical School," *Artificial Intelligence in Medicine*, vol. 3, no. 4, pp. 203-209, 1991.

36. Crocker, David H., *Standard for the format of ARPA internet text messages*, University of Delaware, 1982.

37. Cybulski, Jacob L. and Reed, Karl, "A hypertext based software engineering environment," *IEEE Software*, vol. 9, no. 2, pp. 62-68, 1992.

38. Davenport, G., "Bridging across content and tools," *Computer Graphics*, vol. 28, no. 1, pp. 31-32, 1994.

39. Denning, Peter J., "The Fifteenth Level," *Proceedings ACM Sigmetrics Conference on Measurement and Modeling of Computer Systems*, pp. 1-4, ACM Press, New York, 1994.

40. Diaz, Lily, "PathMAC: an alternative approach to medical school education at Cornell School of Medicine," in *Hypertext/Hypermedia Handbook*, ed. E. Berk and J. Devlin, pp. 488-492, McGraw-Hill, New York, 1991.

41. Dillon, Andrew and McKnight, Cliff, "Towards a classification of text types - a repertory grid approach," *International Journal of Man-machine Studies*, vol. 33, no. 6, pp. 623-636, 1990.

42. Eason, Ken, "Designing Systems to Match Organizational Reality," in *People and Computer V: Proceedings of the Fifth Conference of the British Computer Society Human-Computer Interaction Specialist Group*, ed. A. Sutcliffe and L.

MacAulay, pp. 57-69, Cambridge University Press, Cambridge, England, 1989.

43. Egan, D. E., Remde, J. R., Gomez, L. M., Landauer, T. K., Eberhardt, J., and Lochbaum, C. C., "Formative Design-Evaluation of SuperBook," *ACM Transactions of Information Systems*, vol. 7, no. 1, pp. 30-57, 1989.

44. Egido, Carmen, "Videoconferencing as a Technology to Support Group Work: A Review of its Failure," *Second Conference on Computer-Supported Cooperative Work: CSCW '88*, pp. 13-24, ACM Press, New York, 1988.

45. Ellis, C. and Nutt, G., "Office information systems and computer science," *ACM Computing Surveys*, vol. 12, no. 1, pp. 27-60, 1980.

46. Emery, F. E. and Trist, E. L., "The Causal Texture of Organizational Environments," *Human Relations*, vol. 18, pp. 21-31, 1965.

47. Engelbart, D. C., "A conceptual framework for the augmentation of man's intellect," *Vistas in Information Handling*, vol. 1, pp. 1-29, Spartan Books, Washington, DC, 1963.

48. Engelbart, D. C., Watson, R. W., and Norton, J. C., "The Augmented Knowledge Workshop," *Proceedings of the Fall Joint Computer Conference, 42*, vol. 42, pp. 9-21, AFIPS Press, Reston, Virgina, 1973.

49. Fagan, M. E., "Design and code inspection to reduce errors in program development," *IBM Systems Journal*, vol. 15, no. 2, pp. 182-211, 1976.

50. Finholt, T., Sproull, L., and Kiesler, S., "Communication and performance in ad hoc task groups," in *Intellectual Teamwork: Social Foundations of Cooperative Work*, ed. Jolene Galegher, Robert E. Kraut, and Carmen Egido, pp. 291-326, Lawrence Erlbaum Associates, Hillsdale, New Jersey, 1990.

51. Fish, R. S., Kraut, R. E., and Chalfonte, B. L., "The VideoWindow system in informal communications," *Proceedings of the Conference on Computer Supported Cooperative Work*, pp. 1-11, ACM Press, New York, 1990.

52. Fujikawa, M., "CD-ROM: present state, future prospect, and problems.," *2nd International Conference on the Effective Use of CD-ROM Databases*, pp. 3-18, ISACO, Japan, 1990.

53. Furuta, Richard, Plaisant, Catherine, and Shneiderman, Ben, "A Spectrum of Automatic Hypertext Constructions," *Hypermedia*, vol. 1, no. 2, pp. 179-195, 1989.

54. Galegher, J. and Kraut, R. E., "Computer-mediated communication for intellectual teamwork: A field experiment in group writing," *Proceedings of the Conference on Computer Supported Cooperative Work*, pp. 65-78, ACM Press, New York, 1990.

55. Garfield, Eugene, *Citation Indexing: Its Theory and Applications in Science, Technology, and Humanities,* John Wiley and Sons, New York, U.S.A., 1979.

56. Gerbner, George and Haigh, Robert W., *Communications in the twenty-first century,* Wiley, New York, 1981.

57. Ginsberg, A., "A unified approach to automatic indexing and information retrieval," *IEEE Expert*, pp. 46-56, October 1993.

58. Glushko, Robert K., "Transforming Text into Hypertext for a Compact Disk Encyclopedia," *Proceedings of CHI'89*, pp. 293-298, ACM Press, New York, May 1989.

59. Goldman-Segall, R., "Interpreting Video Data: Introducing a 'Significance Measure' to Layer Descriptions," *Journal of Educational Multimedia and Hypermedia*, vol. 2, no. 3, pp. 261-281, 1993.

60. Goodenow, Ronald K. and Carpenter, Sam K., "Designing and Implementing a Rural Telemedicine Project: Issues and Learnings," in *Medical Multimedia*, ed. Roy Rada and Claude Ghaoui, pp. 53-69, Intellect Books, Oxford, England, 1994.

61. Goodman, Danny, "Hypercard," *MacIntosh Today*, pp. 60-64, August 11, 1987.

62. Goodman, S. E., Press, L. I., Ruth, S. R., and Ruthowski, A. M., "The Global Diffusion of the Internet: Patterns and Problems," *Communications of the ACM*, vol. 37, no. 8, pp. 27-31, August 1994.

63. Gouma, Pelagia-Irene, Deakin, Anthony G., White, Barbara, and Rada, Roy, "A Study of the Evolution of a University Research Department Facilitated by a Groupware System (MUCH)," *Journal Intelligent Systems*, vol. 4, no. 1-2, 1994.

64. Green, James L., "The Evolution of DVI System Software," *Communications of the ACM*, vol. 35, no. 1, pp. 52-67, 1992.

65. Greenbaum, J., "In search of cooperation: An historical analysis of work organization and management strategies," *Proceedings of the Conference on Computer-Supported Cooperative Work*, pp. 102-114, ACM Press, New York, 1988.

66. Greenberg, Saul, Roseman, Mark, Webster, Dave, and Bohnet, Ralph, "Human and Technical Factors of Distributed Group Drawing Tools," *Interacting with Computers*, vol. 4, no. 3, pp. 362-392, 1992.

67. Greenfield, P., "Language, Tools, and Brain: The Development and Evolution of Hierarchically Organized Sequential Behavior," *Behavioral and Brain Sciences*, vol. 14, no. 4, p. 308, 1991.

68. Greif, Irene and Sarin, Sunil, "Data Sharing in Group Work," *ACM Transactions on Office Information Systems*, vol. 5, no. 2, pp. 187-211, April 1987.

69. Gronbaek, Kaj, Hem, Jens A., Madsen, Ole L., and Sloth, Lennert, "Cooperative Hypermedia Systems: A Dexter-Based Architecture," *Communications of the ACM*, vol. 37, no. 2, pp. 65-74, 1994.

70. Grudin, Jonathan, "Perils and pitfalls," *Byte*, vol. 13, no. 13, p. 261, 1988.

71. Grudin, Jonathan, "CSCW: The convergence of two disciplines," *ACM SIGCHI Conference on Human Factors in Computing Systems*, pp. 91-98, ACM Press, New York, 1991.

72. Grudin, Jonathan, "Groupware and Social Dynamics: Eight Challenges for Developers," *Communications of the ACM*, vol. 37, no. 1, pp. 92-105, 1994.

73. Gutek, B. A., "Work group structure and information technology: a structural contingency approach," in *Intellectual Teamwork: Social Foundations of Cooperative Work*, ed. Jolene Galegher, Robert E. Kraut, and Carmen Egido, pp. 63-78, Lawrence Erlbaum Associates, Hillsdale, New Jersey, 1990.

74. Haas, Norman and Hendrix, Gary, "An Approach to Acquiring and Applying Knowledge," *Proceedings of the First Annual Conference on Artifical Intelligence*, pp. 235-239, American Association Artificial Intelligence, Stanford, California, 1980.

75. Hahn, Harley and Stout, Rick, *The Internet Complete Reference*, McGraw-Hill, Berkeley, California, 1994.

76. Halasz, Frank and Schwartz, Mayer, "The Dexter Hypertext Reference Model," *Proceedings of the Hypertext Standardization Workshop*, pp. 95-133, National Institute of Standards and Technology Special Publication 500-178, U. S. Government Printing Office, Washington, DC, 1990.

77. Handy, Charles B., *The Age of Unreason*, Hutchinson, London, 1989.

78. Hansen, Wilfred J and Haas, Christina, "Reading and Writing with Computers: A Framework for Explaining Differences in Performance," *Communications of the ACM*, vol. 31, no. 9, pp. 1080-1089, September 1988.

79. Hardman, Lynda, Bulterman, Dick C. A., and Rossum, Guida van, "The Amsterdam Hypermedia Model: Adding Time and Context to the Dexter Model," *Communications of the ACM*, vol. 37, no. 2, pp. 50-62, February 1994.

80. Harnad, S., "Rational Disagreement in Peer Review," *Science, Technology, and Human Values*, vol. 10, no. 3, pp. 55-62, 1985.

81. Harnad, S., "Scholarly Skywriting and the Prepublication Continuum of Scintific Inquiry," *Psychological Science*, vol. 1, pp. 342-343, 1990.

82. Harnad, S., "Post-Gutenberg Galaxy: The Fourth Revolution in the Means of Production of Knowledge," *Public-Access Computer Systems Review*, vol. 2, no. 1, pp. 39-53, 1991.

83. Hayes, Frank, "The Groupware Dilemma," *UnixWorld*, vol. 9, no. 2, pp. 46-50, February 1992.

84. Hayes, John R., Flower, Linda, Schriver, Karen A., Stratman, James F., and Carey, Linda, "Cognitive Processes in Revision," *Advances in Applied Psycholinguistics*, pp. 176-240, Cambridge University Press, Cambridge, England,

1987.

85. Hewett, Tom, "The Drexel Disk: An Electronic 'Guidebook'," *People and Computers III*, pp. 115-129, Cambridge University Press, Cambridge, England, 1987.

86. Hewett, Tom, "Update on the Drexel Disk: Handout for SIGGraph 1990 Annual Conference," *Technical Report from Department of Psychology*, Drexel University, Philadelphia, Pennsylvania, 1990.

87. Hewitt, Carl, "Offices Are Open Systems," *ACM Transactions on Office Information Systems*, vol. 4, no. 3, pp. 271-287, July 1986.

88. Hiltz, S. R., "Collaborative learning in a virtual classroom: Highlights of findings," *Proceedings of the Conference on Computer-Supported Cooperative Work*, pp. 282-290, ACM Press, New York, 1988.

89. Hirschheim, R. A., *Office Automation: a social and organizational perspective*, John Wiley, Chichester, England, 1985.

90. Hirschhorn, Larry, *Beyond Mechanization*, MIT Press, Cambridge, Massachusetts, 1984.

91. Hopper, Mary, "Courseware Projects in Advanced Educational Computing Environments," *Ph.D. Thesis*, Department of Education, Purdue University, Lafayette, Indiana, August 1993.

92. Houdeshel, George and Watson, Hugh J., "The Management Information and Decision Support (MIDS) System at Lockheed-Georgia," *MIS Quarterly*, vol. 11, no. 1, 1987.

93. Huber, G. P., "The nature and design of post-industrial organizations," *Management Science*, vol. 30, pp. 928-951, 1984.

94. Intel, "The Audio Video Kernel: the Foundation for a Portable, Extendable Multimedia Environment," *White Paper*, Multiteq Ltd, Aylesbury, England, October 1992.

95. International Standards Organization, *Information Processing - Text and Office Systems - Standard Generalized Markup Language (SGML)*, ISO 8879, Geneva, 1988.

96. Isaacs, E. A. and Tang, J. C., "What video can and can't do for collaboration: a case study," *Proceedings of ACM Multimedia'93*, pp. 199-206, ACM Press, New York, 1993.

97. Ishii, H., "TeamWorkStation: Towards a seamless shared space," *Proceedings of the Conference on Computer Supported Cooperative Work*, pp. 13-26, ACM Press, New York, 1990.

98. Iya, Sandhya and Akhilesh, K. B., "Technology as perceived by R&D team leaders: an analysis," *R&D Management*, vol. 22, no. 3, pp. 265-276, 1992.

99. Janis, Irving L., *Victims of Groupthink: A Psychological Study of Foreign-Policy Decisions and Fiascoes,* Houghton Mifflin, Boston, Massachusetts, 1972.

100. Jense, G. J. and Kuijper, F., "Applying virtual environments to training and simulation," *Annual Meeting of the Applied Vision Association,* University of Bristol, England, 1993.

101. Jirotka, M., Gilbert, N., and Luff, P., "On the social organization of organizations," *Computer Supported Collaborative Work-CSCW '92,* pp. 95-118, ACM Press, New York, 1992.

102. Johansen, R., "User approaches to computer-supported teams," in *Technological Support for Work Group Collaborations,* ed. M.H. Olson, pp. 1-32, Lawrence Erlbaum Associates, Hillsdale, New Jersey, 1989.

103. Johnson-Lenz, P. and Johnson-Lenz, T., "Post-mechanistic groupware primitives: rhythms, boundaries and containers," *International Journal of Man Machine Studies,* vol. 34, no. 3, pp. 385-418, 1991.

104. Kahle, B., "Electronic Publishing and Public Libraries," *alt.wais Sun. Dec. 29, 06:58:19,* 1991.

105. Kahn, Robert Louis, *Organizational stress: studies in role conflict and ambiguity,* Wiley, New York, 1964.

106. Kane, Beverly, "LIMES: A hypertext advisory system," *Artificial Intelligence in Medicine,* vol. 2, no. 4, pp. 193-204, 1990.

107. Katz, R., "The effects of group longevity on project communication and performance," *Administrative Science Quarterly,* vol. 27, pp. 81-104, 1982.

108. Kling, Rob, "Cooperation, coordination and control in computer-supported work," *Communications of the ACM,* vol. 34, no. 12, pp. 83-88, 1991.

109. Kompella, V. P., Pasquale, J. C., and Polyzos, G. C., "Multicast Routing for Multimedia Communication," *IEEE/ACM Transactions on Networking,* pp. 286-292, June, 1993.

110. Kraut, Robert, Galegher, Jolene, and Egido, Carmen, "Relationships and Tasks in Scientific Research Collaborations," *Human-Computer Interaction,* vol. 3, no. 1, pp. 31-58, 1987.

111. Kreiner, Kristian and Schultz, Majken, "Informal Collaboration in R&D. The formation of Networks Across Organizations," *Organization Studies,* vol. 14, no. 2, pp. 189-209, 1993.

112. Krol, Ed, *The Whole Internet: User's Guide and Catalog,* O'Reilly & Associates, Sebastopol, California, 1992.

113. Landow, G. P., "Hypertext and collaborative work: The example of Intermedia," in *Intellectual Teamwork: Social Foundations of Cooperative Work,* ed. Jolene Galegher, Robert E. Kraut, and Carmen Egido, pp. 407-428, Lawrence Erlbaum Associates, Hillsdale, New Jersey, 1990.

114. Leiner, Barry, "Internet Technology," *Communications of the ACM*, vol. 37, no. 8, p. 32, August 1994.

115. Lenat, Douglas B. and Guha, R. V., *Building Large Knowledge Bases,* Addison-Wesley, Reading, Massachusettes, 1990.

116. Lewis, Brian T. and Hodges, Jeffrey D., "Shared Books : Collaborative Publication Management for an Office Information System," *Proceedings Conference on Office Information Systems*, pp. 197-204, ACM Press, New York, 1988.

117. Leyland, P, "Reading Notes," *What's New in Computing*, pp. 21-3, March 1994.

118. Liberman, Kristen and Rich, Jane L., "Lotus Notes Databases: the Foundation of a Virtual Library," *Databases, 16, 3*, pp. 33-47, June 1993.

119. Ligon, Helen H, *Successful Management Information Systems,* UMI Research Press, Ann Arbor, Michigan, 1978.

120. Likert, Rensis, *New Patterns of Management,* McGraw-Hill, New York, 1961.

121. Little, Thomas D. C., "Time-based Media Representation and Delivery," in *Multimedia Systems*, ed. John F. Koegel Buford, pp. 175-200, ACM Press, New York, 1994.

122. Lotus Development Corporation, *A Quick Tour of Notes*, Cambridge, Massachusetts: Lotus Development Corporation, 1991.

123. Lovelace, R. F., "Stimulating creativity through managerial interventions," *R & D Management*, vol. 16, pp. 161-174, 1986.

124. Luther, Arch C., Sen, Prodip, and Buford, John F. Koegel, "Architectures and Issues for Distributed Multimedia Systems," in *Multimedia Systems*, ed. John F Koegel Buford and John F. Koegel Buford, pp. 45-63, ACM Press, New York, 1994.

125. Mackay, W., "More than just a communication system: Diversity in the use of electronic mail.," *Proceedings of the Conference on Computer-Supported Cooperative Work (CSCW '88)*, pp. 344-353, ACM Press, New York, 1988.

126. Malone, T. W., Grant, K. R., Turbak, F. A., Brobst, S. A., and Cohen, M., "Intelligent Information-Sharing Systems," *Communications of the ACM*, vol. 30, no. 5, pp. 390-402, 1987.

127. Malone, T. W., and Crowston, K.,, "What is Coordination Theory and how can it help design cooperative work systems?," *Proceedings of the Conference on Computer Supported Cooperative Work (CSCW '90)*, pp. 357-370, ACM Press, New York, 1990.

128. Massey, Doreen, Quintas, Paul, and Wield, David, *High Tech Fantasies: Science parks in society, science, and space,* Routledge, London, 1992.

129. McKnight, Cliff, Dillon, Andrew, and Richardson, John, *Hypertext in Context,* Cambridge University Press, Cambridge, England, 1991.

130. Michailidis, Antomios, Rada, Roy, and Wang, Weigang, "Matching roles and technology for collaborative work: an empirical assessment," *Wirtschaftsinformatik*, vol. 35, no. 2, pp. 138-148, 1993.

131. Miller, M. J., "Multimedia - cover story," *PC Magazine*, vol. 11, no. 6, pp. 112-123, 1992.

132. Min, Zheng and Rada, Roy, "SHyD -- a Model for Bridging Text and Hypertext," *Proceedings 21st Annual Computer Science Conference*, pp. 418-424, ACM Press, New York, 1993.

133. Min, Zheng and Rada, Roy, "MUCH Electronic Publishing Environment -- Principles and Practices," *Journal American Society Information Science*, pp. 300-309, June 1994.

134. Mittman, Benjamin and Borman, Lorraine, "Bibliographic Retrieval and Data Management Systems: Precursors of Personalized Data Base Processing," *Personalized Data Base Systems*, pp. 3-33, Melville Publishing, Los Angeles, 1975.

135. Mowery, D. C., "Industrial Research, 1900-1950," in *The Decline of the British Economy*, ed. B. Elbaum and W. Lazonick, pp. 189-222, Clarendon Press, Oxford, England, 1986.

136. Nardi, B. A. and Miller, J. R., "Twinkling lights and nested loops: Distributed problem solving and spreadsheet development," *International Journal of Man Machine Studies*, vol. 34, no. 2, pp. 161-184, 1991.

137. Nass, Richard, "Competitive Video Compression-Decompression Schemes Forge Ahead," *Electronic Design*, pp. 82-90, June 1994.

138. Newcombe, S. R., Kipp, N. A., and Newcombe, V. T, "The HyTime Hypermedia/Time-based Document Structuring Language," *Communications of the ACM*, vol. 34, no. 11, pp. 67-83, November 1991.

139. Nunamaker, J. F., Dennis, Alan R., Valacich, Joseph S., Vogel, Douglas R., and George, Joey F., "Electronic Meeting Systems to Support Group Work," *Communications of the ACM*, vol. 34, no. 7, pp. 40-61, July 1991.

140. Nyce, James M. and Kahn, Paul, "Innovation, Pragmaticism, and Technological Continuity: Vannevar Bush's Memex," *Journal American Society Information Science*, vol. 40, no. 3, pp. 214-220, 1989.

141. Olson, Judith S., Olson, Gary M., Storrosten, Marianne, and Carter, Mark, "How a Group-Editor Changes the Character of a Design Meeting as well as its Outcome," *Proceedings Computer-Supported Collaborative Work '92*, ACM Press, New York, 1992.

142. Oppenheim, C., "CD-ROM: An introduction to the technology and its potential applications," *Proceedings of Advanced Information Systems - AiS '91*, pp. 69-75, 1991.

143. Orlikowski, Wanda, "The Duality of Technology: Rethinking the Concept of Technology in Organizations," *Organization Science*, vol. 3, no. 3, pp. 398-427,

August 1992.

144. Parkin, Frank, *Max Weber,* Routledge, London, 1988.

145. Pava, C., "Organizational Architecture for Distributed Computing - the next frontier is systems design," in *Technological Support for Work Group Collaboration*, ed. M. H. Olson, Lawrence Erlbaum Associates, Hillsdale, NJ, 1989.

146. Pavitt, K., "Sectoral patterns of technical change: towards a taxonomy and a theory," *Research Policy*, vol. 13, pp. 343-373, 1984.

147. Poynton, Charles A., "High Definition Television and Desktop Computing," in *Multimedia Systems*, ed. John F. Koegel Buford, pp. 383-402, ACM Press, New York, 1994.

148. Price, Charlton R., "Conferencing via Computer: cost effective communication for the era of forced choice," in *The Delphi Method: Techniques and Applications*, ed. H. A. Linstone and M. Turoff, pp. 497-516, Addison-Wesley, Reading, Massachusetts, 1975.

149. Price, Charlton R., "MHEG: An introduction to the future international standard for hypermedia object interchange," *Proceedings of ACM Multimedia'93*, pp. 121-128, ACM Press, New York, 1993.

150. Pye, R., Bates, R. J., and Heath, L., *Profiting from Office Automation; Office Automation Pilots*, Department of Trade and Industry, London, 1986.

151. Quarterman, John S., *The Matrix: Computer Networks and Conferencing Systems Worldwide*, Digital Press, Bedford, Massachusetts, 1990.

152. Rada, Roy and Barlow, Judith, "Document Creation in Offices," *Computing Technologies: New Directions and Applications*, pp. 43-74, Ellis Horwood, London, 1989.

153. Rada, Roy, "Guidelines for Multiple Users Creating Hypertext: SQL and HyperCard Experiments," in *Computers and Writing: Models and Tools*, ed. Patrik Holt and Noel Williams, pp. 61-89, Blackwell/Ablex Publishing, 1989.

154. Rada, Roy, "Hypertext Writing and Document Reuse : the Role of a Semantic Net," *Electronic Publishing*, vol. 3, no. 3, pp. 125-140, August 1990.

155. Rada, Roy, Acquah, Sharon, Baker, Beverly, and Ramsey, Phillip, "Collaborative Learning and the MUCH System," *Computers and Education*, vol. 20, no. 3, pp. 225-233, 1993.

156. Rada, Roy and Carson, George S., "Standards: the New Media," *Communications of the ACM*, vol. 37, no. 9, pp. 23-25, 1994.

157. Rada, Roy, Michailidis, Antonios, and Wang, Weigang, "Collaborative Hypermedia in a Classroom Setting," *Journal of Educational Multimedia and Hypermedia*, vol. 3, no. 1, pp. 21-36, 1994.

158. Rangan, P. Venkat, Vin, H. M., and Ramanathan, S., "Communication Architectures and Algorithms for media Mixing in Multimedia Conferences,"

IEEE/ACM Transactions on Networking, vol. 1, no. 1, pp. 20-30, February, 1993.

159. Rice, Ronald and Shook, Douglas E., "Relationships of Job Categories and Organizational Levels to Use of Communication Channels, Including Electronic Mail: A Meta-Analysis and Extension," *Journal of Management Studies*, vol. 27, no. 2, pp. 195-229, March 1990.

160. Riggins, David, "Design Tips," *Net Happenings*, david.riggins@tpoint.com, August 31, 1994.

161. Roberts, Hillary J., "MRPII - Follow the Yellow Brick Road," *Proceedings of the 25th European Conference on Production and Inventory Control*, pp. 173-180, Birmingham, England, 1989.

162. Robinson, M., "Through a lens smartly," *BYTE*, vol. 16, no. 5, p. 177, 1991.

163. Rodden, Thomas, "Supporting Cooperation in Software Engineering Environments," *Ph.D. Thesis*, University of Lancaster, January 1990.

164. Rodden, Thomas, "A survey of CSCW systems," *Interacting with Computers*, vol. 3, no. 2, pp. 319-353, 1991.

165. Rossum, G. van, Jansen, J., Mullender, K. S., and Bulterman, D. C. A., "CMIFed: A presentation environment for portable hypermedia documents," *Proceedings of the First ACM International Conference on Multimedia*, pp. 183-188, ACM Press, New York, August 1993.

166. Rushton, Chris, Ramsey, Phillip, and Rada, Roy, "Peer Assessment in a Collaborative Hypermedia Environment: A Case Study," *Journal of Computer-Based Instruction*, vol. 20, no. 3, pp. 75-80, 1993.

167. Scardamalia, Marlene and Bereiter, Carl, "Knowledge Telling and Knowledge Transforming in Written Composition," *Advances in Applied Psycholinguistics*, pp. 142-175, Cambridge University Press, Cambridge, England, 1987.

168. Schmidt, Kjeld, "Riding a Tiger, or Computer Supported Cooperative Work," *Proceedings of the Second European Conference on Computer-Supported Cooperative Work*, pp. 1-16, Kluwer, Amsterdam, 1991.

169. Searle, John Rogers and Vanderveken, Daniel, *Foundations of illocutionary logic,* Cambridge University Press, Cambridge, England, 1985.

170. Seppala, Pentti and Salvendy, Gavriel, "Impact of Depth of Menu Hierarchy on Performance Effectiveness in a Supervisory Task: Computerized Flexible Manufacturing System," *Human Factors*, vol. 27, no. 6, pp. 713-722, 1985.

171. Shannon, Claude and Weaver, W., *The Mathematical Theory of Communication*, University of Illinois Press, Urbana, Illinois, 1949.

172. Shneiderman, Ben and Kearsley, Greg, *Hypertext Hands-On!*, Addison-Wesley, Reading, Massachusetts, 1989.

173. Simon, Herbert A., *Models of Man,* Wiley, New York, 1957.

174. Smith, H. T., Hannessy, P. A., and Lunt, G., "The activity model environment: An object oriented framework for describing organizational communication," *Proceedings of the 1st European Conference on Computer Supported Cooperative Work,* Computer Sciences Company, Slough, England, 1989.

175. Sorgaard, P., "Object Oriented Programming and Computerized Shared Material," in *ECOOP '88: European Conference on Object-Oriented Programming; Lecture Notes in Computer Science 322,* ed. Gjessing, Stein and Hygaard, Kristen, pp. 319-334, Springer-Verlag, Berlin, Germany, 1988.

176. Stefik, M., Bobrow, D. G., Foster, G., Lanning, S., and Tatar, D., "WYSIWIS revised: Early experiences with multiuser interfaces," *ACM Transactions on Office Information Systems,* vol. 5, no. 2, pp. 147-167, 1987.

177. Stefik, Mark, Foster, Gregg, Bobrow, Daniel, Kahn, Kenneth, Lanning, Stan, and Suchman, Lucy, "Beyond the Chalkboard: Computer Support for Collaboration and Problem Solving in Meetings," *Communications of the ACM,* vol. 30, no. 1, pp. 32-47, 1987.

178. Stewart, V., *Change: The challenge of management,* McGraw Hill, New York, 1983.

179. Stotts, P. D. and Furuta, R., "Petri-Net Based Hypertext: Document Structure with Browsing Semantics," *ACM Transactions on Office Information Systems,* vol. 7, no. 1, pp. 3-29, 1989.

180. Strawn, John, "Digital Audio Representation and Processing," in *Multimedia Systems,* ed. John F Koegel Buford, pp. 65-108, ACM Press, New York, 1994.

181. Swets, John, "Effectiveness of Information Retrieval Methods," *American Documentation,* vol. 20, no. 1, pp. 72-89, 1969.

182. Tanenbaum, Andrew S., *Computer Networks,* Prentice-Hall, Englewood Cliffs, New Jersey, 1989.

183. Tapscott, D., *Office automation: a user-driven method,* Plenum Press, New York, 1982.

184. Tichy, W., "Design, Implementation and Evaluation of a Revision Control System," *Proceedings 6th International Conference on Software Engineering,* pp. 58-67, 1982.

185. Toffler, Alvin, *Powershift: Knowledge, wealth and violence at the edge of the 21st Century,* Bantam Press, New York, 1990.

186. Trainor, R., "Computers, arts based teaching and rising student numbers," *CTISS File,* vol. 13, pp. 3-6, 1992.

187. Trumble, S., Cesnik, B., Kidd, M., Connoley, G., and McPheea, W., "Primary Health Orientated Computer Users' System: overcoming the isolation of rural doctors with computer based communication," in *MedInfo 1992 Proceedings,*

ed. K. D. Lun, P. Degoulet, T. E. Piemme, and O. Rienhoff, pp. 84-90, North-Holland, Amsterdam, 1992.

188. Twiss, Brian C. and Weinshall, Theodore D., *Managing Industrial Organizations,* Pitman, London, 1980.

189. University of Brighton, *Academic Development Plan,* Faculty of Information Technology, 1992.

190. US Market Intelligence Research Company, *Software World,* vol. 21, no. 4, p. 9, 1987.

191. Vaughan, Tay, *MultiMedia: Making it Work,* McGraw-Hill, New York, 1993.

192. Viller, Stephen, "The Group Facilitator: A CSCW Perspective," *Proceedings of the Second European Conference on Computer-Supported Cooperative Work,* pp. 81-95, Kluwer, Amsterdam, 1991.

193. Walz, D. B., Krasner, H., and McInroy, J., "Groupware research and technology issues with application to software process management," *IEEE Transactions on Systems Management and Cybernetics,* vol. 21, no. 4, pp. 704-712, 1991.

194. Watabe, K., Sakata, S., Maeno, K., Fukuoka, H., and Ohmori, T., "Distributed multiparty desktop conferencing system: Mermaid," *Proceedings of the Conference on Computer Supported Cooperative Work (CSCW '90),* pp. 27-38, ACM Press, New York, 1990.

195. Wayner, Peter, "Inside QuickTime," *BYTE,* vol. 16, no. 13, 1991.

196. Wilson, Dave, "Wrestling with multimedia standards," *Computer Design,* vol. 31, no. 1, pp. 70-88, 1992.

197. Wilson, P., "Computer supported cooperative work (CSCW) - origins, concepts and research initiatives," *Computer Networks and ISDN Systems,* vol. 23, no. 1-3, pp. 91-95, 1991.

198. Winograd, T. and Flores, F., *Understanding computers and cognition: A new foundation for design,* Ablex, Norwood, New Jersey, 1986.

199. Winograd, T., "Where the action is," *Byte,* pp. 256A-256F, December, 1988.

200. Witten, I. H., Thimbleby, H. W., Coulouris, G., and Greenberg, S., "Liveware: A new approach to sharing data in social networks," *International Journal of Man Machine Studies,* vol. 34, no. 3, pp. 337-348, 1991.

201. Yankelovich, Nicole, Meyrowitz, Norman, and Dam, Andries van, "Reading and Writing the Electronic Book," *Computer,* pp. 15-30, October 1985.

Index